To

Frank

with love and respect –

the planner. the dreamer

Paul O'Dwyer

COUNSEL

FOR THE

DEFENSE

THE AUTOBIOGRAPHY OF

PAUL O'DWYER

SIMON AND SCHUSTER
NEW YORK

Published by Simon and Schuster
A Division of Gulf & Western Corporation
Simon & Schuster Building
Rockefeller Center
1230 Avenue of the Americas
New York, New York 10020

Manufactured in the United States of America

1 2 3 4 5 6 7 8 9 10

Library of Congress Cataloging in Publication Data

O'Dwyer, Paul
Counsel for the defense.

Includes index.
1. O'Dwyer, Paul 2. Lawyers—New York (City)—Biography. 3. City councilman—New York (City)—Biography. I. Title.
KF373.038A3 340'.092'4 [B] 79-13936
ISBN 0-671-22573-1

Contents

This book had been completed—its errors of fact eliminated, its spelling and syntax corrected and every name mentioned in it checked for accuracy—when it was submitted to the publisher. Certain expressions which had followed me across the Atlantic, however, had burrowed their way into the manuscipt, and those of the Ivy League whom the publisher had assigned to ensure that the final product would meet the exacting standards of the critics had been puzzled. The meaning, they said, was sometimes obscure, and quaintness was no substitute for purity. Some of those expressions were banished, others left in for flavor.

"There is one more item," said John Cox. "You have omitted a dedication." "I've seen these and they are mostly private messages of affection and inappropriate," I said. "Just as you say," he replied. I thought I detected a faint sigh of relief—one page less. "But maybe," I ventured, "a page of explanation would be a relevant substitute." The man who had already reduced 2,000 pages of a delivered manuscript to 350 showed no enthusiasm. "It's a bit unorthodox," was the way he put it. By way of final resignation he added magnanimously, if critically, "But it may be in keeping with some of the rest. We'll see."

Two days later he agreed, without enthusiasm, that I could write whatever I wanted, not to exceed two pages. What follows comes to you without restriction of any kind.

It was my fortune, good or bad, to come to New York when the inflation of the twenties was well on its way to its destructive zenith. But it provided me with a job and a chance to study and to observe my new country on a spending spree that I was sure would never end. Then, before the ink on my immigration papers was dry, I saw mismanagement and greed take over and, with little regard for mankind, topple us to the ground, while millions among us groveled for food and shelter. Our newly elected leader lashed out at the privileged and he closed all the banks, and the faith he engendered kept us going.

The struggle for a more equitable distribution of the products of labor was a logical consequence of the economic collapse and I had no chance and no desire to avoid the battle. The emotional efforts to create a more equitable society began to develop dangerous proportions. But the new leadership had sufficient reverence for our traditions to halt the excesses which might have destroyed our most treasured rights. We accepted as much of the new revolutionary gospel as would blend with our political past and personal liberty became, if anything, more secure.

Soon we were subjected to a new test. Madness had taken over Europe, cradle of our culture, and the poisons let loose found their way into our saloons and private clubs and onto our street corners. Many of our citizens who knew little of our own past became infected and mouthed the doctrine of hate. Respect for our political progenitors inspired us as we beat back the misguided fools and struggled to reestablish sanity.

The war was won and, although the sacrifice was great, our behavior had been in keeping with the best within us. Yet at the very hour of success, with our emotions high, we looked for other enemies and found them, next door, and we made war on the free and the brave. Beloved Columbia was in greater danger than she had even been before. The memory of our Founders and the framework they had created was our only defense against men who had lost all perspective, and in the end bigoted men and women were destroyed by the Bill of Rights which they had sought to undermine.

The time then came for us to pick up where the Founders had left off and we, as full partners in their Revolution, were privileged to play a significant role in extending to twenty percent of our fellow citizens the personal liberties which had been assured by law and solemnly pledged to all long ago. And we gave our energies to make "All men are created equal" a true measure of our national commitment.

No sooner was the one challenge over than another arose. There was too much nobility in an awakened people to allow the nation born in opposition to oppression to make war against a peasantry twice already in this century brutally assaulted by colonialism—a war without moral justification or sanction of the people.

It took awhile but again the people prevailed. And before long the power of an angry people cleansed our highest office.

So if there is to be a tribute, I know those nearest in kin and closest in affection won't mind if I speak with the utmost admiration about my comrades in these enterprises, and if I say a word of gratitude to the people of New York, the wonderful city into whose midst I came and in which I found a new freedom of spirit. I want especially to mention all those who, recognizing that ours is far from a perfect society, were not content to accept the premise that, because it is better than the others, there is no need for improvement.

CHAPTER ONE

Beginnings

MY BIRTH in 1907 was not regarded as a blessing in my family. I was the eleventh and last O'Dwyer in an already overcrowded five-room house, and while I know my deeply religious mother proclaimed me to be a gift from heaven, I doubt that the other members of the family subscribed to her view.

We lived in Lismirrane, a seventeen-house country village which was part of the parish of Bohola. Today, as then, Bohola has a post office, a substantial parish house, a less pretentious house for the curate, St. Mary's church, and three pubs that do their best business on Sunday during the two hours following the second Mass. Lately it has acquired a monument. In front of the church gate stands a statue of Martin Sheridan, a gift from New Yorkers who had emigrated from the parish and surrounding area. Among the major contributors were Bill O'Dwyer, former mayor of New York, Gene Tunney, former world heavyweight boxing champion, Bill Keary, former president of the Empire State Building Corporation, and John Conwell, whose claim to fame arose from the lawsuit he started against Canon O'Grady, the Bohola parish priest, for back wages before Conwell bid adieu forever to his native heath.

Older Bohola immigrants in America knew Sheridan when he won many track and field athletic contests for his adopted country in 1904, 1908 and 1909. Sheridan was beloved all the more because of an incident that occurred in London in 1908. During the parade of the U.S. team, prior to the start of the Olympic games, Sheridan refused to dip the American flag as he passed in front of the king's box.

Bohola is about in the center of County Mayo, in the west of Ireland, Gaelic in tradition and name. *Mayo* means "plain of the yew tree." Centuries ago invaders, first Normans and then English, found that the woods gave refuge to attacking rebels, so the forest was cut down. There were no yew trees by the time I was born, and very few of any others. Mayo had been overpopulated for many centuries. It has supplied more immigrants to the world than any other area of equal size, with the possible exception of certain parts of Sicily. At different times the landlords tried to drive small farmer-tenants off the land in order to make Mayo a great grazing preserve. The natives' resistance took many forms, the least militant of which was ostracism. The treatment Mayo farmers gave to an English land agent, Captain Boycott, for his tyrannical eviction of tenants, supplied another word to their acquired language.

A generation before my birth the surname in every household of the village was McNicholas—five Patrick McNicholases, three Jameses, and one or two Michaels. The villagers avoided confusion by dropping the surname and referring to a family by the father's first name. Sometimes it was necessary to add the grandfather's name. My maternal grandfather was one of the five Patrick McNicholases. We never heard much about his father, but we knew a great deal about his mother, Peggy, who was widowed when she was quite young. Her children were referred to as if "Peggy" were their surname. Peggy spoke only Gaelic, and her sons grew up with Gaelic as their mother tongue. My mother was bilingual, but during her childhood a campaign against the use of Gaelic wiped out the language in one generation. During my childhood everyone in the neighborhood tried to learn to speak it again. I became part of the nationalist movement, and after three years in secondary school I could speak this expressive and poetic language reasonably well. During the long winter nights I would converse with my mother by the fireside in Gaelic.

Seventy years ago Gaelic-speaking neighbors in Bohola had large families and lived on plots of land of five to twenty acres. Somewhat earlier, greedy landlords used to charge an additional rent for each building besides the main cabin, and the size of the windows too had something to do with the assessment. The tendency, therefore, was toward small dwellings with few and tiny windows and as few outside buildings as possible. Up to the First World War it was common to find people and cattle sharing the same shelter.

The farmer was attached to the land on which he lived even though he did not own it. Oftentimes, influenced by equal affection for two sons, he would split up his sparse holding and give each heir a parcel. The smaller acreage could not possibly provide sustenance for the new family and the farmers were forced to work at least part of the year on larger farms in England and Scotland.

My grandfather Pat McNicholas was expected to look for a wife who had a dowry, for in 1860 it was unthinkable to choose a mate without one. But Pat preferred a cultured woman who would share his humble circumstances. That was to be his dowry.

To supplement his income he set up a country shop. It was stocked with a few farm implements, some simple provisions such as flour, oatmeal and salt, and kerosene. Around Christmastime oranges and raisins were added to the list, thereby providing the children's stockings with unforgettable luxuries. Two Clydesdale horses pulled a tank of kerosene periodically past his door to supply the oil that was destined to light the lamps of the villagers during the long winter nights. The other merchandise he had to get in whatever way he could. Pat bought his flour in Ballina, a seaport fifteen Irish miles away, and drove a mule team to haul shop supplies. The cotton bags in which the flour came were often made into women's undergarments and many a Mayo girl carried the label "Maid of Erin" on her back.

Along his return journey Pat-Peggy stopped at local inns to rest the animals and refresh himself. Penelope Caffrey worked at one such wayside hostelry. Penelope was a young woman of rare charm. She had inherited the knowledge of the use of herbs to cure body ailments and she had learned to play musical instruments, but she had no dowry and there was no rush of matchmakers to knock at her father's door. Pat had the field all to himself. He and Penelope were married and had many children and, having settled in the village of Lismirrane, prospered in a material sense. However, tuberculosis, then the scourge of the Irish, sadly hit their household and took three full-grown members of the family. Another, Bridget, was thin and was suspected of having also been tainted. But she outgrew her malady—if she had ever had it. She was a bright girl, and after completing her formal education at the local school, she continued to study at home, and was finally appointed as assistant schoolteacher in an adjoining village.

In Lismirrane a new school was built and the parish priest advertised in the Dublin papers for a teacher. Patrick O'Dwyer, born in County Cork, one of nine children, and newly graduated from the recently established Drumcondra College in Dublin, answered the advertisement and traveled by stagecoach to Bohola.

Pat-Peggy's break with the dowry tradition had come to plague his family. Consistency required him to resist giving away a dowry with his daughters, and there were three of them who equaled his wife in beauty and charm. Ann was redheaded, Mary flaxen-haired and Bridget as dark-maned as night, but the want of a dowry had stranded all three. By chance the young teacher from Cork cared as little for the dowry custom as did Pat-Peggy.

Bridget McNicholas, she of the raven hair, the assistant

teacher, married Patrick O'Dwyer, whose Gaelic forebears had been Duivers. *Duiver* means "black one," and no attempt was ever made to explain whether black referred to the honorable ancestor's hair, skin, past or character.

It was not much discussed but my paternal grandmother's name was Catherine Norcott. Later, when I asked my sister Katty about it, she volunteered the information that old man Norcott was a planter and a judge and had delivered the most severe sentences to the Irish accused who came before him. When his daughter Catherine married John O'Dwyer she was cast out of the family. She had little choice but, as Shaw observed, influenced by the weather, to become more Irish than the Irish themselves.

As planners, the young teachers failed to earn a passing grade. There was an old Irish saying: Before you marry, be sure of a home wherein to tarry. The young couple showed no respect for the proverb. They moved into Pat-Peggy's already crowded home. A year passed before they bought four acres of land and built the house in which we eleven O'Dwyers were born. A three-room cabin with a roof of oat straw, the house was sufficient for their early needs, but soon it was necessary to build an addition. Slate had been introduced as a more appropriate, although more expensive, roofing, and with the passage of time a new two-story slated addition became attached to the cottage. A stairway to the upper floor zigzagged amazingly from the kitchen of the old portion to the bedroom of the new. The O'Dwyer home with slates on half the roof was looked upon by the occupants with pride and by neighbors with envy. The local carpenter referred to the crooked stairs as evidence of his genius. And for a quarter of a century to follow, the "master's house" remained half thatched and half slated. With a kind of elegant disorder, it came to symbolize the growing family. Over the fireplace hung a picture of the patriot Robert Emmet at the dock accusing the government that had recently condemned him to death. We had come to pay it no heed. The tinkers who came begging felt it would serve them to inquire about it. "And, ma'am," they would say, "are they going to hang the poor *gossur?*" Having disarmed my mother, they would proceed to beg "a dropeen of milk for the child." Their appeal to patriotism was unnecessary. It was the custom in our village never to let even the despised tinkers leave the door without giving them something. Oftentimes the beggar was better off than the giver, but for insurance, the tinker asked his alms "in the honor of God, ma'am."

Sean O'Casey referred to Irish schoolteachers as "the shabby genteel," and that is what they were. They were expected to set a pattern for dress, personal appearance and behavior. In school their children were expected to do better than anyone else, and usually, I think, they did. And although the teacher was respected in the community, he was underpaid then as now. His boots were polished by one or other of his children and his wife saw to it that his "front" and his cuffs were starched and ironed and his suit brushed each morning.

The Irish National schoolteacher was employed by the Board of Education but had no tenure. Under the British system (and now the Irish system) education was supervised by the predominant religious sect in the area and the religious leader became the school manager. So the teacher was hired by the parish priest and could be discharged at his whim, and the parish priest might be full of whims. My mother was one of the casualties of this system. After she had taught in a nearby school for ten years, she had to take a brief leave to have her baby. In a few weeks she had sufficiently recovered to return to her job, but the parish priest had placed a family friend in her place, with not even an attempt at an explanation.

My father, with two or three others, worked secretly to organize a branch of the Irish National Teachers Organization, the first real union of professionals in what was then known as the British Isles. Its chief aim was to wrest from the parish priest his right to discharge teachers without cause. After a long struggle the organizers succeeded, shortly before the First World War. A hearing and the right of counsel for all charges became imbedded in their terms of employment. The union paid the suspended teacher his full salary until the hearings had been completed and a decision reached, and it also paid the legal fees and other expenses. In light of some of the labor gains in the last forty years, these accomplishments may seem trivial, but no union had ever achieved so much against such great odds. With the union organized, my father's head was lifted a little higher and he walked with a bolder step, and Father O'Grady grew meaner and more frustrated.

The discord between the clergy and the O'Dwyers went beyond the issue of educational reform. Although we felt a deep religious commitment to the Catholic Church, at the same time the resurgence of national feeling fostered a grave suspicion of the clergy. To avoid schisms that had weakened the Church at another period, such ambivalence, while discouraged, was tolerated. Nevertheless it was not uncommon for townspeople to ridicule the "odd" one such as P. D. Kenny, the local writer, who "rejected the church because he had a fight with the priest."

The higher up the clerical ladder, the more the suspicion seemed warranted. The Council of Bishops could always be relied upon to take appropriate disciplinary action against recalcitrant Catholic youths who joined any freedom movement. Between 1916 and 1920, through the official act of the Bishops of Ireland, young people were excommunicated or on the eve of a military engagement denied absolution and confession because of their association with the Sinn Fein Movement. *(Sinn Fein,* meaning "we ourselves," symbolized abandonment of the age-old hope of help from France or Spain.)

My father was as much in sympathy with the young as he was hostile to the clergy and, owing to the latter's performance, perhaps eventually more so. The more the forces of revolt came to the fore, the more our pastor, Father John, by now a canon, persisted in using the pulpit as a political sounding board, often branding the young freedom soldiers murderers. He had no word of criticism for the Black and Tans, a makeshift military operation recruited from British jails. (They got their name from the fact that they were hastily provided with whatever clothing could be scrounged up for them—some black, some khaki.)

My father was required to say certain prayers in school, but his prayers somehow got mixed up in politics—there was a special emphasis on the prayer that implored God "to defend us in battle against the wickedness and snares of the devil." We all knew who the devil was. The prayers ended with the hope that God would "look kindly on Ireland's struggle and bring confusion to our enemies." As for Ireland's friends at home and abroad, the master requested the Creator to see to it personally that "their shadows never grow less." It was as far as he could go in making God a partner in our sedition.

The master encouraged the young people in the neighborhood to study. To those who showed promise he became a private tutor after they had completed their schooling. He was paid extra for that by the pupils' parents. He initiated a program of adult education, and migratory workers back from England for the winter were offered further instruction under the dim light of the kerosene lamp. He liked to teach geography, and the British failures at the Dardanelles were now beginning to excite the pupils' attention. The straits on the school map were indicated by one line without evidence of separation. "Here are the Turks," quoth the master, "on both sides, and the British are trying to get through." Quoth the pupil from the mountainside, "They'll never make it." The master was good at mathematics and would survey the odd-shaped fields for farmers who rented land from each other. As his sons grew, each in turn held the surveyor's chain and learned the craft. The neighbors came to him to draw up certain agreements, such as marriage contracts. On occasion he would act as bookkeeper for local merchants.

Here and there in Bohola you could see the ruins of

abandoned dwellings—mute evidence that hunger and the battering ram, the landlord's dread demolition machine, had overcome their occupants during famine and eviction. The old famine songs were seldom sung. It was in the States that they survived. During the Depression, when the American left began to revive old working songs, I heard some of them for the first time.

> The potatoes they grow small, they grow small
> over here, over here.
> The potatoes they grow small and we ate them
> one and all
> And we ate them skins and all—over here.

It was my father's custom to send to the nearest town for the *Freeman's Journal* or the *Irish Independent.* The papers belied their titles; their slanted news favored Great Britain. They arrived by train from Dublin to the local newsdealer. More than half the residents of our village were unable to read English, but the master read the contents and explained their message to the assembled neighbors sitting in the O'Dwyer kitchen as he held the paper close to the light of the kerosene lamp. My mother was the lone objector, and she took silent exception to some of the personal habits of some of the guests. We had no spittoon, and many a visitor, as he faced the open fire, missed the mark.

Because the Black and Tan atrocities concerned all of us greatly, our house was a meeting place each evening. News of the destruction of Tan outposts was met with an assortment of sounds and gestures. One neighbor would thump his knee; another, looking ceilingward, would whistle. Grim silence accompanied the news of the capture of an Irish Republican Army soldier. Dark memories of past wrongs came to stand by the immediate injustice and filled the room with hate. Memories of the Penal Days were revived. During the evening someone would recite snatches of the poetry of Thomas Davis,

Protestant political leader of the Young Ireland Movement of 1842. A favorite quotation described their wrongs:

> They bribed the flock, they bribed the son
> To sell the priest and rob the sire,
> Their dogs were taught alike to run,
> Upon the scent of wolf and friar.
> Among the poor or on the moor
> Were hid the pious and the true
> While traitor knave, and recreant slave,
> Had riches, rank and retinue.

My father, for all that he was small in stature, was reputed to have been an athlete in his youth. He passed none of his prowess on to his children. Of the six sons—William, James, John, Frank, Thomas and Paul—only Thomas showed any sign of excelling in athletics. He died of peritonitis at eighteen. Thomas was nearest to me in age, about four years my senior. I remember telling my parents about finding cigarette ashes beside the chair on which Thomas was seated in a neighbor's house. Tommy denied the charge. My father accepted his denial and lectured me about telling tales. He made reference to something Joseph did to his brothers in the biblical story. I thought it strange that he did not think much of Joseph, who seemed to be our favorite.

Tommy always made a likely candidate for any accusation. My father seemed to overlook the smoking rather conveniently. I thought he felt that the evidence lacked substance, but I think in truth the decision was meant to be a lesson to the "informer." In another incident Tommy did not fare so well. Jack Nappy was a man in his eighties. He had been a Fenian, and that made him something special. The Fenians were members of the secret revolutionary movement initiated by Civil War veterans in the United States, who felt that with the war's end their acquired skills should be put to work for the cause of Irish freedom. Old Jack was working in the potato pit in a nearby field. The cold winter weather had congealed the raised and frozen clay that covered the potatoes stored in pyramidlike mounds. To get at the potatoes it was necessary for old Jack to crouch on his knees, with his head into the mound and the seat of his corduroy britches pointing toward the road. The temptation was altogether too great for a boy passing by on the way from school. His aim was accurate, and a pebble connected truly with Jack Nappy's behind. Jack's buttock stung and his dignity was shattered. Withdrawing his head from the pit, the old man saw a boy retreating. The scholar was wearing a gray jacket. That day my brother was wearing a gray jacket. The old man came to the house to complain, and my father reviewed the evidence and arrived at the conclusion that, despite his denials, Tom was the culprit. He administered a thrashing to him in another room while we all waited in pain. My mother did not interfere. She neither justified nor chided the father of the household. The culprit was not my brother but another boy, coming from another school that day, who had worn a gray jacket.

On another occasion, however, my father defended my brother Jack, who was falsely accused of mischief during Sunday Mass. As was the custom, many of the boys stayed at the back of the church under the gallery, close to the door, the place where casual worshipers fulfilled the requirements, descending on one knee and technically avoiding the sin of disobedience of the First Precept of the Church. They came late, about the middle of the first Gospel, and (scarcely measuring up to their obligations) left in the middle of the last. During the elevation of the Host all is silent and profound. To the worshipers it means that at that moment a wheat wafer becomes flesh—not symbolic but actual—and the wine in the chalice becomes actual blood. With the last bell signaling that the Consecration has been completed, the suppressed coughing breaks out like a series of motor explosions, with cylinders missing. At the moment when all heads were being raised, someone took a piece of plaster from the back wall and, during the diversion, tossed it at a man who was known to be a chronic complainer. The victim looked around and thought he saw Jack. He protested against the "blackguardism of the master's son," and when Mass ended he rushed with his complaint to the canon. God's servant could not have been more delighted. That Sunday became the canon's day as well as God's. He committed his sense of moral indignation to paper. He said he thought it outrageous that one who was charged with the duty of teaching proper behavior to the neighbors' children was setting so poor an example by failing to control his own, even in the house of the Lord.

Investigation disclosed that Jack was at another Mass that Sunday, and nobody would believe that Jack would have gone to two. A hand-delivered answer dispatched to the parish priest branded the charge as lies and contained the further announcement that the accusations, oral and written, could be satisfied only in an appropriate action in a court of law against both accusers. With the same dispatch, the pastor of our flock threw another poor sheep to the wolves. He said he was sorry for the error and would gladly testify before the court, if necessary, that such an accusation had indeed been made by the parishioner, who was now guilty of the further offense of embarrassing his parish priest. The parishioner, now abandoned by his protector, came to the house in panic proclaiming he was a poor man and had not meant to falsely accuse Jack. Suing him would place him in jeopardy of losing his house and small holdings of land, his only means of livelihood for his family. I doubt very much if my father had ever had any intention of suing, but with the canon out of the way, there was no further point to it. In any case, my mother knew the wife of the accuser and would have worked against any lawsuit.

Children in the area were required to work. We did not have any hobbies. From an educational standpoint, the O'Dwyer children may have lived in a different atmosphere from that of the other children who attended the three-room school. But apart from that, we had to do the things that other kids in a country area had to do. Our parents had no money. As a matter of fact, we had outstanding bills in most mercantile establishments in two adjoining towns, and when payday came, a few shillings would be allotted to the ones most neglected at that point. None of us was paid any sort of allowance for our work in the fields, and we helped to bring in the vegetables and potatoes and the hay and oats for the animals. We had a milch cow and a horse (half Arab and half Connemara) and trap (something like a sidecar). We had no farm machinery, and most of the work was done by hand.

There was need of raising fuel for the harsh winter months. The "turf" came from the bogs, which contained a semidecayed vegetation, the accumulation of a million years. It had to be turned over to the sun and further cured. As we worked at this on windy days, chemical-filled dust irritated our eyes so much that we could hardly see. We worked with bare feet, and the bog oozed up between our toes. It was supposed to cure corns. As a boy I brought out the dry turf with a donkey and cart, usually borrowed from a neighbor, and took it home. Every boy, no matter who he was, was expected to perform these chores. I didn't consider it burdensome and we never thought that type of child labor caused any measure of ill health. On the contrary, it seemed to be beneficial to physical development. Work was one's contribution to one's continued existence as a member of a family. I don't remember really liking field work; I don't remember resenting it either.

It was the custom for the community to come to the aid of any landowning widow until her children grew strong enough to take over, particularly during harvest time, when the oats, if not taken off, will shell on the field and become useless. All the neighbors, friendly or unfriendly, would gather one day to plant the seed or bring in the harvest for the widow. The gathering was referred to as a *mehil.* No widow's children starved.

Life in a rural community in Ireland had its difficulties. Almost everyone was in debt at some time or other, but it was customary for adult children to pay off the parents' debt, and local shopkeepers, recognizing the custom, extended credit and lost nothing by it. My family was no exception. The monthly paycheck was juggled to pay a mite to several merchants who had more patience than hard business judgment. Small farmers, of necessity, were also migratory workers. In England the Mayo small farmer, turned migratory laborer, worked hard and long hours and slept on hay beds in barns; the food was poor and the living conditions were atrocious. But he came back to Bohola each year with sufficient money to help keep the family going for at least another year. His stay at home was not idle. He prepared his own acreage for spring tilling and in season sired another child. Martin, a child in the master's class, was one of nine children. He was paraded out for his performance in front of the class, and as the story was repeated, he was conscious of the punch line. "How many children in your house, Martin?" the master would ask. "Nine, seyr," came the reply. "Name them, Martin, and give their ages." "John is twelve, Mary is eleven, Michael is ten, Pat is nine, Luke is seven." At this point there was an interruption. "Luke is seven?" "Yes, seyr," Martin would say. "That year me father schtayed in England."

The pleasures for young people consisted of country dancing. Before World War I this took place in the kitchen of a country house, with the melodeon, the flute and the fiddle providing the music. After the war, interfering "Yanks," who had accumulated some money in America, or Irishmen returning from some years in England set up dance halls throughout the country. It was a way of making a dull life more tolerable. The clergy concluded that the behavior at the dances led to sin and such institutions were unworthy of Holy Ireland. They set out to condemn them from the pulpit, and when that didn't work, some of the more aggressive took to the roads at night to break up couples in loving embraces.

Children were required to tip their hats to the priest, and the habit grew through boyhood into manhood. But the dance halls as well as politics raised questions, and some of the people began to doubt the potency of the priest's curse.

In the fifth century, when the Christian missioners came from Brittany, they found a people believing in a hereafter and worshiping Beal Tinne, the Gaelic god of sun and fire. The Christians did not attempt to destroy the custom of praying one day each year around the fire. They continued the custom and in the course of time moved the day from May 1, the day of the god of fire, to June 21, St. John's Day. St. John's Day and night had special significance and rated next to St. Patrick's. It was celebrated at every crossroads with a bonfire. As children we gathered sticks and all manner of discarded wood and augmented this with turf contributed by the neighbors. At night people came to look at the fire, sit on the adjoining sod fence and talk about current news and old legend. Each St. John's Day our neighbor built a small fire in front of her house and said her rosary as she walked around it. The Christians did not destroy the circle, the symbol of the sun god. They simply put a cross in the middle of it and the Celtic cross was born.

Contrary to popular belief, the famous Irish wake was not a happy occasion. The custom was to supply a number of clay pipes to visitors. Children filled the pipes with tobacco while the body of the deceased was being washed by neighboring women. Both of these customs were unexplained and undoubtedly had pre-Christian origins. When a visitor came he took a pipe, said "God rest the dead" and proceeded to light it. Sometimes the clay extracted the moisture from his lip and the skin stuck to the stem. Later it was said to create skin cancer. Women keened over the body, and the appearance of a relative at the "corpse house," or wake, was the signal for all the women to converge and keen in unison. It was a crying song of praise, and the most persistent theme chided the deceased for leaving. The older ones used Gaelic and others interspersed English with Gaelic. "Why Did You Die?" became the title for a well-known folk song, sung by no less an artist than John McCormack.

Once I was near our house at night and heard people in song down along the river. Pat-Tom's wife was on her deathbed. The song persisted. I told other boys what I had heard. The word spread through the village the following day that I had heard the banshee cry. (Sometimes when death came to a well-known Milesian family the banshee would come to wail against the night wind.)

Stories of persons having seen ghosts were common and nobody disbelieved them. Some were less affected by the stories than others, but it was a brave man who walked the mile or two alone to his home after a night of visiting or talking. Storytelling was a fine art, and in an area officially denied education it had been responsible for the survival of local history. People pointed to the spot a few hundred yards from our house where the female hedge teacher had taught the rudiments of education to some of the children whose parents could spare them from the field and could contribute the food that she required as her tuition. The school was a leanto under a turf bank, with rude heather grass and oat thatch the only protection from the rainy southwest wind. The Catholic Emancipation Act in 1829 saw the beginning of the end of the hedge school.

Our family was large even by Mayo standards. Ten children grew up to maturity; one died in infancy. We enjoyed little privacy and we never felt a special need for it. We did not think there was any hardship in a whole bunch of boys' sleeping together in what now seem to be extremely crowded conditions. There was no inside plumbing; rainwater from the roof provided for the washing, and water hauled from the common well some distance away took care of the table. Nobody had time to spoil anybody in our household and lack of funds was enough to prohibit pampering. We were taught not only to look after ourselves but also, more important, to look after one another.

Whatever money my father earned he spent on the education of the four girls. The sons did not show much inclination for staying around. William, the firstborn, was guided toward the priesthood. Two years of study at the Irish College of the University of Salamanca in preparation for Holy Orders failed to diminish his interest in the Porteros' daughter. Finally, fearing the shame that abandonment of his calling would bring to the family, he decided not to return to Ireland, then or ever. He set sail from Cherbourg and went to America. My mother's dreams were shattered and my father was angry. We children could never understand why. The growing anticlericalism should have made Bill's decision most welcome. In retrospect, we think it was felt that the education was wasted and that in payment for it Bill should have returned, become a teacher or a doctor and helped out the rest of the growing family. We were forbidden to bring up his name in conversation and grew up knowing little about him. I don't believe that my father's attitude would have been different if he had known that one day Bill would be mayor of a town bigger than London, an ambassador equal in importance to the emissary to the Court of St. James's, chairman of an Allied Control Commission governing Italy, and a general in the army, the equal of British General Wilson, whose father had sacked Cork City. Happily, about six months before his death in 1920, my father received a conciliatory letter from Bill, and some of the atmosphere of resentment lifted.

My sisters were more dependable and easier to deal with. After initial training at home they were sent to teachers' training colleges in Great Britain. (The Irish schools were full.) All four became schoolteachers, and all taught abroad before returning to Ireland.

Whatever I knew of my father did not come from any confidence entrusted to me by him. Irish fathers, whatever their feelings, rarely got close to their sons. This was a phenomenon peculiar to Ireland; no such inhibitions attached to the emigrant Irishmen raising families in America. My father spoke very little about himself or his people, even about his experiences. I had to learn from observation or gossip. From his earnestness in the classroom I became aware of his firm belief in education. From his conversations with neighbors at paper-reading time I discovered his commitment to national freedom. His resolute resentment of the clergy was ever clear.

I knew he was fond of the people around the village and that, unlike my mother, he had no snobbishness in his character. Nevertheless he was not above using the newspaper to play tricks on his less erudite neighbors. "What was that about the world champion?" a neighbor asked as old Tom Martin came into the garden where they were stacking hay. "Yes," said my father, pretending not to know that old Tom was within earshot, "it states right here that before ten thousand people in Philadelphia, Irish Tom McNicholas knocked out his opponent and is to be picked instead of Jess Willard to meet Jack Johnson. He's sure, it says, to be the next heavyweight champion of the world." The old man began to shake his head. "What's the matter, Tom?" said the neighbor. "Didn't you hear the master read out of the newspaper about your son's great success?" (Irish Tom had, in truth, never met with any success and was reputed only to be some sort of sparring partner around gymnasiums in Philadelphia.) "The next champion of the world," mused old Tom. "I'm thinking of the terrible hurt later to my poor son when some young one bates him."

Later that month, when the Mollineauxs came to spend a holiday at our house, my father was provided with another opportunity to hoodwink the neighbors. My sister May had a room in their home in Newcastle on Tyne, where she taught school. The word got around the village that Mollineaux was a Freemason. A Mason had some special deal going with the devil.

"Is he a Freemason, Master?" one of them asked my father.

"Is he a Mason?" repeated the master. "Well, yesterday Ena and Bruno [our two dogs] were in the kitchen. Mr. Mollineaux lifted his hand and made two horses out of them and put the two lads on their backs, and in no time the horses have disappeared and the dogs are there again." News of this feat of black magic spread.

At about the same time a neighbor was stealing some of our cabbage. A few days after the horse story my father innocently remarked that Mollineaux had told him that he would show who was stealing the cabbage, and the larceny temporarily ceased.

The master was a student of Shakespeare and, as children in the seventh grade, we were required to act out parts of *The Merchant of Venice* and *Hamlet.* We knew our lines by heart. Later, in New York, I could speak with authority as to whether the Bard had not produced in the former an anti-Jewish treatise. In school I felt that Shylock was a mean-spirited old Jew, and when Jessica married a Christian and left her father, I was all for her and felt it was good enough for him. I thought his plea "Hath not a Jew hands, organs, dimensions, senses . . .?" was an argument too easily overcome. The Bard was too clever by far to have presented so weak a case and would have worked up a better one if he had not been somewhat tainted. I applauded what happened to Shylock in court, and I thought Portia's plea was magnificent. Shylock was the only Jew I knew.

My father died of pneumonia when I was thirteen, and according to custom, his body was taken to the chapel of St. Mary's church a day before the funeral. The funeral was the largest seen in Bohola, and its size outraged the canon. There was no embalming. Putrefaction had begun and liquid from the coffin fell on the chapel floor. The gravediggers were volunteers, and no one thought to clean up the wet spot when the coffin was taken away, whereupon the canon dispatched a message to my sister May demanding that she remove the "drippings from your father's coffin." His note was delivered as we returned from the grave. In our village people closed ranks when death came, and any one of a hundred neighbors along the path the messenger had taken would have attended to the problem. It was a crushing note and the canon had his revenge. I thought of some way of getting even, but it was a sacrilege to hit a priest, and a sacrilege was the worst kind of sin. No priest would grant absolution from it; you had to walk all the way to Ballaghadereen, a long trip, to tell it to the bishop, and you couldn't be sure how he would respond. I finally was pacified by the very prospect of the journey, and instead of plotting revenge, I read Moore's lyric from the songbook on the piano and dreamed about what could have been if the canon had not been the Lord's anointed.

Oh Monarch
Though sweet are our home recollections,
Though sweet are the tears that from tenderness fall,
Though sweet are our friendships, our hopes, our affections,
Revenge on a tyrant is sweeter than all.

After my father's death my mother arranged to have May remain in Bohola to take up the vacancy in the school. May was never asked if she wanted to do it; it was taken for granted that she would perform in the best interests of the family rather than in her own. The fact was that she had come to enjoy life in Newcastle on Tyne and never wanted to return to Ireland. Dutiful, as daughters were supposed to be, she offered no protest.

But the canon did not want May back in Bohola teaching school. One O'Dwyer to make his life unpleasant had been enough, he thought, and he wasn't going to have another if he could help it. While the decision hung in the balance my mother sought an audience with Bishop Morrisroe at the chancery office in Ballaghadereen. It was a palatial castle built in the early nineteenth century, with a long private drive from the main road to the elegantly decorated heavy wooden door at the main entrance. It was a big event for her. She bent one knee to kiss the bishop's ring and to thank him for the audience. He had come from Charlestown and knew who she was. The bishop, she reported later, listened to her with much interest and sympathy. He overruled the canon and my sister became the assistant teacher in my father's school. Thereafter, until the canon's death, she was to feel the resentment born of his frustration.

May remained in Bohola, married a teacher from another

school and retired a few years ago, leaving our house and four acres of land vacant for the first time in seventy years. There is a sad and plaintive song called "The Old House." It depicts the ruins of what once was a joyous place. I thought of the song and bought the place from my sister. It had too much in it, I couldn't let it go. It was torn down and replaced a few years ago by the O'Dwyer-Cheshire Home, now used as a permanent residence for thirty handicapped patients as part of the Cheshire Trust.*

During the time I was growing up, and long before women had the right to vote, there was much agitation for women's rights in various countries, and the echo was heard, though faintly, in our village. My mother played a part in the struggle, which was led by two Protestant women named McManus. Their family's fortune had been squandered in London by male members of the household. Only a shell of an ancestral house remained, in which the two unmarried sisters lived, with diametrically opposite views about Ireland. They had fine manners, old but elegant clothes and good horses. Miss Emma refused to believe that their days as "gentry" were numbered; Miss Lotty understood what the struggle of the people meant. She wrote several books on the subject, was eternally loyal to Ireland and threw herself completely into freedom's cause as a sort of local Countess Markievicz.

Miss Emma, equally true to her own beliefs, wanted women to make their abilities felt in the social and economic life of the country, and my mother, who had taught until just before the birth of her seventh child, became secretary of the organization

*Leonard Cheshire, Wing Commander in the RAF and British observer of Hiroshima and Nagasaki, used his own home to help an army veteran dying of cancer. With help in short supply, he went to the local hospital to learn how to care for the dying man. There are now one hundred and sixty such homes across the world, each locally operated and tending thirty wheelchair patients suffering from chronic illnesses. There are seven in Ireland; Bohola's is the first in the western province of Connaught.

Miss Emma headed. Their conflicting views on the Anglo-Irish ascendancy did not prevent the two from working together, and they made constant appeals to the local women to get themselves out of bondage.

This secretarial work, an occasional song at the old harmonium in our house, Sunday Mass in Bohola and its social aftermath, and a trip to Swinford and Kiltimagh, market towns a few miles away, once a month on payday were my mother's only diversions from the drudgery of rearing children. No doctor had attended her when she gave birth to her brood. The obstetrician was a midwife named *Brigeen na broig* ("Little Bridget of the One Shoe"). She lived alone in a hut four miles away. Brigeen and her equipment seemed to be the antithesis of all the hygienic, masked nurses and disinfected instruments that I have seen in maternity wards since then. On reflection, I marvel that there were no serious repercussions for mother or children.

Bean an Kark gibboch nuar a hogan she a hall is the saying. Translated, it means: The hen is slovenly when she is raising her young. I can't say this was true in our home. My mother's pride in her personal appearance would not have permitted it. Besides, it would have ill become the secretary of a women's organization devoted to cleanliness in the home to be out of step with her own oft-expressed slogan, Cleanliness is next to godliness.

Another of my mother's expressions served as a warning against any sign of sexual revolt. She was at once a very gentle and an austere person. "I hope there is no dirt on you that water cannot wash off," she would be heard to say. This, a scolding for a threatened and most regrettable possible injury to the soul, was meant to strike at the conscience.

In my youth sex was verboten, both as a subject for discussion and as an activity. We learned about sex from the animals—dogs and bulls and the stallion that impregnated the waiting mares in Michael Murphy's yard every market day. On that occasion the walls of the yard were lined with the young. It was a show we were forbidden to see and one we never missed. But in spite of such lessons we children gained no insight into the origin of our own species. We were taught and we believed that we had been found under a head of cabbage. It never occurred to us that the instincts of the farm animals were the same as our own. The discovery in puberty came as a shock, all the more shameful as the activity was so furtive and shrouded in secrecy.

All of Ireland was affected by Jansenism and had been tainted with it for centuries after the doctrine had been declared heretical. Because Irish seminarians had to be smuggled out to France, Spain and Italy to be trained for the priesthood, the Irish hierarchy preached a most intolerant Catholicism. This doctrine traveled with the famine ships to Boston, New York and San Francisco. (It was not always so. Before the Penal Laws this hard line, with its severe attitude toward sex, was not typical of Irish Christianity. When Con O'Neill, powerful head of the O'Neills of Ulster, had a child by Mrs. Kelly, the wife of a Drogheda blacksmith, the British overlords, in keeping with their own customs, would not recognize this firstborn. O'Neill, however, insisted, and finally Henry VIII conferred on Matthew O'Neill in 1558 the title of Baron Dungannon. But that was long before the Penal Laws made it necessary for young Irish clerics to be trained abroad.)

In this connection, I recall being awakened by my mother at five o'clock in the morning when I was about twelve. Our neighbor Martin Brennan was at the door. I was sent running in my bare feet across the fields to the neighboring village to carry the message to Mrs. Brennan's mother that she was needed. Maria Brennan was in labor, about to have her first baby. But I was told nothing about that.

An unmarried girl who became pregnant was made to suffer indescribable shame. The disgrace applied equally to the man, and he too was shunned by neighbors and friends. There was no place thereafter for either of them, and each bore the stigma for as long as he or she stayed in the neighborhood. Such scandals were referred to for generations, long after the miserable miscreants had fled the scene.

It was assumed that men and women of the parish were virgins when they married, and they married late—men averaging about thirty-five and women twenty-seven or twenty-eight. How young people behaved after they left was another matter, and the release that Irish immigrants experienced in other cultures—well, that's another story!

My mother was handy with scissors and needle. Using what would seem to have been the first Singer sewing machine, she turned my father's clothes inside out and remade them for the boys to wear. Not until I went to secondary school did I wear my first tailor-made suit from "Dummy" Kilgallon, the mute tailor who lived a mile away. By that time my father was dead and there was no suit to turn inside out.

Bridget O'Dwyer made certain the girls learned to play the harmonium and piano. But trying to get musical appreciation into the boys was a failure, and the project was abandoned. Among the brothers, only Bill pursued a training in music, and the rest of us were limited to the Jew's harp. The girls had good voices and sang light opera and semiclassical songs. They looked down on folk music as being too common, and great stress was laid on the undesirability of singing through the nose, a style to which other villagers were given whenever they got together to perform. Theoretically, the girls also were required to clean, bake, knit, sew and wash clothes. But Katty, the oldest, was unteachable and never learned to cook or do housework until her marriage at sixty.

Katty's salary as a teacher made her a very eligible candidate for the post of farmer's wife, but her disposition and training prohibited it. She knew that as such she would be expected to feed the chickens and pigs as well as to teach. So she spurned the amateur matchmaker who sought her out and instead took up learning in a serious way. After her teaching apprenticeship in England she returned to teach in the home school—the canon by then had given up the fight—and continued her education at the National University in Dublin, earning several higher degrees. At her retirement she married Tom McCaffrey, a widower from Dundalk, and moved there to complete a lifetime of excitement and happiness.

Bridget O'Dwyer always felt that her children were better—were required to be better. And we were to be judged by our deeds, not our looks. "Handsome is as handsome does," she would say. She was a proud person, proud that her mother was cultured, proud that her father was industrious and sober, and she sought to transmit that pride to us. It was class consciousness with more than a little snobbery. But we accepted what she taught without question. Rebellion was unthinkable, to all but Bill. I didn't envy my oldest brother; I thought he was unjust and didn't play the game. He had left us.

My mother was respected by everyone who knew her, and her poverty never got in her way. She had a unique gift for making the best of things. She would prepare the main meal on Fridays as if it were any other—usually potatoes, some variant of creamed onions, no meat. Thursday was market day in Kiltimagh and the tinkers sold salt herrings for a penny apiece. (We were too far from the seacoast for fresh fish.) You could smell the herrings before you entered town. I have never been sure whether it was the Galway herrings or the Church's approval of fish as a Friday substitute that accounted for my aversion. All through my life I have found fish distasteful.

But my mother never seemed to care. After the meal was over, still seated at her customary place at the head of the table, she would cross herself reverently and, eyes cast upward, invariably thank the Creator for all He had provided. "Thanks be to God for this lovely meal." It had an air of faith but no ring of truth. It was pure propaganda and went down no better than the onions.

CHAPTER TWO

Growing Up in Ireland

WHEN I was seven, approaching my First Communion, Father Denis O'Hara, the curate at St. Mary's, stopped me outside the chapel, where I was taking instruction. He introduced a visiting English priest. "Paul," Father Denis said to me, "should Ireland help to fight the Germans?" I said, "Yes, Father." "Why?" said Father Denis. "Because," I said, "the Germans are killing nuns and orphans in Belgium."

Beginning in 1914 the British talked, and the Irish media repeated stories, about "little Belgium" and the rights of nations great and small to be free and to enjoy self-determination. They also talked about Germans who had, according to the recruiting sergeants, "butchered nuns and killed Catholic orphans in Belgium." By 1915 the country accepted this propaganda. The people were anti-German and accordingly pro-British. Belgium seemed like Ireland, a small Catholic country. (We knew nothing of the Belgian Congo.)

To help recruitment the British awarded the Victoria Cross to Private Michael O'Leary, a young Kerry private, and brought Michael's old father to the fair of Macroom. "And now," said the recruiting sergeant, "we give you, all the way from Kerry, the father of that sterling, that courageous, that brave Irishman, the wearer of the prized Victoria Cross. I am speaking of course of Private Michael O'Leary, and his father is here to tell you how he feels about the filthy Hun." The old man stood proudly in the crowded square. "I'm telling ye," he said. "Sign up and fight to bate the Kayser, and if you don't, he'll come over here and he'll do to ye fot the English did long ago." The crowd roared with laughter. The ballad singer got in the mood and sang about what happened to Pat Sheehan, blinded in the service of Lord Cardigan, the general who charged the "light brigade" into the jaws of death at Balaklava.

Then Irish youths—dear countrymen,
Take heed of what I say,
For if you join the English ranks,
You'll surely rue the day.
And whenever you are tempted
A soldiering to go,
Remember poor blind Sheehan
Of the Glen of Aherlow.

The appearance of O'Leary senior aroused no special Irish pride either. There had been little spirit of nationalism since the latter part of the nineteenth century, and Yeats, decrying it, wrote: "Romantic Ireland is dead. It's with O'Leary in the grave."

Then, on Easter Monday 1916, a handful of Irishmen, among them James Connolly, the radical labor leader, Patrick Pearse, the poet, professor and Gaelic scholar, and other writers, teachers and poets, led insurgents into central Dublin and issued their now historic proclamation. Therewith the Rebellion, after some false starts and leadership disagreements, commenced, taking the British military by surprise. The newspapers came from Dublin to Bohola bringing the news: the famed Dublin post office was in the hands of the rebels, and British gunboats were leveling Sackville Street. I remember my father telling the people gathered round to hear that it was "foolish for a small group of men to take on the Empire." But take it on they did and held the post office for a week. Then the long guns leveled the area and ended what came to be called Easter Week. The rebels totaled 1,100 men, including Connolly's citizen army, which marched under the new banner, the Plow and Stars.*

If the British had not arrested and, a week later, executed the leaders, the Easter Rebellion probably would have remained an obscure, futile, senseless, hopeless incident. As it was, British reaction triggered resentment and revived memories of accumulated wrongs, and young men looked for buried Fenian rifles and ballad singers resurrected "The Croppy Boy."

> It was early, early in the spring,
> The birds did twitter and they did sing.
> The birds did flitter from tree to tree,
> And the song they sang was "Old Ireland Free."

I saw some of the rifles, then over fifty years old. The barrels seemed to be as long as fishing poles. Jack Straw, the ballad singer, sang to farmers in the square in Kiltimagh, "Who fears to speak of Easter Week? Who dares its fate deplore?" In no time at all the Black and Tans were in full swing, and American Quakers again were investigating military atrocities.

But abstract ideas of freedom and liberty come slowly to a country people and the fighting did not spread soon to Bohola. Children of merchants, teachers and laborers were the ones most interested, in both the Rebellion and the subsequent War

*Connolly had been a labor agitator in America prior to 1914. He left New York that year for Dublin, changing places with James Larkin. Connolly headed the Irish Transport Workers Union, the first union in Ireland, and led the first strike, of tram-car operators, in Dublin. He was later executed for his role in the Easter Rebellion. Larkin, who took Connolly's place in New York (during the hysteria following World War I), was convicted of sedition and sentenced to Sing Sing. He was later pardoned by Governor Smith, returned to Ireland, and was elected to Parliament, where his son now serves.

of Independence. But finally come it did, and involved the neighbors' children. The Bohola Volunteers trained in our yard.

As fierce reaction to conscription set in, the Jack Straw sales of the ballad about Mrs. McGrath and her son Ted took an upward swing, and Jack himself sometimes sang it when the constables were not about. The song started with the recruiting officer, who gave the brave *gossoon* the "Queen's Shilling."

"Oh, Mrs. McGrath," the sergeant said,
"Would you like to make a soldier of your son Ted.
With a suit of blue and a fine cocked hat,
O Mrs. McGrath, wouldn't you like that,
With my rye aye, foll the diddle aye, toory oo ry oo ry aye."

After many intervening verses Mr. Straw got to the point of Ted's return:

Then up steps Ted without legs, and in
their places were two wooden pegs.
She kissed him a dozen times or two, saying
"Holy Moses, it isn't you."

And then the "too ry aye" merely provided the pause. The impatient crowd started the next verse before the tramp could catch his breath.

"Arah! were you drunk or were you blind, when you
left your two fine legs behind,
Or was it walking upon the say, cut your two fine
legs from the knees away, with my too ry aye."

The Royal Irish Constabulary were on the watch for such seditious rhyme. They constituted the local civilian police force in Bohola. The insignia on the blue uniform and the flat-topped hat was a harp topped by the Crown. At different times the R.I.C. were liked, tolerated and hated. At times when they constituted the intelligence agency of the Crown they were peelers, named for Lord Peel, the British prime minister who first recruited them. And at those times the ballad singer found insistent demand for "The Peeler and the Goat," and to promote sales at the cattle fair he furtively sang it:

> The Peeler went out one night on duty and patrolio.
> He met a goat upon the road and took him for a strollero.

The arrest of the goat on sedition and the goat's subsequent prosecution were bound to delight the country people as much as they annoyed the officials.

I had two brothers, Frank and Jack, who were conscription (draft bait) material. Jack joined the Volunteers, which soon after the Rebellion changed its purpose and became a force on which the British could no longer count. Frank meanwhile went to England to work. He was sixteen and very tall and in England he took a man's job. In the course of it the draft caught up with him and he skipped back to Ireland, the conscription officer at his heels.

Sergeant O'Connor, from the Bohola barracks of the R.I.C., shortly afterward came to our house one Sunday afternoon. He was believed to be an unusually enthusiastic informer. "God save all here," said the sergeant, using the anglicized native idiom. "God save you, kindly sergeant," said my mother, answering in kind. "What brings you to my door?" my father demanded from outside, as if he didn't know. "I'm looking for a tramp," said the sergeant. The insult may not have been intended, but it made no difference. The blood drained from my father's face and he turned to enter the house. My mother shouted to the sergeant to get out if he valued his life and ran to where she knew the gun was hidden. A moment later the constable burst through the door in full flight, and cycling down the road, hardly noticed my brother Frank playing "pitch and toss" with a bunch of other boys.

But my father had gone as far as he could go without risking his job, and my brother's presence at home became a definite threat to my father's livelihood. Jack put up with friends in other parts until, a constabulary having begun to search for him and other Volunteers, he left for England and later New York, where Bill and Jim awaited him. Soon after Jack left, the heat was on the Bohola Volunteers, and the drilling and Morse Code practice left our yard for safer, more secluded places.

Jim had left for New York in 1912, when he was eighteen. From that base he had worked on luxury liners as a bartender, while his oldest brother, Bill, carried hod for the construction of the Woolworth Building. When Jack joined them they were living in Hell's Kitchen in the apartment of a Mrs. Losty, a Kildare woman.

On one occasion Jimmy had left his German ship at Southampton on its way to Germany and had come home to visit. His German boss had told him to take the week off and catch the ship on its return. In the meantime, however, Archduke Ferdinand was murdered and the First World War broke out. Jim always believed that his boss knew the war was coming and had befriended him. As a British subject, he would have been in danger of being interned. In any event, he returned to New York, worked for another employer, eventually was drafted and served in France. Bill took an exam for the New York Police Department and abandoned the hod for a nightstick. Jack found a job on the New York waterfront, and Frank joined them in New York.

When the Home Rule Act of 1912 was passed in London, it did not immediately take effect. In 1914 its implementation was further postponed, until after the war—a maneuver that had worked several times before and that the Irish regarded as British treachery. By election time in 1918 the Easter Week leaders had become martyrs. Eighty-two percent of the population voted for Sinn Fein; the party carried every constituency but one.

It was during the elections—I was then eleven—that I became

a courier of sorts. I remember preparing crudely written signs on boards and nailing them to trees by the side of the road in front of our house. We proclaimed our commitment to Eamon de Valera, the Sinn Fein candidate, who was running for the East Mayo seat in the new Irish Parliament. (He was an American citizen, born in New York of a Spanish father and an Irish mother. He had been one of the leaders of the 1916 Rebellion, but his life had been spared when all other leaders were executed. The British did not want to risk executing an American citizen lest it interfere with America's entry into World War I.) De Valera had become our hero, and all the more because he had been a mathematics professor at Blackrock College. I took his name, Eamon, in confirmation, but in 1932, disillusioned by his poor civil rights record, I regretted it.

The Sinn Fein party had not been expected to win Mayo, because the people were devoted to John Dillon, a local merchant, who had been a very popular leader. He was, however, committed to a dominion form of government, and that gradualist approach was overtaken and crushed by subsequent events. The execution of the 1916 leaders had brought about a great change. "A terrible beauty was born" was the way Yeats described it many years later. The old Nationalist party, of which Dillon was a leader, was devoted to eventual freedom, but without separation from Great Britain. They continued to preach patience and a "constitutional" approach. They said that all good things would come, that one could not expect his rights overnight. They were convinced that right was on their side and they would accomplish their ends by peaceful means in time. It was the Irish version of America's gradualist approach to the demands of its blacks for fair and equal treatment.

But the people would not listen to the Nationalists anymore. The dominion party had lost its credentials. Two years before, John Redmond, their leader, had recommended conscription of Irishmen to serve in the British Army in France. Many saw

Redmond's act as a betrayal, and the poet Dora Sigerson had penned her warning, "Conscription."

> There is a shadow on the head I love,
> There is a danger lurks thy path upon,
> It murmurs low as coos the mating dove,
> It calls in gray and gathered clouds above,
> For thee, for thee Kathleen ni Houlihan.*

Bohola too had begun to think once more of Kathleen ni Houlihan. Outside the chapel gate young men and old signed pledges to resist conscription even with their lives. "If we are to die, let us die in Ireland" was the way they put it. What started out to be agitation against serving the Crown on foreign soil wound up in guerrilla warfare.

As kids, we were in the middle of it. The Black and Tans were going up and down the roads in open-throttled Crossley tenders, rifles poised on both sides. They rode roughshod over the populace, burning homes of suspected patriots, killing, destroying and hunting. Young people with ideals took to the hills.

In the hilly countryside in 1918–20 guerrilla engagements increased each passing week. Young men gave up their lives as if they were "worthless trifles." The Tans scored in Mayo, killing John Corcoran, a popular local leader. When the truce came in 1920, and with it the treaty between Lloyd George and rebel leader Michael Collins, Ireland's emissary to the peace table in England, Erin was maimed. Six of the nine counties of the historic province of Ulster were severed from Ireland, to remain subordinate to Great Britain. "It is a stepping-stone," the negotiators said. But many Irishmen rejected it, and the civil war was on. The holdouts—De Valera was the leader—

*In other days it had been treasonous to love Ireland; thus Irish poets and songwriters referred to Erin by many a name, one favorite being Kathleen, or Kathleen ni Houlihan (daughter of Houlihan).

said, "Those who gave their lives in the struggle for independence did not do so to settle for a dismembered nation."

The new Irish Free State government took the same British Crossley tenders, the same British guns and the same British ammunition that had so recently been used against them. Now Irishmen killed each other with weapons of the Black and Tans. It was disgustingly savage. Yeats never said it, but his terrible beauty had died an ugly death.

When my father died in 1920, his teaching post was taken by the husband of the canon's niece, so my mother sent me to another school, three miles away. For about a year I studied with my father's friend Pat Clark and his wife. They prepared me for secondary school, teaching me mostly mathematics, English and religion. I excelled in the last, taking the class prize in a competition. (In spite of my heritage of anticlericalism I was awestruck when the bishop made the presentation.)

I was taught very little, however, about the history of Ireland. We youngsters knew about the 1916 rebellion because it was current, but we knew almost nothing about the rebellion of 1798, which followed the revolutions in France and America. We knew all about Daniel O'Connell, the nineteenth-century fighter for Catholic Emancipation, but nothing about the Young Ireland Movement, which gave so much idealism to Ireland and so many leaders to the world. Even Wolfe Tone, now called the father of Irish republicanism, was only a name, and the patriotic Presbyterians who fought with him were unknown. The Irish, who suffered so much under the heel of English rule for centuries, had an amazing capacity to be parochial themselves.

In school I was somewhat better than an average student but by no means the pride of my family. We were constantly reminded that we had an obligation to excel, in school as elsewhere. It was a matter of duty and we accepted it. I don't recall that I was mischievous, and there weren't many disciplinary problems at home. Fishing the clear streams was perhaps my favorite recreation, but it was allowed only on Sunday, when my enjoyment of it was hampered by my mother's visits with her friend Mrs. Keary after Mass. Mrs. Keary was one of two widows who operated pubs in Bohola. While my mother sat in the Keary parlor, having a glass of wine and some biscuits and exchanging gossip, I waited and watched and watched and waited outside, calming the horse and polishing the trap and harness. By the time we finally got home all the other boys in the village had already gone fishing or hunting, and I had to trail behind, missing what seemed to me to be the best part of the day. To complain was unheard of. My mother's visits with Mrs. Keary were entirely nostalgic.

I did not participate much in athletics. I was undersized and underweight. (It was only after I arrived in the United States, in 1925, that I grew to my present height of five feet seven and a half inches.) My brothers claimed it was the climate that brought about the welcome dividend. In secondary school, at St. Nathy's College in Mayo, I hung around the sidelines, waiting for the football to come my way, while bigger boys played. Often I waited throughout the full half-hour sports period without getting a single shot at the ball.

St. Nathy's was the only high school in the diocese and was about twenty miles from our home. The yearly fee of 40 pounds (about $100) was prohibitive for all but teachers' and shopkeepers' sons and priests' nephews. The small farmer's son, no matter how bright, had no such opportunity as I. I think my mother prevailed upon the president of the college to take me in for 30 pounds. My father at the time of his death was earning about 120 pounds a year (about $300). Even the 30 pounds, therefore, was a tremendous financial burden on my mother and my two working sisters.

St. Nathy's at one time had been a British military barracks and later became the local training school for clergy. (A few of the favored students filled the needs of the diocese at home. The others were sent to far-off climes—Africa, China, the Philippines, South America and the southern, western and southwestern United States.) We who were not inclined toward the priesthood were not pushed into it, but we suffered under the same discipline and deprivation as the novitiates. We were not permitted off the grounds from the time we arrived for term until we left for vacation—with one exception. On Sundays we could walk, two abreast, through the town and out into the country for about two hours. Priests took care of our discipline, religious worship and education. Each day began with Mass, followed by a breakfast of tasteless gruel and exercises in the yard. Then we attended classes until evening, when we spent a few hours in supervised study, a prefect enforcing strict order and silence. Even those who were not naturally so inclined studied to fight the boredom.

Adjoining the east side of the grounds was a small Church of Ireland chapel and cemetery. It was a sin for us to set foot in the place or go on the grounds. Occasionally on Sunday the Anglican minister came. He wore a wide-brimmed hat, much like a Spanish priest's, and rode in a "back to back" horse-drawn carriage. If we happened to meet him we were required (out of some kind of professional courtesy) to tip our skull caps in his direction, as we would to a woman or priest. It seemed a strange act of deference to make to one who preached in a church we were forbidden to enter under pain of falling from grace.

We came to the institution aching with homesickness. We were children of lower middle-class or upper working-class families and had rarely if ever been far from home. Confronted with the severe restrictions and abominable food, we came to believe that home was the greatest place on earth. We counted every day until term's end, when we could return to our families.

I went through a behavior change at St. Nathy's. I was punished quite often—an angry box on the ears—for what seemed to me trivial infractions, and after a while I learned to fight back in my fashion. On one occasion I was chosen to complain about the food. The president of the school told me I had no right to complain, because I was living there partially through the generosity of the school. His comment stung because it cast me among the impoverished, and in Ireland poverty is a crime for which there is no defense. A few years later, while I was working on the Brooklyn waterfront, I sent the school ten pounds for every year I was there, to clear the record. This represented the difference between the yearly tuition and what my mother paid. The president wrote back thanking me for my gratitude. I was not grateful; I was getting rid of pent-up resentment.

The civil war broke out shortly after I entered St. Nathy's. Among the students, cliques developed—the I.R.A. against the Free Staters. There were gang fights—some of the boys sent to Dublin for brass knuckles—but the school authorities remained in control. Home, on the other hand, became a hotbed of sedition. At one point there seemed to be enough explosives in our backyard to blow up half of Ireland. The civil war came home to us as the Black and Tan skirmishing never had, since our place became a way station for fugitive patriots, similar to the Underground Railroad during America's Civil War. My sister Joe, who was teaching in Newcastle on Tyne, arranged to hide those who escaped to England, which was then the safest place for a fugitive to be. The English knew little of the atrocities their armies perpetrated, and like Americans reacting to charges against Lieutenant Calley during the war in Vietnam, they would not believe reports, no matter how clear the proof.

The first post–civil war election, in 1924, furnished another example of clerical intervention in the affairs of state. The priests had returned to the side of the Crown, or its Free State satellite, urging the people to support the new government. It was a corrupt election; power was brought to bear unstintingly against those who had supported the republicans, and most people were intimidated.

I recall preparing to take some neighbors to the polls. I had harnessed the horse. My sister May, by this time teaching at my father's school, came upon me. "What are you trying to do," she challenged, "drive us out of our jobs?" Many teachers had not received their salaries for the year because they were known to be republican sympathizers. May knew very well that had I been seen taking people to the polls, she too might have lost her salary. That would have put an unbearable economic burden on the family.

So I went to the polls and watched at a distance and tried to vote. The rule was that one could vote if one was listed in the enrollment books. There was one male O'Dwyer listed, and I was now the only male O'Dwyer in the village. I proclaimed that it was obviously my registration. An objection was raised and I was rejected. I was then seventeen.

That election merely established officially that the cause had failed; avarice took over the Irish government and many patriots fled. A new breed of Irishmen filled places at the top. The Irish were bequeathed the British Civil Service, which was a greater blow than all the harrowing effects of the Black and Tans. Finally greed began to infect those on the run. Like certain Confederate Civil War veterans, some became brigands and held up banks and robbed trains, all in the name of patriotism.

Partition corrupted the people, too. The division of Ireland, having no geographical justification, crystallized religious differences and set them in cement, to do extensive damage in years to come. Protestants and Catholics had always found it difficult to get along with each other in the North, but the partition institutionalized their hate. Whereas the North moved toward cruel, officially proclaimed and directed discrimination, Trinity College, Dublin, which had been the bastion of imperialism, became a great Irish institution; and the *Irish Times,* previously the organ of the ascendancy, became a great literary Irish newspaper and much more responsive to Irish culture than the other national organs. Moreover, although a few confirmed unionists left for Great Britain, those Anglo-Irish who stayed remained in possession of their considerable estates and have them to this day.

Miraculously, my family suffered no retribution after the

election. There were no other male O'Dwyers around and I was too young for the authorities to pursue. They knew our home had been a shelter for fugitives, but they knew also that my mother would have put up anyone of any persuasion in the same position. The tendency is strong in Ireland to help a fugitive. My mother was part of the tradition. The Free State army raided our home on several occasions, took the place apart and drove their bayonets into the haystack. But every time they came, a warning preceded them, and any visitor was over the hill and far away by the time they appeared.

I graduated from St. Nathy's in 1924, when I was seventeen, and went on to Dublin University, quite unprepared for the experience. I knew nothing about the university's atmosphere, in which no one seemed to care whether a student attended classes or not, and there was no orientation or briefing on what one might expect. Going to Dublin was a mistake.

I lived in a boardinghouse of the O'Connor sisters. Their family were neighbors from Mayo, and they went out of their way to be kind, but I was not happy. I was a stranger in Dublin. Only years later did I discover that I had been in the midst of a great cultural revolution and in a place full of history.

Politics had died. Freedom's cause was destroyed, and to make it worse, corruption in public life became evident on every side. Power and might had prevailed, and most people resigned themselves to believing the justice people sought was simply unattainable.

At this time my sister Joe was still teaching in Newcastle. My sister Linda, closest to me in age, was qualifying in a teacher-training school in Scotland, and my two other sisters, May and Kathleen, both teaching in Bohola, were largely supporting Linda and me. My situation was becoming untenable.

About the same time I received a letter from my brother Frank in New York. He offered a way out of my lonely existence and the threat of failure at exam time. Frank told me I could come to New York, study law at night and work during the day. "You won't be a drain on the family," he wrote, "and our sisters can marry once they don't have to pay for your education. You won't be a burden on anyone." I really had not thought of myself quite as a burden and my sisters had never mentioned their dilemma, but I concluded that Frank was probably right, and I began to make preparations to leave Ireland and emigrate to the United States. "Don't tell anyone you're coming," he said, "or they will resist it." I thought about that and couldn't do it. I broached the subject. Frank had been right. My sisters wouldn't hear of it, but my mother supported me when she saw that I wanted to go. It was while I was driving her to confession on a Saturday during Christmas vacation. "There will come a time," she said, "when you will be here and I will be gone. I don't want any of my children to suffer because of my selfishness."

In order to migrate, one needed the approval of the American consul and references from any three of the following: a banker, solicitor, parish priest and sergeant of the new police force, the Guarda Siochana (Civilian Guardians). I would not go to the canon, and it was just as well. Concurrently, my neighbor Tom Byrne's son Johnny planned to go to Chicago. Johnny was not on the best of terms with the canon because Johnny had joined in the Freedom Movement, but the canon gave him the letter. Suspicious, Mrs. Byrne steamed it open. "To Whom It May Concern" was the noncommittal greeting. It continued, "John Byrne has asked for 'lines,' which I gladly give him. It is a cheap price to pay for his departure from my parish, which I fondly pray will be permanent. His leaving will be a pleasurable event." The next Christmas Johnny's father dropped the letter on the church's collection table for transmittal to the canon as his annual gift.

There was a custom, which must have grown up in the famine of 1848, that was known as the "American wake." It occurred on the eve of an Irish emigrant's departure for the United States. In those days most emigrants never returned; hence the term "wake." My relatives and neighbors gathered in the house, stood around and encouraged me. They said such things as, "Well, you're going to be with your brothers, so it will be just like home." I knew that that was not true, but I smiled just the same. The older people were saddened, and I had mixed emotions. I feared going to America, but I knew there was nothing for me in Mayo. I did not like Dublin; I did not like the university. I did like Mayo, but I had to move on, and "Besides," I told myself, "everyone has done it." The people mostly talked about their own kin. "Wasn't young Johnny-Amby [that would be John Brennan, the son of Ambrose, to distinguish him from another John Brennan] the head of the fire brigade in St. Louis?" and "Wasn't Ellen Seamus doing so well in Malden, and the Dunleavy boys, weren't they getting along fine with their uncle in Detroit?" "Sure 'n you'll be seeing them all at Mass," remarked the oldest of the group. Detroit, Malden and St. Louis seemed to be adjoining towns in that far-off friendly land that had done so well by their children. The evening ended with the expressed hope that I would soon return to stay. Unmentioned, but understood, was the hope that I would return well heeled.

The neighbors left about midnight. Each one pressed a coin into my hand. The sum came to seven dollars in all, a tremendous amount for the poor of our parish to part with. My mother had purchased a new suit for me, tightly fitted and in keeping with the latest Irish style. It was a blue serge suit and the bottom of the jacket barely came to my hips.

The next morning my mother and sisters accompanied me on the trip to the railroad station by pony and trap. There were periods of silence when we faltered in making the best of it. At the station my sisters cried, and my mother didn't. It wasn't manly to cry, so I didn't either—until the train left the station. Then I did. I felt bereft and terrified.

As the train moved south I tried not to think of my mother and sisters, my neighbors and friends, and to look forward to what lay ahead. The plain that is Mayo receded and an old fort appeared where the Milesians, or was it the Firbolgs, or no, no, it was the Tuatha De Danann, had built round towers dating from a time long before the Christ of Galilee walked by Lake Tiberias. Who put the limestones on the tower, one on the other? I wondered. My mind wandered to the Irishtown, where the Land League was born less than fifty years before Captain Boycott made nearby Ballinrobe famous. Ballinrobe and Ballintubber—yes, there was the nursery rhyme, and at seventeen I could remember it still:

Shake hands brother—You're a rogue and I'm another,
You were hanged in Ballinrobe and I was hanged in Ballintubber,
I broke the rope and ran home to my mother.

Scores of Irish towns and villages begin with "Ballin" or "Bally," anglicizations of the Gaelic word *Baile,* meaning "community" or "village." Ballinrobe, the Mayo town that prompted my musings, means "village near the Robe River," and Ballintubber "village of the well," the holy well of St. Patrick. (Ireland is spotted with holy wells. John Mitchell, the Protestant patriot and anticleric, wrote: "Ireland is noted for its priests and Holy Wells. The sooner the former are at the bottom of the latter, the better off Ireland will be.")

Ballintubber had additional significance. It contained a ruined monastery, "a broken chancel on a broken cross." I recalled that from the fifth to the twelfth century Ireland's kings and chieftains had created monasteries and endowed them with large estates. While some monks worked the fields, others taught and produced illuminated manuscripts. Then the Normans and the English destroyed almost all the monasteries.

At Ballintubber there was such a monastery. Whether it had been erected around the legend of the well or the legend created to bring attention to the monastery is unsettled. Cathal O'Connor, king of Connaught in the early thirteenth century, with a mind to providing a fire escape when his time came to shuffle off his royal coil, provided the money and the artisans to build an abbey and cloister at the edge of the well. Pilgrims traveling to Croaghpatrick, the holy mountain where, legend holds, Patrick fasted before he drove the snakes into Clew Bay, stopped off there to rest and refresh themselves and to warm up for their more serious devotions on the mountaintop. The monastery was complex and the craftsmanship superb. The masonry, even on the outside, was of limestone, with finely chiseled images. Their uniqueness was their undoing. To Cromwell and his followers, graven images meant idolatry and a perversion of Christianity which had to be destroyed. On special orders from the Protector, the Roundheads came, breaking the statuary and throwing it to the ground. Ireland's was a sad history, I thought.

The train clicked along from Cork to Cobh and I thought of John Locke, the poet:

O kindly generous Irish land, so leal, so fair, so loving,
No wonder the wandering Celt must think and dream of thee
in his roving.

Locke described Cobh as "leaning her back up against the hill and the tip of her toes in the ocean."

The sight of Cobh brought an end to my musings; it was obvious John locke had not seen Cobh as I was seeing it. It was a garrison town now, filled with cheap hotels living off the emigrants, and a few better hotels catering to those returning. The shipping agent in Kiltimagh had done the booking for me, which at the time we thought was nice of him to do. But when I got to my hotel I wondered. The place was crammed with emigrants and teeming with British troops as well. The latter were not there to set sail.

Tom Clancy, the folk singer, maintains his song "The Holy Ground" refers to Cobh. "The Holy Ground," he says, has little to do with God. "It has to do with the liquor and willing-women section of Cobh." Forty years later I heard Tom sing the song at Downey's in New York at 3 A.M.: "And still I live in hopes to see the Holy Ground once more." He may. I do not.

Maybe it was my mood on that April day in 1925, but I

couldn't shake the thought that everyone in Cobh was interested in the few shillings in my pocket—the prostitutes, the old women selling tin shamrocks, mottoes and shillelaghs to take to relatives and friends, the man in half a uniform who insisted on taking my bag whether I liked it or not.

The Cunard and White Star lines had made fortunes at Cobh, and the companies laid down the rules. If you had a second-class ticket you did not need to be deloused, but if you held a steerage passage, the boy, the girl, the clothes, the hair were laundered before you reached the tender. Third-class passengers were obliged to have a haircut and the barber was part of the conspiracy. "If you slip him a shilling, you will get a neat trim," my brother Frank, who knew the ropes, had written. "But if you fail to do so, you will arrive here bald." As a matter of absolute precaution, Frank had sent me a second-class ticket written by James Boylan, travel agent from Hell's Kitchen.

I met a friend, Pat Shannon, just before I sailed, and we compared notes. Pat had been sent to Dublin by his travel agent to get a visa clearance and had stayed at the Globe Hotel. Pat had never before been out of his native village or seen electric lights. "When I got into my hotel room," he told me, "someone quenched the light, but there was no one in the room." (At the Globe and elsewhere the current was shut off at night.) "In about five minutes a girl opened the door. She didn't have a stitch on her and she tried to get into bed. I told her it was my bed, but she kept trying to make me lie down, and I shouted and she ran out. Dublin is a quare place," he concluded as he set out for Chicago—of all places.

CHAPTER THREE

America

THE CROSSING to America was uneventful in all but one respect. I shared quarters with an Ulster Protestant, the first I had ever met. David Scott was an older man, perhaps twenty-three or twenty-four, and he was on his way to Pittsburgh to work in a steel mill. He suggested some rules on our first encounter. "Look, you're probably Catholic," he said, "and I'm Protestant, but now that we're on this journey together, do you mind if we forget about it for the time being?" On Sunday we arose together. He said, "If you want to go to Mass, it's going on in the lounge. As for me, I'll skip the service and walk around the deck." I wanted to say, "I'll walk with you," but habit held me back. I went to the lounge. By the time the week was over I liked Scott very much. I thought he was very civilized, and I remember how refreshing I thought it was to bridge the gap.

On the boat the Englishman in charge of the bath stood outside the cabin each morning and said in an accent I recognized but found jarring, "Your bath is ready, sir; will you have a bath, sir?" I wasn't sure I needed one every morning. It seemed an unnecessary ritual; my bathing habits in Mayo had been confined largely to an occasional swim. Within a few months I understood that almost incessant bathing is a guarantee and obligation of American citizenship.

Most of my fellow passengers were prospective immigrants, meeting for the first time. We thought of our journey as strange, not a happy outing to America. The myth that all immigrants were full of hope was just that, a myth; none of us believed the streets of New York were paved with gold.

To while the time away we walked the decks. At other times I frequented the third-class quarters, because second class, where I was staying, was stuffy and first class was even more so. In steerage there was a lot more life. A girl from Galway played the melodeon and a youth from Sligo taught us to sing "Muirsheen Durkan," a siren song that called Irishmen to San Francisco in 1849 and the historic significance of which was lost on us.

In the days I went a courtin',
I was never tired resortin',
To the ale house and the playhouse
And many a house beside.
I told my brother Seamus,
I'd go off and get right famous,
And before I'd return again,
I'd roam the world wide

So goodby Muirsheen Durkan,
I'm such a tired of workin'.
No more I'll dig the praties,
No longer I'll be fooled.
For as sure as my name is Carney,
I'll be off to Califarny where instead
of digging praties,
I'll be diggin' lumps of gold.

Soon we joined in the chorus of another popular emigrant song, "I'm Off to Philadelphia."

When they told me I must leave the place
I tried to keep a cheerful face,

To show my heart's deep sorrow I was scorning,
But the tears will surely blind me,
For the friends I lave behind me,
When I'm off to Philadelphia in the mornin'.

With me bundle on me shoulder,
Sure there's no one can be bolder,
And I'm lavin' dear old Ireland in the mornin'.
For I lately took a notion,
For to cross the Briny Ocean,
And I'm off to Philadelphia in the mornin'.

On April 21, 1925, I arrived in New York with twenty-five dollars in my pocket, a single suit of clothes—on my back—and a straight razor. (When my brother Frank saw the suit he told me to discard it; it did not fit the going style and was too heavy for the climate.) I barely noticed the Statue of Liberty and nobody told us much about it. But the harbor looked magnificent.

Frank claimed me at the dock (U.S. immigration requirements had been completed in Ireland) and took me to Mrs. Maguire's Irish boardinghouse at 103rd Street and Columbus Avenue, where he and Jack were living. Frank was working as a truck loader in Washington Market, the wholesale depot for all incoming fruits and vegetables, and Jack was employed as a checker on the waterfront. Jimmy by then was a fireman, and Bill had just graduated from law school; both were married and settled down on their own. All were very kind in their way, but my relationship with them was less intimate and more formal than that with the half of my family I had left behind.

I was fond of Jack, whom I remembered practicing the Morse Code with a young man named Walsh from the other side of the parish. I was closer to Frank, who was nearest to me in age and unselfish and considerate. But our deepest respect and affection were reserved for Jimmy. He was the family favorite. He had written home regularly and sent more money than he could properly afford. (I had first seen him when I was seven, when he visited us in 1914 at the outbreak of World War I, and last seen him when I was nine or ten, when as an American soldier he was furloughed so that he could visit his parents in Ireland.)

They were all at Mrs. Maguire's to greet me that first night—Jimmy, Jack and Frank. But not Bill. Time passed and Jimmy became embarrassed. Bill had done it again. Here everyone was waiting and waiting. Frank and Jack made fun of Jim's distress. Finally the outer gate opened and in came my oldest brother. He was a stranger to me. He had left Ireland eighteen years earlier, before I was born. He had not kept the ties that otherwise bound us. It was unpardonable for an immigrant to ignore the plight of those left behind. It was a sin.

The introduction was awkward. Bill looked nothing like the rest of us. He had a gold tooth that showed when he smiled. He spoke in a loud voice, as Americans do. He used strange expressions and had lost his Irish accent completely. The encounter wrought no change in our relationship either. We talked for a while and he assured me he would find a job for me. I got the impression he meant it but didn't see why he needed to give me that assurance. Wasn't that what brothers were for?

Two days later I went to work in a garage. Bill had spoken to a precinct captain and the captain had recommended me. My job was to distribute automobile parts to the mechanics, but the parts confused me and I never could learn to differentiate the various nuts and gaskets. I had been there only a few days when I overheard someone refer to me as a "donkey," a derogatory term for an Irishman. Later he said it directly: "Look, donkey, when I want a gasket, I want you to hand it to me; don't throw it down on the floor. Now pick it up and hand it to me or I'll tan your ass." Eventually I learned that in America hurling verbal abuse is expected and I conformed. But not until I had threatened more than one Yank with violence.

After about a month the boss said to me, "Look, kid, you're a nice kid, but you're really not suited to this kind of work," and that undid my career as a stock clerk. I found that the *World* had the best employment ads. I answered one for a stable boy, and the boss, assuming that I, being Irish, knew all about horses, gave me the job. In fact, I knew how to ride bareback; I knew how to plow, harrow, drive a horse in harness. But I knew nothing about the refinements of saddle riding as practiced in riding stables. I lasted one day, but on this occasion owing to Mrs. Maguire's insistence that I couldn't live in her boarding-house if I worked in a stable.

Thereafter my brothers suggested that I not work for a while. Jimmy thought I needed time to get acclimated. Frank told me to take it easy, that there was no reason to rush. But the fact that I was living off them began to bother me. So again I consulted the *World* and found an advertisement for an elevator operator at 807 Riverside Drive. I met Dick Ryan, the superintendent, who was a County Clare man. He asked me how old I was, how long I had been in the country and what county I came from. I felt good that out of seven applicants for the job I was hired. But I didn't know whether my success was due to my qualifications or my standing as a fellow Celt. Jimmy Lyons of Hell's Kitchen, one of my coworkers, set me straight. "That cheap Irish bastard hired you because you were the only one to fit the uniform."

I loved the work (there were no gaskets to keep track of) as long as none of my friends saw me on the job in my uniform. I did not want word to get home to Ireland that I was working as a "lift" operator and accordingly avoided showing my face at the front of the building. In Bohola it was expected that my brothers by now would have sufficient prestige in America to convince a bank or similar institution to avail themselves of my talents. In fact, I too shortly yielded to the same kind of expectation—to become a lawyer. I determined to quit my job and go back to school.

Sitting by the elevator one day in late summer (I worked

alternate day and night shifts), I was foolish enough to tell Jim Lyons about my plan. It must have sounded either pretentious or crazy to him, my going back to school before I had been six months in the country. As I finished my story I got a signal to take the elevator to the sixth floor. There was a troublesome tenant on that floor and I prepared to get there without delay. But Jimmy stuck his foot in the elevator door. "Paulie, my boy," he said, putting on his best brogue, "when you're a big lawyer, I want you to do me a favor." I didn't know how to handle this. "When that happens," he said, "if you need a chauffeur, will you have me in mind?" He then removed his foot and I closed the door. But as the elevator ascended, the shaft rang with the explosion of a Bronx cheer.

My heart sank. Was the plan so impossible? Was I reaching beyond my depth? The blues lasted till Mrs. Maguire put the lamb stew on the table and began to chatter about a strange Ireland where she had been a little girl in Portumna some fifty years before. I talked to my brother Bill. After all, he had made it in a modest way. I didn't say anything about my misgivings. We had come to know each other a little better. He would take me on his rounds while he investigated insurance claims, pending his admission to the bar. Listening to his optimism gave me courage—until Harry Gluckman spoke to me.

Of all the tenants in the house where I worked, Harry Gluckman was the most special, friendly, talkative. He wanted to know where you hailed from, were you living with your parents, and did you like your work. After learning of my ambition he became even more loquacious. "Paul O'Dwyer," he would say, "member of the bar of the Empire State of New York." My experience with Jimmy Lyons was still troubling me. I heard Harry once, I heard him twice; the fifth time was too much. "Mr. Gluckman," I said, "you are a big man and I don't think you should be doing this." He looked surprised. I said that I thought he was pulling my leg. "Young man," he said seriously, "I have seen many a young Jew and many a young

Irishman come to this country and from a humble beginning become successful. I was not joking with you." I felt immeasurably better.

When fall came I enrolled as a prelaw student at Fordham. Classes were held in the Woolworth Building. I had never learned American history and I really had to bend to it. It was inevitable that I would eventually become impressed with the story of the Revolution and the American form of government, although in the beginning my reactions were varied and not always favorable. It seemed unexplainable to me that while immigrants poured into the United States to enjoy its standard of living, native whites languished in poverty in the South. The contradiction in our giving munificent foreign aid while letting poor whites remain illiterate and hungry was difficult to understand. (The injustice to the Negro community was not even discussed and I did not then think about it.)

All I knew about America was what I had picked up between April, when I arrived, and September, when I started school. I understood that all kinds of people lived here—blacks and whites, Jews and Gentiles, Catholics and Protestants, Italians and Irish—and that more often than not they didn't get along. I myself had conflicting feelings. I found myself clinging to my Irish identity because it gave me an edge over an Italian, and to my Catholic identity because it gave me a favored position over a Jew. I was aware too that being white put me in a class in which I was, even as a noncitizen, ahead of a black American citizen of long standing.

Meanwhile the *World* was not producing suitable opportunities for me, and Bill sent me to see Captain James Skehan at the East Thirty-fifth Street station house. The captain sent me to the Farmers Loan & Trust Company at Fifty-fourth Street and Fifth Avenue. I saw the boss there and told him I was going to night school. "The bank," he said, "requires the services of every employee for late-night work for several days at the end of each month. That is the time we must balance our books. I'm afraid you won't suit." I called Captain Skehan and he sent me back again to the bank. The boss said that since my object was to be a lawyer he would send me to Mr. LeBlanc, one of the lawyers in a very large law firm that handled the bank's account.

"Mr. LeBlanc is away in Europe," the secretary said, "and will not be back for two weeks." In two weeks I returned. Mr. LeBlanc said he was pleased to meet me. The Fifty-fourth Street manager of the Farmers Loan & Trust Company wanted to extend every courtesy to Captain Skehan for the many courtesies the captain was extending to them. "That's the way it is in this fine city," he assured me. "We try to help one another," he said, pausing, "whenever possible. Now, how much money do you believe you are entitled to?" "I need seventeen-fifty," I said. It seems Captain Skehan's courtesies were not that valuable. "We pay ten dollars a week to our clerks," said Mr. LeBlanc. I begged leave to go since there was nothing more to be said. He called me back. Hope rose in my breast again. "Young man," he said, "I don't want you to take offense, but if you want to be an American lawyer, you must learn to speak like one. I know this advice will help you."

I went back to Captain Skehan. He extended protection as well to the Susquehanna Silk Mills at Thirty-second Street and Madison Avenue and he believed that they could use an extra man in their shipping department. He felt, however, there was something wrong with my approach. The captain came from Tipperary and was a strict disciplinarian. He had been in the army for several years before joining the Police Department. "Go outside," the captain directed me, "and come in and make believe that I am Mr. Rebein, to whom I am sending you—he is the head man of the shipping department of Susquehanna—and tell me what you want." I went out and returned. "Mr. Rebein," I began, "Captain Skehan sent me to you." He motioned me to a chair beside him. I sat down. He did not speak. I nervously crossed my leg over my knee. "Hah," said the captain, triumphant in his discovery. "You shouldn't cross your leg." I didn't cross my leg when I saw Mr. Rebein and I got the job.

At the packing bench next to mine was Timmy Sullivan. "Do you know where Bandon is?" he asked me. "I do," I replied, adding, "They say that even the pigs in Bandon are Protestant." I knew immediately I had said the wrong thing. "My father was a Corkman," Timmy said, "and he was no pig and no Protestant." "I meant no harm," I said. "My father was a Corkman too, and he came from Tullahlease"—and that repaired the damage.

Mr. Rebein, our German boss, was a hard man. When he wasn't around, Timmy would softly sing working-class songs of the previous century when his father worked for John Crimmins, the contractor. That was before the Irish workers had gotten to be "uppity Micks" and still asked only two dollars a day. Crimmins, however, soon put them in their place. He sent for a shipload of Sicilians and started them at one dollar a day, and that was the beginning of an episode that was to last another half century.

"I come from Bandon," Timmy would half say, half sing, with more than a trace of a Cork accent:

> I come from Bandon, I had a hard time landin'.
> I went to work for Crimmins diggin' a ditch.
> To hell with Bandon and the trouble landin'.
> Fill up the cart you son of a bitch.

The year after landing I joined the Mayomen's Association. It had come into being after the American Civil War, with the purpose of helping immigrants from Mayo find employment. Its function was to teach me *Robert's Rules of Order*. "You must first listen," said Michael Barrett, the wise man of the association, "and then learn, and later speak when you know what you're talking about." The admonition was hardly necessary since there was little to learn and less to talk about, except when the bills were read out and when constant reference was made to *Robert's Rules of Order*. "How does an Irish leader behave?" I asked my promoter. "Watch Rody Kennedy," he said, "and you will see how to run a meeting."

The meeting, of the St. Patrick's Day Parade Committee, took place in the Yorkville Casino; Rody, a vigorous octogenarian, had been chairman of the committee for forty years. For four decades the pattern had not changed and the rules of the parade were as rigid as those of the meeting: no clay pipes, no pigs, no green hats, no drunks, and no Mrs. O'Leary with her donkey.

But something disturbing had come into the meeting and the old man, for the first time, was rattled. John O'Connor,* of Kerry, was the owner, editor and publisher of the *Irish Advocate,* and he had two young daughters, Elise and Pearl. At an early age they had taken to horseback riding and the hunt. They thought it would be a good idea to have horses at the parade, and that was not out of order. But lady equestrians—that was too much for Rody. He issued an edict summarily rejecting the request. He felt this was the unquestioned prerogative of an Irish chieftain.

The O'Connor girls had other ideas. They would have none of his arbitrary decisions and had suggested that Rody was what we would now call a male chauvinist pig. Through the power of the press and their own personalities they had attracted the ears of the members of the committee, and they determined to fight it out then and there.

After a heated discussion it became obvious to old Rody that he was about to lose the battle. He banged the gavel. "Enough," he said. "I can see by now this move is well organized, and I bow to the inevitable." There followed a significant pause. "I will entertain a motion that on St. Patrick's Day, on Fifth Avenue, the ladies will be mounted."

*John O'Connor was the grandfather of actor Carroll O'Connor.

I left work at Susquehanna at 5:30 P.M. and got to Fordham by 6 o'clock. A doughnut and coffee generally tided me over until I got back to Mrs. Maguire's boardinghouse at 9:45. She kept dinner warm for me. Every Irish boardinghouse keeper had a soft spot in her heart for the greenhorn, and many a young man, taking advantage of her affection, left owing money. Mrs. Maguire wrote to my mother. She said she would look after me as if I were her own and assured my mother there was no need to worry: I was a nice, polite, mannerly boy.

My brothers Jim and Frank paid the $75 tuition for my first semester. Thereafter I became disillusioned with myself and my life and I let out my resentment on them. Frank, who shared my room, bore the brunt of it. All the warmth of teen years abruptly ended; the weaning process had begun. I made up my mind to take no more money and arranged with Fordham to pay tuition by the month. My brothers knew my next tuition payment was due and assumed I was balking. Jim came to my room one evening to give me the $75. I wouldn't take it. I had saved the monthly installment of $19.25.

The two things I liked most in America were strawberry ice cream sodas, which Jack introduced me to in a drugstore on Columbus Avenue, and the twelve-hour cruise on the Hudson Day Line to Bear Mountain. Frank took me on the latter one Saturday in early June. I found, to my delight, that it was easy to get acquainted with the young people aboard and, despite the differences in our cultures and customs, easy to get on with them. I shed some of my reticence (even with the girls) for the first time, forgetting my shyness in my pleasure in the music of the ukulele, the singing, the beauty of the river and the beauty of the girls.

A few days after I finished my year of prelaw at Fordham, the dean called the class in and advised us that we should not rely thereafter on going to the Evening Law School at the Woolworth Building. "Other applicants from all over the country," he explained, "are better qualified—some with two, three and even four years in college—and Fordham's reputation must take precedence." We had no recourse but to accept the verdict. Some who were exceptionally well connected with the Church were given a spot. The rest of us had to forage for ourselves.

My lack of knowledge of civics and American history had made my study difficult for me, and I soon learned that I had failed my history exam. (I studied during the summer and passed the examination in August; even the dull manner of its teaching could not diminish my interest in the subject.) But in the meantime a calamity overtook the family on both sides of the Atlantic. On June 29, 1926, my nineteenth birthday and the day I was to receive the results of my exams, a second O'Dwyer brother, the most beloved, my brother Jimmy, died. His career was just in the making. The war over, he had returned to New York, joined the Fire Department, married, studied for the lieutenant's exam, and was looking forward to the birth of his first child. On the twenty-ninth he was on messenger duty, but stayed at the firehouse to await word of how I had made out on my exams. An alarm came in and he answered it. A block away from the firehouse the truck on which he was riding collided with a kid riding on a motorcycle. Five hours later Jimmy died in Knickerbocker Hospital. His daughter, Joan, was born three months later.

Jimmy's death brought despair to my mother and sisters in Ireland, and to us in America it was nothing less than a disaster. Jimmy was the force that had kept us together. Indeed, he had been, on both sides of the Atlantic, a concerned, devoted son and brother. Until his marriage he had sent a portion of every paycheck home and after his marriage had sent as much as he could afford.

After Jimmy's death, Bill, Jack, Frank and I waited for his child to be born, and behaved like idiots during her early childhood. Mildred, his wife, a Staten Islander, was unfamiliar with the ways of Irishmen and at first was overwhelmed. But as time went by, she, as well as Joan, became the nearest thing to the unifying force that Jim had been. She was young and attractive, and we urged her to remarry. But she never did.

In the fall of 1926, the whole pattern of my life changed. Since Fordham was closed to me, I enrolled in St. John's Law School in September 1926. St. John's College had been founded much earlier in Queens County by the Vincentian Order of Priests. In contradistinction to Fordham, which was a Jesuit institution, St. John's was designed to accommodate the children of citizens in the lower economic levels. In 1923 a few Irish politicians together with the college heads received permission from the state of New York to establish St. John's Law School. It was a good business and profitable to its sponsors. It provided the means of capturing a few honest dollars from the raft of young Jewish students, the children of East Side immigrants who had crossed the East River into Brooklyn and who were hungering for a legal education. Eighty-five percent of my class was Jewish, and hungering, and so too were several Irish Americans and Italian Americans. The law school was located at 50 Court Street in an old converted office building in Brooklyn. Neither the outside nor inside gave any appearance of being a seat of learning. In short, it had few pretensions. But it did hold out, for those whose options were limited, some hope of entering the professional life of the city. We had no complaint. We paid our money and got the worth of it.*

I found it difficult to pay my room and board and tuition on the $78 a month I had been earning at the silk mill. The Brooklyn waterfront had been my brother Bill's beat as a policeman, and through him I got a job as a checker on the docks which paid me $35 per week. I joined the longshoremen's union, which brought me into the most interesting phase of my life in New York. I was now fully integrated into the life of my

*St. John's College is now the depository of all my papers dealing with the activities in the United States aimed at helping Ireland gain its complete freedom from Great Britain (covering a span of fifty years).

adopted city and became a New Yorker years before I became an American citizen.

I moved from the Irish environment of our boardinghouse on 103rd Street. I rented a furnished room from a Scandinavian family in Brooklyn, and during the next three years learned to appreciate the fine qualities of these most civilized people who had moved so far ahead of other Europeans and Americans in dealing with health and social problems. My room was located a few blocks from the waterfront and a half hour (on the Culver Line) from the law school.

My duties as a checker required me to keep track of wooden cases of merchandise that were delivered to the docks in trucks, lighters and barges. We got quite an education in geography by osmosis, as the merchandise came from all parts of the world.

My brother Jack was on the waterfront at about the same time as I. He was a lighthearted fellow and people liked him. He soon left the waterfront and, with a friend from Ireland, opened a speakeasy at Sixty-fifth Street and Broadway. It was on the ground floor of a brownstone house, three steps below the street. It had a long bar and a place to store the ice. Speakeasies were illegal, but his partner had been a cop and knew how to deal with inquiring revenuers.

Jack did not have even the small investment necessary. He borrowed money from Frank, the family banker, but promptly forgot the indebtedness. I had to take a hand to see that Frank was paid back his hard-earned money.

Jack became restless again, and toward the end of the twenties he entered the prizefight business. He acquired a couple of pugs with no prospects of success. Everyone knew that but Jack. As far as he was concerned, all of his stable were sure to be champions. From the speakeasy profits, Jack had acquired a man to drive him around, another to rub the boxers down, and a trainer. All the money he had made in the speakeasy went into the boxing ménage. Once the family, out of loyalty, went to St. Nick's Arena to see one of Jack's boxers perform. Our champion was knocked out in the first round. He might have been lucky at that—all the good fighters were controlled by gangsters. Jack then opened up a restaurant and bar in Brooklyn with Andrew Gallagher. But by then the Depression had begun and the halcyon days of the twenties were ending. Unknown to us, Jack's own days were ending too.

My coworkers on the docks were an assortment of gangsters, toughs and the most kindly, loyal and gentle people. Some had so little regard for human life that their behavior could be described only as savagery. Others were frightened immigrants, victimized by racketeers. The great majority, like myself, were workers simply making a living.

I liked most of my Italian fellow workers and remember in particular how unjustly they were treated in 1927. The other longshoremen for the most part reveled in the trial of Nicola Sacco and Bartolomeo Vanzetti, who were about to be executed in Massachusetts. Seven years previously the cobbler and the fish peddler had been arrested and indicted by the Commonwealth for the murder of a paymaster and a guard in South Braintree. Both defendants admitted that they were anarchists-pacifists, but denied any complicity in the crime. The year 1920 was a bad one for anyone espousing a cause called by such strange names. The country was then at the apex of one of its periodic repressive binges, and the Commonwealth had not had more satisfying victims since the Salem trials. No one today doubts that those gentle idealists were convicted and executed for a crime they did not commit, but in the shack at the head of Pier 3 on the day of their deaths their fellow countrymen heard every kind of vengeful epithet. In the face of the onslaught they remained silent and so did I; we were aliens. We had not learned that America did not deny us the right to claim Sam Adams and Thomas Paine and Thomas Jefferson and James Otis as our brothers. There was then no Italian-American society to protest against the legal lynching of two defenseless immigrants, made martyrs, in our America.

Another kind of discrimination meanwhile threatened at St. John's. I and some of my Irish classmates had gravitated toward one another and formed a group to study. Sheehan, Fitzgerald, Hanley and I met each night after class at Fitzgerald's flat on Montague Street. We talked about the law, we talked about girls (I covered up my inexperience with veiled references to haystack episodes in Mayo which, had they ever taken place, would have condemned me to ostracism, transportation and exile), and eventually we talked about joining a fraternity. At first I was not sure exactly what a fraternity was, but when I discovered that Jews were excluded, I knew it was not for me. It sounded too much like "No Irish Need Apply." Besides, my brother Bill's associate Oscar Bernstien had already become a close friend. Happily, that was the end of talk about the fraternity.

Thereafter we broke up the clique because we weren't getting anywhere with studying, and I then began to study with some Jewish friends. My introduction to politics began with one of them, Ben Shorr, who asked, "Do you want to join a club?" "A fraternity?" I asked uncertainly. "No," he said, "a Democratic club, a young Democratic club." "Sounds fine with me," I replied, and the Kings County Young Democratic Club thenceforward was made up of thirty-five Jewish classmates and me.

I had mixed feelings about the Democratic party. I had been told in Mrs. Maguire's boardinghouse that Woodrow Wilson was anti-Irish and a fraud, that his commitment to the right of self-determination had stopped at Ireland's shore. Nevertheless, Irish Americans were Democrats. Republicans had shown no interest in their needs, and the Democrats had nominated and elected an Irish mayor. In the twenties the Irish were still mostly workers. There were few conservatives among them and it was to be expected that "Irish Catholic" meant "liberal Democrat." We had all heard the story about the ward heeler who told his boss that O'Brien had become a Republican. "That's a damned lie," the boss had said. "I saw him at Mass last

Sunday." Anyway, it was no serious commitment to a political philosophy that brought me into the Democratic party, and the catalysts who ushered me in were all Jews.

The Kings County Young Democrats took themselves seriously. We could not, of course, operate without a constitution and bylaws, and when the question of qualification for membership came up, Ben Shorr rose to his feet. "I propose we take into membership only American citizens." (I was to learn that in the formation of a truly American association exclusion is the first order of business.) I pulled Shorr's coattail. "I'm not a citizen, Ben," I whispered. "Have you your first papers?" he asked hurriedly. "That I have," I told him. "Mr. Chairman," said Ben to Chairman Sol Eisenrod, "on reflection, I believe we should also admit those with first papers." The motion carried—my first lesson in pragmatic politics.

The next lesson was less edifying and ended in our removal from the clubhouse. We had a strange idea that a Democratic club should make decisions democratically. The district leader at that time was Kenny Sutherland, a Brooklyn Democratic boss ensconced in a private office who passed down judgment to his people, who often waited hours for it. We went to see him and said that we would like to have a hand in the choice of candidates for endorsement and in other decisions. He replied that this should not concern us, and when we sought to discuss the subject further he had us literally thrown out. Moral: club members may help on primary day and pull the voters out to vote for the candidate of the boss's choice; they may also stand and wait, and, if favored after several years of faithful service, may be rewarded with a plum. I did not return to politics for ten years.

During my summer vacations from law school I went to sea. The second summer, as an ordinary seaman, I sailed on the *Harry Luckenbach,* with a crew of Scandinavians, to the West Coast. We passed through the Panama Canal on my twenty-first birthday and sailed north to San Pedro, California, where Pete

Hanson, a Dane, took me under his wing. "Come on, Irish," he said. "Let's get out of here. It's backbreaking work from here up to Oakland." So we collected our advances—$12.50 in my case—and headed for Los Angeles. Pete taught me to hitchhike and ride the rods.

In Los Angeles Pete and I parted and I contacted some Mayo people. One of them offered me a job and promised to get me into Loyola Law School. But my roots were already sunk in New York and I turned the offer down. Moving on to San Francisco, I put up in a hotel on the edge of Chinatown. I expected to see pigtails everywhere but saw only a few. The new culture was fascinating. I went to a dance at the Red Branch Knights Hall (oldest Irish fraternal society) and to a Gaelic-football game at the Irish Park. I also spent almost all of my money.

When the time came to return I tried to ship out, but there were no jobs and I was forced to turn to Pete the Dane's bag of tricks. I began on the highway to Sacramento. Hitchhiking was easy, although less reliable than the rails, but both provided excellent lessons in geography. I passed by Sutter's Mill, where men mad with greed had destroyed the successful Swiss immigrant and where Sam Brannon, the Mormon, came afoul of the same lust, losing half his flock to the gold rush and finally losing himself.

Automobiles going over the Sierras became fewer and fewer, and the time came, as Pete had said it would, to try the freights. I came across a number of hoboes crouched near railroad tracks. I knew what they were up to and joined them. When the train slowed down, all went aboard, double time, and I with the rest. The gondola, or empty coal car, we ended up in was hot, and I was told by other hoboes to keep my head down until we were safely past the slow-down area. Once moving, we left the scorching gondola and climbed onto the platform surrounding a tank car. With three engines pushing, we crossed the Sierras to Emigrant Gap, passing the divide where the Donner party had been stranded in snowdrifts in 1847.

A few miles from Reno my fellow passengers gave the "all out" sign before the train pulled into the marshaling yards. We camped nearby and the next day, a few miles east of the town, embarked again. As the train approached, slowing down for a bend, heads appeared from the sagebrush and ragged bodies scrambled aboard, safe now from the Reno yardmen.

The road from Reno took us to Salt Lake City, where on the Main Street I bought copies of the *Irish World and Industrial Liberator,* the Irish American weekly that had taken a radical stance in the days of the Molly Maguires and that boasted it had never missed an issue since it first voiced the protest of the Knights of Labor. I took a room, washed off the grime of the road, and the following day visited the Mormon Tabernacle.

East of Cheyenne I ran into a group of Texas cowboys on their way to the Cheyenne rodeo. They invited me to spend the night with them at their improvised campsite. They cooked dinner and breakfast over an open fire and shared both meals with me. The experience was unforgettable.

The only untoward event occurred at North Platte, Nebraska, where I ignored Pete's advice "Don't ever try it alone." Sure enough, I got lost in the railroad yard, and, as the price of my rescue by company dicks, had to purchase a coach ticket to Council Bluffs, Iowa.

The following summer I shipped out on a banana boat bound for Tela, Spanish Honduras. On July 4 we docked about a half mile from the town. The mate warned us that Honduran rebels were threatening a revolt on American Independence Day and cautioned us to return to the ship on time or be left behind.

We went to the local *cantina,* where the whiskey, beer and women were. A Russian sailor named Vassily from our crew was more interested in the revolution than in any of them. He pressed the barkeep for news: How was the people's *revolución* progressing?

The word *revolución* attracted the attention of some barefooted soldiers stationed in a corner and armed with Springfield rifles. Vassily insisted that the *patrón* give him an account of the battle against *imperialismo.* Alas, the talk of revolt was premature, and Vassily remained in seclusion when we pulled in the plank and set sail.

It seemed a shame too, considering that United Fruit had fenced off the entire length of Tela's beautiful beach for the use of its own officers and friends.

I graduated from law school in 1929, just in time to join the Depression job seekers. Moreover, I ran into difficulty qualifying to take the bar exam; I had not been in the country long enough to be a citizen and citizenship was a requirement. I went to Bill with the problem and he asked State Senator Philip Kleinfeld to see what could be done. Bill and he drew up a petition and Judge Benjamin Cardozo (then an associate judge of the state Court of Appeals) signed the order that allowed me to take the exam. But after passing the bar I had to wait two years—until I became a citizen—before being admitted to practice.

In the interval I went to work for the law firm of Cohen and Lieberman at five dollars a week, serving summonses, typing complaints and conducting investigations. I also settled my first case there. Hymie Shornstein, the Democratic leader in Brooklyn, owned the franchise for the Brownsville Bus Company. One of his buses had knocked over a peddler's cart, spilling the notions all over Pitkin Avenue. The peddler was Mr. Lieberman's uncle. I served a summons on Mr. Shornstein. The summons demanded that the bus company pay thirty-five dollars to the peddler for the damage he had sustained. Hymie, who could not read or write although he was a close personal friend of the Roosevelts and Lehmans, asked me to explain the contents of the summons to him. "The peddler is a *gonif,*" he responded angrily. "There isn't thirty-five dollars' worth of notions on all of Pitkin Avenue. Call your boss," he demanded, "and tell him I'll give him three dollars." I told Hymie that the offer was insulting. But finally I felt obliged for my own protection to do as Hymie said. I called the boss and, in language I made sure Hymie could hear, communicated the offer and my determination to reject it. "Find out if he'll make it five dollars," said my boss in what I felt was surrender. I grudgingly relayed the counteroffer. "Young fella," said Hymie, "you are a *goy* mit a Yiddishen *kop*. You have settled a case." It was the highest tribute paid to a Gentile that year on Pitkin Avenue.

At the end of that service I was obliged to serve a *sub pro* on a woman who owed money to Lieberman's brother, a doctor. A *sub pro* is a demand, following judgment, that the debtor pleading inability to pay appear and testify under oath about his assets. The lawyer's hope is that, out of carelessness, the hunted one will appear sporting a diamond ring or other luxurious item, thereby betraying the falsity of his claim of abject poverty, or alternatively, that he will ignore the *sub pro* and thereby be in contempt of court. Invariably the debtor who has hidden his assets is wise enough to show up. Only the "shnook" fails to appear. The lady who was the object of my pursuit lived in an isolated area of Flushing, as yet not urbanized. I was required to cross a stream and pursue a path through some woodlands in order to track her down. She was living in a shack put together with tin cans. She was frail, little and red-haired. "Oh, I owe the doctor money," said the widow, "but I have no money to pay. I wish I had. Dr. Lieberman is a good man." I rocked on my heels. Two small raggedy kids came running up with a belligerent dog. The dog growled at me. The widow reproved him and asked me not to mind. I told her I was sorry but that I was required to serve the process. "No sense in my going to court—I have nothing," she repeated. I begged her, "If you show up and tell them you have no money, you will be all right. Please, you must go." I found myself talking as if I were her lawyer. "Otherwise you will be in contempt of court." On the way back to town I understood that my advice was not called for and that I was really on her side. Worse, I was unhappy that I had served the paper at all. I worried about the problem for days. Then I quit my job and that ended the turmoil.

I was admitted to the bar in April 1931, but it soon became obvious to me that I was not ready to practice. Besides, the country had plunged into the depression that was to last until World War II. I thought I should see more of the world. I applied to my friend Captain Michael Brennan, a remarkable man from Carrigaholt, County Clare, who had for several years skippered Admiral Byrd's sailing vessel on the expedition to the South Pole and was then port captain of the American Republic Line, a United States Shipping Board enterprise. "I thought you were a lawyer," Brennan said reprovingly. "I would also like to be a sea captain," I said jokingly. "You have neither the muscle nor the head," he boasted, towering over me, "but a hitch at sea will do you no harm." He gave me a job on deck on the *S.S. Collbrook* and I shipped out for Rio de Janeiro, Santos, Montevideo and Buenos Aires.

When I got back to New York I was still uncertain about my future as a lawyer. I put up at the Seamen's Institute on South Street, hoping to sign on board a ship bound for the Orient, but by that time the bottom had fallen out of shipping as well. The Depression was in full swing and there were no jobs to be had anywhere. All the while my brothers were unhappy. Frank particularly felt I should make use of my law degree. Diplomatically he opined that my experience at sea would help me immeasurably should I have occasion to represent injured longshoremen or seamen. And, indeed, my knowledge of ships and docks came to my aid later in many a courtroom skirmish.

CHAPTER FOUR

The Depression

IT WAS not the thought of courtroom triumphs that lured me away from the sea. It was a plan Bill presented that acted as the greater magnet. He proposed sending me back to Ireland to help him in an adventure on which he had embarked.

The middle twenties witnessed the last great wave of immigration from Ireland. At the time of the stock market crash 25 percent of the population of greater New York was Irish-born or of Irish extraction. The Irish were then the second- or third-largest ethnic group in the city, almost a quarter million of them having come into New York in the wake of the Irish civil war. As a result, there was a resurgence of interest in Gaelic football* and hurling. Celtic Park, out in Woodside, Long Island, and later Inisfail Park, at 240th Street and Broadway, were crowded with Gaelic football and hurling fans every weekend.

*Gaelic football is somewhat like association football (soccer) with a mixture of basketball. In the Gaelic game the round football may be caught in the air, but it must be put into play immediately.

The Mayo Gaelic football team back home had just won the provincial championship, and at the urging of some compatriots, Bill had agreed to sponsor a competition in New York between the Mayo champions and a select New York team. "Sponsoring" such a contest meant paying the expenses and reaping the profits or suffering the losses. "I need you to go to Ireland and make the arrangements for me," he said. "You are closer to those people than I have ever been." While I knew there was truth to what he said, I also felt that my brothers were conspiring to wean me away from a seafaring career.

It was seven years since I had seen my mother and sisters. My mother wrote to me regularly, and if two weeks went by without a reply, I heard about it in a subtle way. In Ireland, eel skins are prescribed as a cure for a sprained wrist. If I had failed to write, my mother's next letter would decry the fact that there were no eel skins in America. She wrote in a fine, clear hand, and generally her letters reflected a firm point of view. They kept me abreast of what was happening to the Irish O'Dwyers.

My sister Linda, nearest to me in age, was by then teaching school in Glasgow, Scotland, where she had been trained, and was awaiting a vacancy back home. Mary Rose, who had taught school in Newcastle on Tyne with Josephine and who had always wanted to remain there, was living in the old home in Bohola and teaching in my father's school. She had married Bernard Durkan, captain of the Mayo Gaelic football team. He too was a schoolteacher. Kathleen, my oldest sister, was also teaching school in Bohola. She had become the most highly qualified teacher in the province and it showed in her work. Her education and the standing of her class were the only things that prevented her from being dismissed. She had an unexplainable resistance to being punctual and was rarely on time for school. Dudley Solan, the principal, admonished her, but finally gave it up as futile.

For years Katty's journeys to the Saturday lectures at the National University in Dublin were equally trying for others.

The train left Kiltimagh Station, two and a half miles from Bohola, every Friday evening at seven o'clock. Everyone around the town knew where she was going and the purpose of her weekly journey. Everyone also knew of her reputation for tardiness, for one particular reason. Each Friday, as seven o'clock approached, "Tidy" Walsh, the railway porter, developed a high state of nerves, keeping one eye on the Bohola road and the other on the eastbound railway tracks, always praying that Katty would get to the station ahead of the train. It never happened. Invariably the stationmaster would be standing on the platform, a ticket in his hand, waiting for the schoolteacher-student to arrive. The engineer would blow the whistle with impatience. The baggagemaster on occasion joined the stationmaster and other passengers on the platform, and "Tidy" would report that he had spotted Katty on her bicycle coming around the corner of Main Street—which, if true, would have constituted a miracle equaled only by the apparition at Knock, eight miles away, where the Virgin had appeared to workingmen in 1879.

The train engineer, unaccustomed to the quaint ways of the West of Ireland, and unsympathetic to Mayo attitudes toward time, felt imposed upon. He frequently threatened to leave without any further delay so that he could get east of the Shannon and away from the scene that made his ulcer hurt.

A month before I got to Ireland he did what he had often threatened to do. He started out on his journey to the nation's capital without clearance from the stationmaster. As the train chugged past the last gate, a local farmer working in the field waved his spade frantically, pointing back in the direction of the station. The engineer made the mistake of looking back. The stationmaster directed him to back up the train. Katty and the train got to the station at the same time from opposite directions. Both left for Dublin amidst applause.

Josephine, who was the third-oldest girl, was teaching in Newcastle on Tyne, where she had schooled. Unlike her sister

Mary, she longed to return to Ireland, but she had not studied Gaelic, and under the rules of the new Irish government, she had to be fluent in Irish in order to qualify for a teaching post in Erin. So she had to content herself with vacation trips home. In England she arranged for lodging for Irish boys "on the run" from British or Irish Free State authorities.

But the news of how matters stood in Bohola was no substitute for a visit, and with a job to do and my way paid, I looked forward to seeing my family and Mayo again.

I had heard other news—about the Special Powers law enacted by the new Free State government to deal with the holdout Sinn Feiners, who wanted an Ireland completely free of England. Plans were under way to abandon jury trials in "political cases." It was distressing to read reports that a new Irish government would resort to tyrannical practices and defile a court of justice so soon after the withdrawal of the British, whom we had so long condemned for this type of government-sponsored oppression.

Alcock and Brown's airplane flight to Galway in 1919 and Lindbergh's solo to Paris in 1927 gave promise of faster travel at some far distant date, but in 1931 the travel time from New York to Mayo was seven days. As the ship approached the Irish coast the Irish passengers were out before sunup to catch the first glimpse of the headlands. Cobh had not improved in my absence. I soon discovered that whereas in New York I was considered an Irishman, in Cobh I had lost that status. I was now a "Yank"—and that was not meant to be a compliment.

I took the train up to Mayo—it seemed to take forever to finish the last ten miles—where all the family were waiting for me. My mother had gotten old, I thought, and the houses seemed small, but knowing how such appraisals irritated those who stayed behind, I held my tongue.

While the going-away scene was always grim, the homecoming was an occasion for joy for the whole village. Invariably the house was newly whitewashed. A lime-and-water combination and even a dash of paint here and there gave evidence that a wanderer had come back.

The neighbors—all of them—came to visit the first night. We sat around the fire and for the most part I listened. It was good manners for one who had seen a large piece of the world to keep quiet about it. Besides, I wanted to hear the old stories again. It was wintertime and the night frosty and the air clear. It was a perfect night for poaching. The river Gwistan flowed on the edge of our village.

As had been the case for hundreds of years, the fishing rights were owned by an absentee Englishman, who hired a local "barger" to chase or prosecute poachers. The barger had also come to visit that night. The poachers from the village were out, walking chest-deep in the cold, cold water, carrying in one hand a blazing kerosene-soaked canvas bag on a stick, to throw light on the salmon as the poacher followed the fish upstream. It was a skilled poacher who could gaff the salmon as it turned sideways to get back downstream to its spawning bed. The village boys figured the barger would stay only for a short visit before returning to duty on the riverbank. But the barger became engrossed in conversation as the evening wore on. Suddenly the door opened and two neighbors came in, each with a fifteen-pound salmon on his shoulder. They were in the kitchen before they observed the barger. Discreetly, he turned away to look into the fire while the salmon and their captors were shuffled into the parlor and out of sight.

I completed an arrangement with the Gaelic Athletic County Board officials without any trouble. However, I had some heated arguments with a former classmate who was now a lawyer in Kiltimagh.

"The jury," he said, "is now a hindrance to justice. Last spring a juror over in Kildare was told plainly that he had better vote to free an I.R.A. man or face the consequences. And we don't know how many more have been intimidated."

"Every tyrant argues that democracy must be assaulted in

order to preserve it," I said. "Don't feel the Irish invented this queer logic." I felt I was being regarded as an intruder, and indeed I was.

The political news was not all bad. De Valera had changed his mind about taking his seat in the Dáil. His party was not in power. He castigated the government and particularly condemned the Coercion Act. His new party, which had cut loose from Sinn Fein, had decided to contest every seat in Ireland in the coming 1932 election. Predictions were that they would win.

When I returned to New York, I sought out Connie Neenan, head of the I.R.A. in the United States. "I suppose, Connie," I said, "that when De Valera gets in he will continue the fight for total freedom." I was too young for the last one but in time for this. "You've grown older, Paul," he said, "but you still haven't grown up. The fight is over for you and me, and if Kathleeen ni Houlihan isn't dead, she's badly wounded." Six months later De Valera and his Fianna Fáil party took over the government of Ireland. Their first announcement was addressed to the Coercion Act. "It is legislation aimed at protecting the public and winning peace," they said. "It shall be strictly enforced." The growing-up process had progressed by a leap.

Meanwhile I reported to Bill that all arrangements for the tour had been completed. All that was needed was the money to pay the bills. Neither of us had any knowledge or experience with banks, and besides, they were failing left and right. Bill had no money. I had no money. But Frank had saved $6,500. He had put it together a dollar at a time from his backbreaking labor in the wholesale fruit-and-vegetable market. He was a hardheaded businessman and did not think much of the venture but gave his money to Bill anyway.

The scheme turned out to be a disaster. The gate receipts from the first two games at the Polo Grounds were assigned for the benefit of Mrs. William Randolph Hearst's pet charity, the Milk Fund, which had been established years earlier to aid ghetto children. The promoter relied on the third game to pay the expenses of the tour. The *Journal American* and the *Daily Mirror,* both Hearst publications, turned cartoonist Burris Jenkins and Hype Igoe loose on the contests, and the other six dailies followed suit as a matter of courtesy.

Cartoons and stories appeared every day in the sports pages and there were feature stories about the players. The enterprise was a great social success and the promoter got all the credit that was due him—and more. On the financial side, things were difficult.

On the first two days the sun shone with unusual brilliance and the Polo Grounds was filled. But on the third day it rained and few showed up, and the team had to leave the next day. Frank's hard-earned $6,500 had gone to glory.

However, within the year, through a kind word from Mrs. Hearst to Mayor Joseph V. McKee, Bill was appointed to the bench as a city magistrate. He had taken the first step in a political journey that was to carry him a thousand miles. Frank was advanced from laborer to buyer in the fruit-and-vegetable business, and I took up the law again. But clients were few and far between. My friends were feeling the pinch and the economy was grinding down—down—down.

Franklin Delano Roosevelt was elected President of the United States and approached his task with commendable candor. "One third of the nation is ill housed, ill fed and ill clad," he said. A new community had sprung up along the edge of the Hudson River directly below aristocratic Riverside Drive. People unable to pay rent put shacks together from driftwood, flattened ashcans and scrap. In the cold winters the community gathered around outside fires to ward off the cold. The new town had become known as Hooverville. Street-corner orators preached revolution. Ben Davis, black leader of Harlem, and Peter Cacchione, Brooklyn Italian radical, were elected to the New York City Council on the Communist ticket.

Legislation favorable to union organizing was enacted in Washington and Albany and old unions took on new life.

Bright, energetic organizers tackled the job of organizing the giant auto and steel industries. The old craft unions were not moving fast enough for them, so they created a new federation known as the Congress of Industrial Organizations. The C.I.O. took within its fold both craft and unskilled workers.

But the laws merely gave paper protection to organizing efforts. Strike-breaking and union-busting remained widespread and brutal. The unions' local enemies were the Police Department and the magistrates' courts. Peaceful pickets, exercising their First Amendment rights, were arrested for disorderly conduct, and the magistrates before whom they were arraigned usually remanded them to jail to await trial unless they produced bail. The bondsmen's fees had to be paid out of the meager treasure of the struggling unions, and the police and judges became partners of management in a conspiracy.

Soon I found myself in the middle of the movement, defending pickets against labor-organizing injunctions and opposing deportation proceedings against foreign-born agitators. My brother Bill was by then one of the magistrates before whom the agitators were hauled. He had the gift of discharging the pickets without antagonizing the police. From his days as a hod carrier he had been inclined to favor the labor struggle and he found no satisfaction in convicting a picket. We never worked together better.

We had not, however, worked well together before. Under pressure from Frank I had joined Oscar Bernstien and Bill in the suite they shared in the firm of Holmes and Bernstien at 26 Court Street, in Brooklyn. After a few months of serving as a lawyer for both of them I realized I would never overcome the subservient role I had to play as the kid brother, so I borrowed $300 from Bill and moved to Manhattan, where I set up my own office at 521 Fifth Avenue, in the middle of the world. After Bill became a magistrate in 1932, I moved back to his office to what seemed to be an established practice. But even then I learned that law is a purely personal business, and I held on to very few of Bill's clients. In six months I owed the firm of Holmes and Bernstien $1,100 for rent. Holmes became impatient for payment, but Oscar pleaded my case, and I received no dispossess notice. Thereafter I won a few accident cases and with the resulting fees paid off my indebtedness.

Oscar Bernstien's father had been a student of the Talmud, a wise man, however poor, who held the Sabbath sacred. Oscar, as a young lawyer seeking employment, had explained that to Everett Caldwell, a stalwart Republican leader of Brooklyn, and Frank Wing Holmes, from New York's northern tier. Oscar made it clear that he could not, out of respect for his father, accept a job that required him to work on the Sabbath. The two partners thought over the situation and hired him at a salary of fifty cents a week less than they had agreed to pay him.

That was in 1907. The sign "No Irish Need Apply" was down by then, but no sign was needed for Jews. They knew the jobs available to them were peddling and tailoring or running a candy store, where the family could take turns between 6 A.M. and midnight. But Oscar was different. He knew that the framework of democracy ensured freedom. He and other young Jews were determined to seize it, and two thousand years of Jewish struggle against discrimination had bestowed on them the energy and ingenuity to do it. (Oscar was himself a brilliant student and a man of great culture, a devotee of literature, theater, science and math. His Yiddish was perfect. I never knew a lawyer who wrote a more skillful brief.)

After a few years Caldwell and Holmes had looked over their files and found that their reliance on Bernstien had been greater than they imagined. They offered Oscar a raise; he promptly refused. They offered him a partnership, and the firm became Caldwell, Holmes and Bernstien, until Caldwell became engrossed in politics. But when the Republicans denied him the nomination for Kings County district attorney, he became disconsolate and died by his own hand. Thereafter the firm prospered as Holmes and Bernstien.

Oscar became my mentor. His greatest contribution to my training was his insistence that nothing, not even the most widely accepted dogma, should be immune from careful scrutiny. He went over my cases with me point by point, questioning my arguments and identifying my mistakes. The Bernstien home also became my classroom—a salon for actors, labor leaders, thinkers, writers, activists and politicians. Becky Bernstien had been a reporter for the *Herald Tribune,* and such writers as Heywood Broun, *The New Yorker*'s Joe Mitchell and novelist Joe Freeman were regular visitors to their rambling apartment on Madison Avenue. John L. Lewis, president of the United Mine Workers of America, and actors Barry Fitzgerald and Eileen Crow, from the Abbey Theatre in Dublin, would drop in. Gus Goetz and his wife, Ruth Goodman, and Genevieve Taggart were friends. Being with the Bernstiens meant rubbing elbows with people such as Jack Fahy or Charles Keith, fresh from their experience with the Abraham Lincoln Brigade in the Spanish Civil War. Bill O'Dwyer also occasionally dropped by after his day in the Coney Island or Brownsville criminal court.

The times colored our discussions. Relief for the masses of distressed Americans was slow in coming, and only the people's faith in Roosevelt sustained them. Reformers were developing new, bold concepts, and there was a sense of freedom with all. The conversation in Oscar and Becky's living room increasingly was given over to social issues—discrimination in public and private housing, anti-Semitism in America, the rise of Hitler, the Russian Marxist experiment, the injustice done to the Scottsboro boys (who recently had been condemned to death in Alabama), native fascism in America, the court decision allowing *Ulysses,* Joyce's masterpiece, to be imported and the far-reaching effect of Judge John M. Woolsey's ruling. Also the effect of the new breweries on the American economy, the future of the five-cent beer and nickel cigar, the inability of American capital to recover, even with Roosevelt's pump-priming and boondoggles, recognition of Russia, establishment of a WPA theater, as well as other things trivial, interesting, profound, provocative and nonsensical. All contributed to the liberal education of one brought up believing that Ireland was alone in its struggle for freedom.

Bill also contributed at that time. He challenged some of my more parochial and self-serving views and set me to thinking. While he was not passionately committed to any social or political philosophy himself, he thought bigotry in any form was indecent. He said that as time went on I would find out things about the Irish that I did not like and many things about other Americans that I did like. I clung to my Irish clannishness. But continuous exposure to Oscar Bernstien's clear thinking was moving me in Bill's direction.

During my apprenticeship at Holmes and Bernstien I accepted a number of indigent cases. After I had proved my capacity to conduct a defense with skill, Judge Algeron I. Nova assigned me as one of two lawyers to a penniless murder defendant. I went to Brooklyn's Raymond Street jail, where my client was awaiting his trial for the premeditated killing of his mistress. He refused to see me, on the ground that I was a cop. Two court-appointed psychiatrists were called in and pronounced him sane. The only defense he believed possible shattered, he then agreed to work with me.

We were ordered to trial before Judge John Fitzgerald, who was stone-deaf. A hearing aid alone gave him a glimmer of what was being said. As was his custom, he had read police reports on the case, and he had come to the conclusion—ahead of trial—that the defendant was guilty of murder and should be electrocuted. Thus the defense was opposed by two prosecutors—one in front of the bench and one behind.

My fellow counsel and I struggled for a plan of attack and prayed for inspiration, but none came. Whatever skill we possessed was nowhere evident. Charlie Cohen, then with his eye on the state Supreme Court, was the prosecutor. A list of convictions was the best qualification for advancement to the bench, and Charlie was not inclined to lose the case. He opened his argument to the jury as follows: "This is a clear case of premeditated murder."

The victim had been the thirty-one-year-old estranged wife of a merchant seaman and the mother of two small children. My client, an unmarried twenty-eight-year-old long-distance truck driver, had met her, fallen in love with her, left home for the first time and moved in with her and the kids. Thereafter he became extremely jealous of her every move—and apparently she made many. He asked the landlord to keep an eye on her activities during his absences, and when he returned from his travels the landlord told him stories of the men who had come by. She did not deny her indiscretions and taunted him with reminders that he was not the only man who acknowledged her special attractions.

On Tuesday he got a gun.

On Wednesday he bought the bullets.

On Thursday he talked to the landlord and told him, "I'm going to kill the bitch!"

On Friday he changed his mind.

On Saturday he shot her dead in the vestibule of the house.

He ran away and, in his panic, hid out in his mother's house, where the police were maintaining a stakeout. When the doorbell rang he ran into the backyard. As he was climbing over the fence, a policeman's bullet brought him down. He confessed his crime and showed the police where he had disposed of the gun and the little bag in which he had kept the extra bullets. Over vigorous objection, which only proved counsel's panic, Cohen read the defendant's full confession to the jury. The jurors' faces showed how badly the defense had been hurt.

This was no instant killing. The defendant had obviously mulled it over, and I knew that the blue-ribbon jury, with its Anglo-Saxon complexion, did not go for *crime passionel;* dispatching the unfaithful mistress is not in the Puritan code.

My client's story that he had struggled with his lover and the gun had accidentally gone off was hopelessly at odds with his announced intention of killing her. The defense was weak, the prosecution relentless, and the judge had closed his mind in an apparently ironclad case.

But sometimes in cases that are so stacked that the lawyers are helpless, there is a Providence that looks in on the scene. It had done so in this case at the time of jury selection. The defense and prosecution had been given twenty peremptory challenges to the jury list, and each side tried to outmaneuver the other in an attempt to get a jury favorable to his client. We could question the prospective juror about his business but not about his race, religion or politics—although in a place like New York City, race and religion are often evident. Halfway through the process James McGuinness was called to the stand. To save time I informed the prosecutor that I had known McGuinness for some time. "Do you excuse him for that reason?" asked the prosecutor. To do so would have used up one of my peremptory challenges. I declined the prosecutor's bait.

Mr. Cohen concluded that volunteering the information was not an act of generosity, and he believed I was trying to get rid of the juror. Cohen took up the questioning. "How well do you know Mr. O'Dwyer?" he asked.

McGuinness answered, "I have been in his company on several occasions."

"What business are you in?" the prosecutor asked. McGuinness said that he was in the insurance business and lived in Flatbush. From his background and calling, lawyers would judge that McGuinness was a man who could be expected to do honor to the blue-ribbon scheme. He was a man from a higher stratum of New York life, an Irish Catholic of the kind then beginning to become conservative and "law and order"–minded.

Mr. Cohen continued, "Would your acquaintance with Mr. O'Dwyer place the prosecution at any disadvantage here?"

"It would not," McGuinness emphatically said.

Now it was my turn. "Would the fact that you know me cause you to lean toward this eminent and aggressive assistant district attorney, lest you incur the criticism of your fellow jurors during deliberation?" McGuinness answered quickly that this fact would in no way affect his judgment. The prosecutor accepted him and so did I. A mysterious and unseen hand was at work.

I did not know McGuinness very well, but I knew a good deal about him from Callahan, Millward and O'Brien, my tennis partners and late-evening friends, who were colleagues of his in the casualty insurance business. McGuinness, they had told me, had had an affair of the heart with a woman who had left him for another man. McGuinness had gone on a six months' drunk and it had been a year before he got himself together again. His experience came to be meaningful.

The trial occupied several days and was an extremely one-sided affair. Both sides summed up, and the judge took over. Perfunctorily he instructed the jury that every man is innocent until proved guilty, and the burden is on the prosecutor to prove his guilt. "He must be guilty beyond reasonable doubt," he stressed, "but you should not seize upon this protective provision to avoid carrying out what might be a disagreeable duty." The jury was then directed to retire and deliberate.

I stayed at the courthouse all night, drinking coffee and waiting for the verdict. When you defend a man, a human being, and you know that the verdict may mean life or death to him, you agonize over every possible mistake. Did you question too much? Did you make the wrong argument? Did you become too aggressive with the judge? Did you carry sufficient conviction in your argument? You talk with those around you, and the hangers-on make side bets on the outcome. After eight hours you're ready to vomit, and you can't let anyone know. It might hurt your standing. Against all odds, you must remain the blasé *lawyer*. So you make your way to the men's room, and you get some relief, and you begin to rationalize. You did your best. And then you begin all over again.

In those days there was no sequestration, and the jurors were kept together, with no sleep, until they concluded their deliberations. Several hours after they went out the jurors returned for further instructions, but Judge Fitzgerald was asleep in his chambers, and they had to return to their room without benefit of his direction.

After twenty-six hours the jury returned a verdict of murder in the second degree. Judge Fitzgerald felt betrayed. He could not legally sentence my client to a term in excess of twenty-five years. He could not contain his frustration. Angrily he turned to the offending panel. "If this is not premeditated murder, I don't know what is!" he shouted. He dismissed the jury without thanks.

The next evening I went to the Italian restaurant where I had previously met McGuinness and he was there. "The first vote," he told me, "was eleven to one for murder in the first degree. I couldn't see killing the poor bastard. After eighteen hours the foreman said the reason I kept voting for acquittal was because I was a Catholic and Catholics are opposed to capital punishment. McCaffrey, the other Catholic on the jury, is sixty-eight years old, and he protested that what the foreman said was not so. That meant there were two of us. McCaffrey was angry at the foreman, so for twenty-six hours we stood ten to two.

"Finally," he continued, "the foreman made reference to my religion again and threatened, 'I will report you when we leave here.' I countered, 'You will have something real to report because I mean to beat the shit out of you.' This wearing-down process got us nowhere—and everywhere." McGuinness said he had finally persuaded the others to go for murder in the second degree. The juror who had been jilted by his lover prevailed.

Business by then had improved to the point where it justified my reaching for a partnership in the prestigious firm of Holmes and Bernstien. I talked over the possibility with Oscar, and with some monetary concession to Holmes, a new partnership was formed, Holmes, Bernstien and O'Dwyer. I was twenty-six years old, and I personally took the announcements to the printer. The letterhead—five thousand sheets—bore the firm name on the most expensive stationery I could find.

I had joined a number of Irish organizations by then and had picked up some clients that way—a few house closings and personal-injury cases. Joining fraternal organizations for business reasons is not always successful, but for a young lawyer in the thirties without wealthy friends it was the only way to succeed. And sometimes it brought unexpected rewards.

The Mayomen's Patriotic and Benevolent Association provides a case in point. There I saw the Establishment at work. The Mayomen, whose average age must have been fifty (mine was twenty-three when I joined), opened their doors to all who came from County Mayo and their descendants. When I was admitted to membership George Ormsby was president. He was also the only Protestant member. Like most Irish American organizations, the Mayomen were nonsectarian, and George was not the sort of man to tell his fellow members that there was a measure of inconsistency in a nonsectarian society's having as its chaplain a Catholic priest.

The Western People, the *Mayo News,* the *Ballina Herald* and the *Connaught Telegraph* were all passed around at meetings, and through those weeklies the members were kept informed of events in the county back home. Soon after I joined, the local papers were filled with a controversy revolving around the new County Mayo librarian. The young woman had come from Dublin and was apparently well qualified for her post. She was, however, a Protestant, and when this was discovered the County Council suspended her. The Dublin government promptly suspended the Council, and the case precipitated a crisis. The matter came on for debate in New York. I took the side of the government, the chaplain took the side of the county, and the membership stood in judgment on both of us. I called on the spirit of Michael Davitt and with that help carried the motion. The chaplain, taking his defeat ungracefully, said he thought my anticlericalism was showing. But the Mayomen thought the charge not disabling, and at age twenty-five I was elected their president.

The association's ball took place each St. Patrick's Day night and in 1933 it afforded another unexpected reward. Eight thousand immigrants had crowded into the 12th Regiment Armory, and one of them was out of place. She was of Galway descent; she was also pretty, and there she was in the middle of the dance floor with somebody else. I arranged an introduction and soon met Kathleen Rohan, my future wife.

Thereafter, with Kathleen on my arm, I visited the family regularly. Things were progressing well. Frank, still a bachelor, was established in a fruit-and-vegetable business, and Bill, by then a magistrate and married, was achieving renown on the bench. Mildred, Jim's young widow, was collecting a pension of a thousand dollars a year, which, together with her small salary, was sufficient for her and little Joan to make ends meet. Jack, less in evidence, had made a go of his Brooklyn restaurant.

Then tragedy struck again. Late one evening in June 1934 Jack and a policeman friend closed the restaurant and went to a nearby eatery for a snack. A few minutes later three hoodlums entered and held up the place. The policeman exchanged shots with one of the gangsters and Jack was hit in the stomach. He died several days later at Holy Family Hospital, a tragedy hideously compounded by the judicial aftermath in which the gunman was tried, convicted and executed.

My mother, who had been in good health up to that time, began to grieve, and died shortly after, at the age of sixty-five, less than a week before I arrived in Bohola to be with her. Somehow I think her death predisposed me to marriage. Strong Irish women influence their sons in many ways, and their death creates a terrible void. I think I fell into that category.

Frank and I were sharing an apartment on Plaza Street in Brooklyn and we had jointly purchased some furniture. We agreed that the one who married first would leave the apartment and furniture. Frank, however, characteristically decided to move out, leaving the furniture and apartment to Kathleen and me. On August 19, 1935, we were married in St. Kazimir's Polish Catholic Church, with Father Kubek officiating, and thereafter made our home on Plaza Street. A year later Frank moved to California, where he married, had a family and became a successful vegetable farmer.

By the time of my marriage I was representing a few unions—Local 33 of the Hod Carriers (who carry building materials to bricklayers), the Sandhogs (the men who build tunnels under rivers, get the bends and die young), the grain workers (whose function it is to load grain on boats for export), and the warehouse workers (who store imported merchandise in waterfront warehouses). The warehouse workers' union was the only integrated union on the waterfront in the thirties. And to the extent that my services were required in the unions' political work, I was pulled back toward politics.

The Depression had brought about new political allegiances, and President Roosevelt, who was not sure he could count on the full support of New York Democrats in the 1936 elections, began to play with the formation of a second party. He sought the advice of two New York masters of the political game, Ed Flynn, the Bronx Democratic chief, and Democratic National Chairman James Farley.

At the C.I.O. meeting in Washington several months later David Dubinsky of the International Ladies Garment Workers Union, Sam Kovenetsky of the Millinery Workers, and Sidney Hillman of the Amalgamated Clothing Workers met with Flynn and Farley. Convinced that an additional line on the ballot would help Democratic prospects immensely, the men knew that, with labor backing, success was virtually assured. Back in New York, the quintet met Alex Rose, an obscure official of the less-than-powerful millinery workers. Rose was given the then innocuous post of secretary-treasurer of the new party, which they called the American Labor party. Louis Cohen, a young political strategist later to become deputy mayor and patronage dispenser under Mayor O'Dwyer, was put to work qualifying the A.L.P. He had a bagful of tricks, and Flynn's wish was his bidding.

A close working relationship developed between the ALPers and the Flynn-Farley combination of Democrats. Union members from New York City spread across the state to gather the necessary signatures to qualify the new party for the ballot. But I stayed out. For all his political wisdom, Jim Farley was unaware what havoc he was creating in his own party. The Democrats won the first round; the American Labor party garnered 275,000 votes for the President, and Rose, Dubinsky and Hillman were elected presidential electors. But the next year the A.L.P. abandoned the Democratic party and backed Fiorello La Guardia, the Republican-Fusion candidate for mayor, who polled 483,000 votes on the line, assuring his election. In the gubernatorial election of 1938 they returned to support Democrat Herbert Lehman over Thomas Dewey (the A.L.P. received 420,000 votes; Lehman won by 64,000 votes), but a year later they supported Dewey, the personification of Republican conservatism, for district attorney of New York County. He was elected with A.L.P. support.

(By 1941 the left and right wings within the A.L.P. were quarreling, and the party began to come apart. The unions, particularly those of liberal persuasion, remained with the party until 1944, but then the left wing and the right wing went their separate ways. Dubinsky was feuding with Hillman, who stayed with the A.L.P. Charging a Communist takeover of the A.L.P., Dubinsky pulled the I.L.G.W.U. out and formed the Liberal party. With that move, the possibility of either a national labor or national liberal party disappeared from the American scene.)

Bill was elected Brooklyn district attorney in 1939, which

meant that I was barred from criminal-law practice in Brooklyn for as long as he was in that office. It was a sensible regulation and I didn't by any means resent it. Unlike many of our fellow New Yorkers, Kathleen and I had prospered during the Depression and had moved from the flat on Plaza Street into a spacious, even elegant, house in Park Slope. We and our two children, Billy and Eileen, loved the house, but with the passage of time we had begun to dislike our surroundings more and more. Irish-Catholic conservatives with their prejudices showing were everywhere around us. A few incidents made it clear that we should think about moving.

One happened at a Sunday-afternoon meeting of the Ancient Order of Hibernians. I was founder of one of its Brooklyn divisions. At the meeting two separate proposals came on for discussion. One was to condemn Mike Quill for being a Communist. I opposed it. Voting was by show of hands. Two hands went up in opposition. The second motion had to do with Father Coughlin. His radio program each Sunday had taken on a more and more anti-Semitic cast. I voiced my opinion that he was the menace and that he should be condemned. This time I cast the only minority vote.

It was clear that were I to remain in those surroundings I would have to surrender to the overwhelming opposition of the rest. It was time to complete my emancipation. We put the house up for sale and prepared to move to Manhattan. The liberalism I was espousing had become embarrassing even to my friends.

Taking a stand in defense of the rights of radicals brought me into association with the left-wing unions and their lawyers. Louis Boudin, then the dean of U.S. constitutional lawyers, was aging and almost blind, but his discussions about Supreme Court interpretations of the Bill of Rights were intriguing. In 1940 I was hired by Boudin and his partners, Sidney Elliot Cohn and Hyman Glickstein, to defend the Fur and Leather

Workers Union,* which was later drummed out of the C.I.O. on a charge of Communist domination. It was a six-week trial in federal court. I was assigned to the defense of Ben Gold, † the union president, and to our astonishment he was acquitted.

The great majority of prominent and well-known corporate and political lawyers in New York belonged to the Bar Association of the City of New York. It was then a reflection of its membership. The less well known National Lawyers Guild, on the other hand, did not have many Establishment lawyers. One of its founders was Frank P. Walsh of St. Louis and another was Louis McCabe of Philadelphia. Both had been in the vanguard of the Irish Freedom Movement twenty years earlier. Walsh, who continued on in active practice into his mid-seventies, had died on the steps of the federal courthouse in Foley Square after having argued an important labor case. Louis McCabe was still alive and an active member of the guild in Philadelphia when the infamous Smith Act prosecutions were commenced.

About the time I was defending the Fur and Leather Workers Union, I was asked by some of my colleagues on the case to join the guild. I soon became the chairman of the guild's Civil Rights Committee, and as such I submitted numerous amicus curiae (friend of the court) briefs in some of the more important Smith Act cases. While doing so I met Louis McCabe, who years later, in 1949, incurred the ire of federal Judge Harold Medina during the trials of the Communist Eleven. McCabe had been sentenced to serve three months for contempt of court in the West Eleventh Street federal jail.

On the morning he was released a special homecoming

* From my F.B.I. file I found out thirty years later that it was this case that brought me to the attention of Director Hoover.

† Ben Gold had admitted to being a believer in Karl Marx and a member of the Communist party. (Later he became head of the Communist party in New York.)

breakfast was arranged by his friends at the Fifth Avenue Hotel. The crusading radical Elizabeth Gurley Flynn was among the nonlawyers who came to welcome Louis back. We were prepared for an account of Louis's travails and a description of the horrors of his term in prison. Instead, McCabe, who, on the occasion, felt like Thoreau at Walden Pond, declared that prison was the place where every decent lawyer should be at that time in our nation's history.

"Friends and colleagues," he said, "my stay at the West Eleventh Street prison was not long, and it had its interesting moments. For instance, one would expect the screws to be Irish, and indeed they were for the most part, but the one assigned to us was a White Russian. I was sure his assignment was deliberate, but if so, the jailers had stereotyped him and did not know what we soon thereafter discovered—that we were guarded by a White Russian comedian. He took it for granted that all of us were confirmed disciples of Karl Marx. As dawn broke around our lonely prison cells, this refugee from the Kremlin would lean his stick against the passageway bars and walk along as it rattled. 'Arise, ye prisoners of starvation,' he would shout. 'Arise, ye workers of the world, and partake of the miserable repast that a decadent capitalist society has prepared for ye—a large glass of orange juice, fresh from the Florida glades, to tickle your taste buds; bacon from the finest Secaucus hogs; coffee grown and cured in Java and roasted to your special taste by wealthy merchants down by the Coffee Exchange; eggs laid yesterday in Hohokus, New Jersey—our adjoining sister state, the Garden State—which boasts the finest chickens to be found in this rich and fertile country; and cream brought here especially all the way from Wisconsin, its congressmen having convinced this administration that the prisoners' rehabilitation process requires a Wisconsin product to aid the condemned in their long road back. Add to all that fresh bread baked last night while you were sleeping and delivered this very morning by Mrs. Dugan herself. Arise, comrades, it all awaits you—the bread and the coffee you get this very morning. The rest must await the Revolution.'"

Leftists at that time were committed and dedicated but for the most part woefully lacking in humor. McCabe was a refreshing exception.

Subsequently, as the country approached entry into the war, I became involved in a different kind of civil rights case. One day I received an unexpected visit from a former courtroom adversary, Joe Casey, a trial lawyer who had been for a long time an employee of the Traveler's Insurance Company. He asked me to consider defending one of several German Bundists about to go on trial on Long Island. I agreed to see them and to talk about representing them. The charge against them was conspiracy to overthrow the state of New York, an accusation I considered farfetched and indicative of the sentiments in the grand-jury room and the prosecutor's office on the eve of the war against Hitler. Before we completed the arrangements, however, the defendants arranged with Joe to eliminate Bernstien's name from the court papers—and that ended our negotiations. "For shame," said Oscar, "you used me as an excuse to avoid doing your clear duty."

CHAPTER FIVE

Wartime

FRANK HOLMES grew old elegantly. His pace decreased, but he continued to function, confining himself mostly to the appellate courts. He had no children or any other relative to take his place, and upon his death in 1939, Oscar Bernstien and I carried on under the firm name of O'Dwyer and Bernstien. My brother Bill was still the district attorney of Brooklyn, and I had no wish to be engaged in practice across the street from the district attorney's office, so my partner and I decided to move our office to Wall Street, in Manhattan. Kathleen meanwhile had selected an apartment at 350 Central Park West, where, thirty-five years later, we still live.

In 1941 my brother Bill had made his mark—as the successful prosecutor of Murder, Inc., an amazingly successful gang of hoodlums who had murdered eighty-five people in the ten years before Bill's election. At the same time, the weakened Democratic party, still suffering from the disclosures of the

Seabury investigation,* was on the lookout for a likely candidate to oppose La Guardia for mayor. The Democrats were very interested in a candidate who could make a respectable showing (no one expected La Guardia to be defeated), which would help them to elect the borough presidents and the rest of the Democratic ticket. Bill's reputation and personal popularity singled him out as the only candidate who could be expected to do better than the candidates put forward in the two prior mayoralty campaigns, and he was chosen. The leaders, however, believing the incumbent unbeatable, thereafter sat on their hands. Bill lost the election by a small margin and La Guardia won a third term. I played an advisory role in Bill's campaign, which I will now describe.

In 1940 I had represented City Councilman Eugene Connolly, Transport Workers Union President Austin Hogan, and several taxi drivers who were attempting to organize the taxi drivers' union. Nine men, all told, had been charged with beating another driver in a Bickford's restaurant after an organizing meeting. The case appeared to be an attempt to intimidate the organizers, as no weapon had been used and no

* While Jimmy Walker was mayor of New York City and Franklin Roosevelt was governor of New York State, with ambitions to be the Democratic candidate for President in 1932, selling a second New Yorker to the country was not going to be easy. Some special event was required to justify the choice of a second Tammany man as the new candidate after the ignominious defeat of Al Smith in 1928. By design or otherwise, that unusual happening took place in 1932 when Judge Samuel Seabury, a very independent Democrat, was appointed by Governor Roosevelt to investigate corruption in New York City. The headlines in the city's seven daily newspapers were responsible for charges being brought against Mayor Walker. The governor had the authority to remove him, and there was no appeal from the governor's verdict. Halfway through the hearings Walker quit and went to England with his girl friend, Betty Compton. Two years later Seabury and his influential friends supported La Guardia.

serious injury inflicted. In the end, all but one driver were acquitted, and he received a suspended sentence.

While preparing the case I got to know the defendant, Councilman Connolly. We talked about the approaching mayoral election. He was a member of the American Labor party, and because I had come to be identified with liberal causes, I was able to meet other members of the A.L.P. At one of our informal sessions I discussed the idea of the A.L.P. withholding support from La Guardia and supporting someone else, not necessarily my brother, but an A.L.P. member, for mayor. All agreed that La Guardia had been less than helpful to labor.

These discussions led to a larger meeting with A.L.P. leaders. The head of the Transport Workers Union, Mike Quill, had been ignored by La Guardia and was in favor of withdrawing his support from the mayor. Congressman Vito Marcantonio also had reason to mistrust La Guardia, his erstwhile friend. However, Marcantonio had reservations about how his defection might affect his future in Little Italy (a La Guardia as well as Marcantonio stronghold). All these dissidents were convinced that if an insurgent candidate were successful in the A.L.P. primary, La Guardia would lose in the November election. The insurgents were, however, in no financial shape to carry out an expensive primary campaign.

We suspected that Democratic boss Ed Flynn of the Bronx might surreptitiously lend his assistance to La Guardia and that Mrs. Roosevelt might openly support him. Flynn and La Guardia were good friends. Flynn, as national chairman of the Democratic party, was the creature of President Roosevelt and might be expected to do the President's bidding.

I asked the A.L.P. leadership how much such a campaign would cost. "About thirty-five thousand dollars, to cover printing in each assembly district. We have the manpower," they answered. I went to my brother with the problem.

Unlike me, Bill had faith in the Democratic leaders and did not want to enter into such an arrangement without their consent. He took the matter up with Irwin Steingut, the Brooklyn Democratic chief, and with the leader of the Democrats in the state assembly. Steingut placed the matter before other county leaders, including Flynn, who reported to Bill that the plan would not work. Bill decided to abide by their decision. Had I known then what I came to know later, I would not have listened to the Democratic leaders and would have gone ahead with the plan on my own.

The group within the A.L.P. with whom I had been negotiating won most of the primary contests in 1941 against the forces within their organization favoring La Guardia, and I am convinced that, had he proceeded with the plan, Bill would have been elected mayor of New York in that year rather than in 1945.

Bill's campaign manager was Dwight Sullivan, a New York lawyer who came recommended by the Democratic leaders. One night at a campaign headquarters I came across a speech Bill was to deliver in which he charged Sam Null with being a Communist. Null was a respected lawyer, a partner in the prestigious labor-law firm of Markewich and Null. "You simply cannot say that," I told Bill, "it's not true," and he agreed to eliminate the offending passage from the speech. But an advance text was given to the press and was published the next day. Bill publicly apologized to Sam, who took the incident in stride. To this day I don't know whether such incidents were a result of carelessness or deliberate sabotage.

As the radical younger brother of the candidate, I was thereafter seldom consulted. However, I was able to convince Bill to speak without written scripts, because by then we had little faith in the canned speeches prepared by party speech writers. Besides, the speeches increasingly were being given to Bill only a few hours before he had to deliver them. I believe that was by design.

As a result of his new, informal style Bill began to draw huge crowds wherever he spoke. But because the leaders regarded

La Guardia as a sure winner, many of the clubhouses remained dark, just as they were when Stevenson ran for President in 1952 and when McGovern ran in 1972.

Toward the end of the campaign, when it was clear that Bill was picking up support and it looked as if he might win, La Guardia became very irritable and took to name-calling. He was furious that Governor Lehman had endorsed Bill, and called the respected governor a *gonif*.*

A few weeks after Bill's defeat the Japanese attacked Pearl Harbor, and the United States declared war on them and the Axis powers. I was past thirty-four years of age. I had an established law practice, a wife and two children, and another child expected soon. Nevertheless the army was taking married men my age, and like many in my in-between group, I felt increasingly uncomfortable about not participating. Finally I talked it over with Kathleen and she agreed that whatever I felt I must do I should do. She did not say what would make her happy and I did not ask.

Having been rejected earlier by Naval Intelligence, I decided to try to join the Coast Guard, and was told to get letters of recommendation from prosecutors and judges, which I did. After a month's wait I was notified to report for an examination. The test was in navigation, a subject about which I knew nothing. I gave the test papers to the proctor and told him that there must be some mistake. He told me that my application had gotten into the wrong hopper, that he would note it, and that I should wait for another call.

The call never came. I knew how to load a ship, and I knew also that some of the Liberty ships listed out at sea because of improper loading and this held up the convoys. Sabotage was suspected, but the more likely reasons were haste, improper checking, sloppy planning on the dock, with little attempt to balance the load, or just plain ignorance and incompetence. I

*The Yiddish word for "thief."

put in a bid to join the Liberty ships or supervise their loading.

In the meantime, if I was going to join the service, I thought that I had better know something about the military way of doing things, so I joined the Fighting 69th New York National Guard. I never made corporal, but Jack Feeney did. He could sing and was a well known Irish tenor. And Terry Long did too. He was a reporter for the *Irish Echo* and could type with two fingers. Our function was to guard the town in case of an attack, and I shudder to think of the fate of New York if it had had to rely on the home guard.

I made another application to the navy, this time to be a gunner on a Liberty ship. It was obvious that the armed forces did not feel a desperate need, and I was never notified whether or not I was accepted.

The draft finally sought me, and I went to the draft board to report. There I was asked if I wanted to appeal my status. I said that I did not but that I wanted one month to wrap up my affairs. On St. Patrick's Day, 1942, I was ordered to take the physical examination, which I passed. "Which branch of the service do you wish?" said the soldier at the end of the exam. "Navy," I said. "Army," he said as he put the final stamp on my papers. At the end of the month, three days before my prospective induction, the army reduced the maximum draft age to twenty-six and I was not called.

Rejection produced mixed emotions in me and a sigh of relief from Kathleen. That I was too old to serve the military was a blow to my ego, but I got on with the practice of law and contented myself with taking orders from an efficient lieutenant in the 69th who had had, evidently, at least one bad experience with either a lawyer or an Irishman.

During the years that followed I fought several wars of my own, one of them against the army. Young Jeremiah O'Donovan Rossa, like many American youths, had enlisted in the army shortly after Pearl Harbor. In 1915 his grandfather, whose name he bore, died after a lifetime devoted to a struggle for Irish freedom which saw him convicted of treason, editing an insurrectionist newspaper, and everywhere revered. The funeral oration by Padraig Pearse at O'Donovan Rossa's funeral is an Irish classic, and the final lines proved to be both inspirational and prophetic:

> The fools, the fools, they have left us our dead and while Ireland holds these graves, Ireland unfree shall never be at rest.

O'Donovan Rossa III had been born the year this Irish leader died, so it was natural that he be given the illustrious name. After service in Alaska, Jeremiah had volunteered for paratroop training and had passed the necessary tests. As a volunteer he was given his choice as to the branch of paratroopers in which he wished to serve. He selected the infantry, but as is so common with the army, his choice was ignored and he was assigned to field artillery. He protested, and the officer in charge took offense at what he felt was unwarranted criticism of army regulations and sentenced the soldier to fourteen days on K.P. O'Donovan Rossa lodged another complaint, and in order to teach him another lesson, the C.O. confined him to quarters. Because O'Donovan Rossa thereafter went to the post exchange, he was imprisoned for six months.

Fate seemed to be with him, however. His outfit was moving to North Africa, and the army manual prohibited shipping a soldier to foreign soil while serving a sentence. O'Donovan Rossa was released and landed with his contingent in Africa, whereupon he was again placed under guard. No new charge had been lodged against him, and when he asked the reason for his detention, he met only hostility or stony silence. One day he and the other prisoners were ordered to dig latrine ditches. He protested and referred to the rules and regulations. A lieutenant was called and the lieutenant repeated the order that the sergeant had previously given. O'Donovan Rossa again inquired about the reason for his being held prisoner, and the lieutenant could not, or would not, tell him.

But under army regulations he had disobeyed a commissioned officer in time of war in a war zone. Two days later he was told that his old sentence had been set aside. "I will now obey the order," he said, but was told that it was too late and a new charge, willful disobedience of a lawful order, was being pressed. A court-martial was hastily put together; O'Donovan Rossa had the benefit of meeting once with his lawyer. The trial was a mere formality, and with unseemly speed the court found the soldier guilty and sentenced him to death before a firing squad.

On review, a higher military court urged the original tribunal to reconsider their sentence. They did and within five minutes reconfirmed it. On June 16, 1943, O'Donovan Rossa wrote General Dwight D. Eisenhower, Commander in Chief of the American Expeditionary Forces in North Africa, explaining his plight and asking for the general's help:

> Sir, I am not a coward. What I ask is a chance to prove myself to my superiors, my countrymen, my family and myself . . . I am not asking for my life, but for something more precious, my good name . . .
>
> There are people at home who believe in me and there are the officers and men in my own battery who believe in me. Give me a chance to prove that I am worthy of that fate.

On July 25, 1943, General Eisenhower replied:

> No person in the military service can defy the orders of superior military authority with impunity. In this respect you were at fault. However, you should have been informed of the reason for your confinement and because the officers were at fault in not so informing you and because of your desire to perform service in the front lines, I have approved a sentence under which you will be

> entitled to be restored to duty within a reasonable time. Thereafter, you are a real soldier. I am directing the Commanding Officer of the disciplinary training center, where you will be confined, to keep me informed as to the character of your conduct. If such conduct is exemplary, your release, for front line service, will be accomplished this year.

The general, however, was not kept informed, and the duties of war made it impossible for him to make certain that his orders were carried out. Smarting under the reprimand from Eisenhower, the officers were determined to get even with O'Donovan Rossa. Mysteriously, he became ill with a tropical ailment and was sent to the hospital, but was soon removed to the brig and placed on a bread-and-water diet for fourteen days. The subtle torture became too much for him to bear; he became despondent and attempted to take his life. Army psychiatrists examined him and he was returned to the United States in a straitjacket and confined at Fort Leavenworth.

I had been president of the United Irish Counties Association, and although I had not seen eye to eye with Irishmen, my relationship with this particular organization had not yet deteriorated and we could share a common outrage in the case of the scion of a man much honored for his sacrifices on behalf of freedom in Ireland. I urged the association to mobilize their thirty-two affiliated organizations to seek redress.

A massive letter-writing campaign ensued. Congressmen, the Clemency Board, the War Department, the Secretary of the Army and countless other public officials were deluged with letters urging intervention. Maureen Mulcahy of the Irish Bureau coordinated the letter-writing campaign, and soon criticism of the army for its barbaric misconduct began to appear in the *Congressional Record.* O'Donovan Rossa had been told he would be given a dishonorable discharge. When we asked for a review of that decision, we were told that never in the history of the army had there been a reduction of a dishonorable discharge.

In January 1946, in the middle of our campaign, we received word that the Clemency Board had reviewed the case and had reduced O'Donovan Rossa's sentence to four years, which was the exact time he had been imprisoned. He was therefore eligible for immediate release. The dishonorable discharge was ordered put aside and was replaced by a "blue discharge." For the first time in the history of the army this unchangeable rule had finally been changed.

During the war people involved in defense industries were exempt from the draft. Two of my clients, young men, were sons of wealthy parents. They had obtained employment in a camera factory and were duly certified by their hard-pressed employers as essential to the war effort. Reporting this fortuitous turn of events to their respective draft boards, the two worked faithfully at their benches, but there came a time when their contract ran out.

They applied for the renewal, which never came, and in the fashion of young men of their station, they got impatient with the hard New York winter and traveled south for the warm weather. But, preoccupied as they had been with their vacation, they neglected to tell the local draft board that there was a change in their status. Some friends, whose kin were at the Bulge, Pantelleria, or hard-pressed Solerno, made an inquiry; the camera factory was visited by government agents.

Soon there was a roundup of draft evaders, and my two clients were unceremoniously hauled before the court on a cold wintry day. They wore deep Florida tans, and no amount of cosmetics could hide the evidence of their southern sojourn. We sought a postponement adjournment for a period sufficient to permit their tans to fade. The parents of these evaders had retained a battery of lawyers. Eddy Levine, a former assistant district attorney, represented two others. Joe Delaney, probably the best criminal lawyer of his day in federal court practice, represented two more.

As we went to trial we found ourselves sharing the counsel table with two other lawyers, representing other members of the draft-evading group. These lawyers had no reputation in the trial field.

We came before Judge Robert Inch, and at a conference the prosecutor offered to allow all defendants to plead to a lesser count. The two inexperienced lawyers accepted the terms, but we were convinced that the indictment was faulty and that our clients were not technically guilty of the charges. The case was severed, and although we conceded the facts as outlined, we disputed the legal consequences. We argued that it was not possible for the draft boards to cast a citizen in the role of a criminal just by promulgating rules that they changed on their own initiative from time to time.

We presented a plain question of law to the court, and Judge Grover Moskowitz, before whom we argued, found our six clients guilty, and sentenced them each to a year in jail. The defendants who had pleaded guilty to the lesser charge meanwhile had been given a suspended sentence. We scoffed at Judge Moskowitz's ignorance; we knew that the judge was not much of a lawyer and that he was probably suffering from war hysteria, which regrettably had taken the place of a sound legal decision.

The Circuit Court of Appeals, we reasoned, was made up of men of better caliber. We prepared our briefs, and with a confidence that bordered on arrogance, argued before the higher court. The government's brief contained a lot of rhetoric and, we thought, was based on the most unprofessional appeal to the patriotism of the court. The circuit court listened quietly, too quietly, we felt, and in a decision that will not be recorded among the great legal opinions of history, the court affirmed the conviction.

Our first reaction was disbelief. How, now, were we going to explain to our clients, who had paid us well, trusted our judgment and followed our professional advice, that our judgment had been inferior to that of lawyers of no repute? We appealed to the United States Supreme Court, but it refused to hear the case.

We were in a fix. Under the rules, we had to return to the sentencing judge for resentencing after the adverse decision. But Judge Moskowitz had died. The resentencing was referred to Judge Inch, whose plea bargain we had rejected at the outset. I knew Judge Inch and had tried a few negligence cases before him. As neither Levine nor Delaney knew him, I was elected to open the discussion with the court. "Judge Inch," I started, "I want to tell you that we are three lawyers who know our business."

"There is no question about it," said His Honor, unable to hide his distaste.

"We are so good that we are better than the judge who tried the case," I continued.

"There are those who would question that statement," answered the judge, who felt obligated to defend a dead colleague's reputation.

"We are so good," I persisted, "that we are even more knowledgeable than the Circuit Court of Appeals."

"Sometimes," he said, "I have felt that way after reading their judgment of reversal, but a sense of propriety would have prevented me from saying so even under the most trying circumstances." The judge was annoyed.

"Well, Your Honor, it's because we are so cocksure of ourselves," I replied, "that we come before you in deep trouble."

His eyes softened a bit. "Pray, tell me about it, counselor," he said.

"There were five lawyers to start," I said, "and we fancied

ourselves better than the other two. Their clients now admire and respect their lawyers and our clients do not. You suspended sentence on their clients, and ours, charged with precisely the same offense, must do a year in jail because they trusted our judgment. Arrogant pride has been responsible for this embarrassing development, but it does not square with justice that clients should suffer because their lawyers thought themselves wiser than the judge before whom they appeared." And I closed with the well-known words "'Pride goeth before a fall.'"

The judge smiled and lit a cigar. He walked to the window barely controlling his laughter. And when he returned to his desk he agreed to a resentencing hearing.

The question by then revolved around what Judge Inch would do with the lawyers. As it turned out, he decided not to impose sentence on us, placed our clients on probation and let them go free.

During the war years the federal government established price controls. Chester Bowles, one of President Roosevelt's brain trusters, headed the enforcement. The scarcity of consumer goods had created a black market, trafficking in which was not universally condemned. In fact, many, perhaps most Americans took pride in their skill in evading the law.

Paul Ross, a friend and colleague from the National Lawyers Guild, was named head of the local price-control board. Corruption and graft were evident on every side. Ross was determined to make price controls work, and he was both strict and severe. His doggedness brought him into conflict with many industries, and their complaints to Bowles continued and multiplied. Powerful interests demanded that Bowles discharge Ross, and the ace enforcer was fired.

People in New York were appalled and came to his assistance. Ross and I met at the guild office. We decided to commence a legal action against Bowles. After the legal papers were served,

Bowles called to ask me to come with Ross to Washington for a meeting with him.

Ross felt that his usefulness was impaired and he could no longer have the same support from the people who had been working for him. But vindication was important. The three of us reached a compromise. The charges against Ross were withdrawn and he was reinstated. He resigned a short time later.

(Subsequently I asked Ross to be the director of research in Bill's 1945 campaign for mayor. After Bill's election Ross became assistant to the mayor. Soon thereafter the Federal Bureau of Investigation informed Bill that Ross was a Communist. Bill consulted me, and I said I had no knowledge that Ross was a member of the party. Bill thought it over and sent back word to the F.B.I.: "I don't know what Paul Ross's political views are, but if the F.B.I. knows anybody else who is as faithful to his obligations as Ross is, please let me know because I would like to hire him.")

Wartime produced other dissidents to be defended. A number of members of the *Clann na Gael* ("The family of the Gael") and Irish Republican Army clubs in New York resented the draft on the grounds that to serve might help Great Britain. Some of them returned their draft notices, attaching notes indicating that as long as the United States was in partnership with a power that held five hundred million persons in subjection, they would refuse to fight.

As could be expected, they ran into trouble because of their refusal. The F.B.I. came around asking questions, believing the Irishmen were somehow involved in sabotage activities. They were not, but they needed legal protection anyway and I supplied it.

American I.R.A. members had been able to break through wartime barriers and communicate with the I.R.A. in Ireland. This was indeed an embarrassment to the officials in Washington, because the country had installed strict censorship. Letters of every kind were stopped; security was so tight that nothing could get through. Yet Scotland Yard was able to come up time and again with an I.R.A. letter that had gotten through. As a result, there was growing pressure here to stop the letters and find the culprits.

Eventually government agents raided the I.R.A. hangouts in New York. They went to see Jimmy Brislane, who ran a saloon at Ninety-seventh Street and Lexington Avenue in Manhattan. He came from County Cork and had been active in the I.R.A. there as a young man. Jimmy still spoke with a heavy Cork accent, which was difficult for people—even the Irish from other regions—to understand. He came to my office to tell me what the F.B.I. had said to him and what he had said to them. When he had finished his story, he said, "What do you think, Paul? Did I answer them right?"

"Well, Jimmy," I answered, "you have confessed yourself into the federal penitentiary for about twenty-five years. But you're safe, because the F.B.I. couldn't possibly have understood your accent."

In any event, these men were never prosecuted. The ones who objected to going into the army were not opposed to fighting for the country. They simply objected to being sent to Europe and fighting alongside British soldiers when their own native land was still under British rule. The men came to me periodically with their draft forms in hand. I composed an answer that would satisfy them and still not cast them in the role of traitors: "I owe my allegiance to the United States and to no other power. I would gladly give my life to defend it. I firmly believe that it is a distinct disservice to democracy that we are fighting side by side with people who continue to maintain 500,000,000 human beings in slavery. I resent our flag being flown with the flag of Great Britain. They are no better than Hitler."

These few sentences satisfied the government. They were an

expression of opinion and not of defiance and mollified officials eager to avoid a confrontation. The authorities found ways of sending these men to the Far East, where they would not have to serve in the same arena with the British.

As the war ended, Americans prepared themselves for a new era, one promising peace and prosperity but also presenting the darker, frightening prospect of hysteria.

CHAPTER SIX

Hysteria

By 1945, the year my brother Bill was elected mayor, the second red scare had begun to be felt in every sector of American life, including the United States Congress. Voluntarily removed from Bill's campaign and administration, I was red-baited constantly. It would have done no good for me to enter a denial. Instead I became more active in the National Lawyers Guild. The country was ready to pursue a scapegoat on which to blame all manner of problems, and American Communists were the prime target. The large C.I.O. unions that had come into existence during the Depression had many left-wingers, liberals and Communists within their ranks and in leadership positions. For some time the unions had resisted demands from industry, the media and religious institutions (mainly Catholic) to purge Communists from their ranks.

The Taft-Hartley Bill in 1947 was designed to reduce further the power of the unions and to bring them to heel. It swept through Congress on a wave of emotion. President Truman, in one of his many courageous acts, promptly vetoed the bill, but the Congress overwhelmingly overrode his veto.

Surrendering to exaggerated fears of constituents, Congress in 1940 had passed the Smith Act. The statute made it illegal not only to advocate violent overthrow of the government but also to be a member of any group that did. The act became the weapon with which the government pursued Communist party members after the war. "Proof" of membership was often spuriously supplied by paid informers. The social and economic effects of the witch-hunt on the victims were horrendous. Many of the country's most talented citizens were reduced to pauperage and many more were publicly reviled. Few Americans questioned the loss of constitutional guarantees.

By the late 1940s the C.I.O. had purged from its midst nine international unions that, the leadership charged, were Communist-influenced. Opportunistic labor leaders took full advantage of the purge to catapult themselves into high union offices, for among the many provisions of the Taft-Hartley Act was one prohibiting a Communist from holding union office. Charges of Communist affiliation were carelessly made by ambitious men, and the mere accusation was enough to brand a rival union leader forever. Many progressive and liberal leaders, who would have been the first to lose their lives under a Communist regime, were damaged or ruined.

In the immediate postwar years few organizations could be counted upon to fight against official repression. The National Lawyers Guild was one of them. I was president of the New York chapter of the guild in 1947, and from 1948 to 1951 I served on the national board of directors. We lobbied publicly against repressive bills as they came before congressional committees that were designed to abridge civil liberties, and we represented in court various clients who got caught in the web of hysteria.

One of the causes undertaken by the guild was a campaign to urge President Truman to rescind his Executive Loyalty Order, which, according to the *New Republic* issue of September 27, 1948, "arbitrarily branded scores of organizations as subversive, purged its strategic departments without adequate safeguards, and added to the hysteria by deportation proceedings." Specifically, the loyalty order was aimed against federal government employees, and again according to the *New Republic,* "two million civil servants" were on the suspect list.

The opposition to the national witch-hunt was weak and diffused. The liberal community was sprinkled with people who, at one time or another, had been associated with the Communist party and had become disenchanted. Others splintered off because of ideological socialist attitudes, and these people developed an irrational hostility toward their former allies. In the early stages they secretly welcomed the attacks, and when they finally woke up, they realized too late that they were being tagged equally with those they had left years earlier.

The Liberal party was sensitive about its past association with the American Labor party. Once I met David Dubinsky, head of the Liberal party and then president of the I.L.G.W.U., in Lindy's restaurant. He berated me rather rudely and publicly for my tolerant attitude toward left-wingers and Communists. After some minutes I cut in to say, "David, I have no compulsion to hate Communists, because I never was one." It was a smart rejoinder, but, politically speaking, I had used poor judgment. It was remembered years later.

In April 1947 I received a rather weak resolution from the prestigious American Civil Liberties Union, opposing only part of the loyalty order. The A.C.L.U. requested that the Lawyers Guild adopt their statement. The acting director of the Union, Clifford Forster, wrote me and said that from their preliminary inquiries they had found no sentiment or intent on the part of government officials to engage in witch-hunting. I replied to the Union's request, saying:

> I believe that the promulgation of the order at this time is in and of itself a threat to civil liberties in America.

> Coming at this time, it will mean that literally millions of government employees will live in fear and dread as long as this order is in existence. If there is enforcement of this order, no matter what precautions are taken, it will, in my opinion, undoubtedly mean a system of witch hunting and spying unequaled in the annals of this country since the time of the Alien and Sedition laws.
>
> Unless all persons interested in civil liberties are heard now to protest against this order in its entirety, the memorable happenings in the days of Mitchell Palmer shall undoubtedly be paled into insignificance by the reign of terror soon to come.
>
> At a recent meeting of the National Lawyers Guild in Detroit, we decided, by unanimous vote, to protest against this executive order in its entirety, chiefly for the reasons I have outlined above. I would be only too glad to join with you or any of your committees along the lines I have indicated.

A few days later I sent another note to the Union:

> No matter how well intentioned some of the government officials in charge of this investigation may be, we can take it for granted that no government employee is going to join either the American Civil Liberties Union or the National Lawyers Guild from here on in, and that would be some indication of the effect that this order will have on the morale of our civil service. In other words, I think that they will have the right to speak freely, at their own risk.

The guild was not able to stem the tide of hysteria, and, if anything, things got worse. President Truman established the Loyalty Review Board, which expanded the purpose of the order from denying federal employment to persons concerning whom there were "reasonable grounds" of suspicion to persons about whom there was "reasonable doubt." To his credit, however, the President refused to turn over the board's records to congressional investigating committees.

In California, writers, actors and actresses were the targets of the purge. In New York, mostly teachers became the victims. Approximately fifty teachers lost their positions by virtue of the state's insidious Feinberg Law. The Board of Higher Education, taking its cue from the state legislature, began to develop restrictive rules against teachers on campuses. The city's Board of Education adopted a loyalty oath for teachers. I appeared before the Board of Education and the Board of Higher Education opposing both of these restrictive measures, and in doing so incurred the ire of Dr. Edward Lodge Curran, the president of the International Catholic Truth Society.

Soon after my appearance I received a letter from Dr. Curran. He was described as "protector of the faith" and spent an inordinate amount of time and effort going after liberals, progressives and suspected Communists. In his letter of September 2, 1947, Father Curran wrote me:

> In the July 12th issue of *The Tablet,* Catholic newspaper of the Diocese of Brooklyn, a letter appeared signed by Thomas Casserly. The caption, under which this letter was printed on the Readers' Forum Page, reads as follows: "Finds P. O'Dwyer Joined Reds on Another Issue." The letter itself makes the following allegations:
>
> 1. You are charged with having presented a memorandum to the Board of Higher Education, "in opposition to an amendment to the Board's by-laws that would deny subversive groups the permission to organize on the campus of any city college."
>
> 2. You are charged with having opposed a ban on the book entitled *Citizen Paine* written by Howard Fast, editor of *New Masses.* . . . The book in question has been described as "lascivious and objectionable" in passages and "unfit for children." You are further charged with having appeared on this occasion and spoken before the Board in company with recognized Communists.
>
> 3. The National Lawyers Guild, which you represented, is likewise charged with having "consistently followed the Communist Party Line" and with even opposing "the taking of a loyalty oath by teachers."

> I should like to know if these facts and allegations are true.

I had made it a practice not to reply to letters or questions of this type, but I had known Dr. Curran, had met him on several occasions, and I did not doubt his sincerity. I was in Ireland when he sent the letter; he wrote again requesting a reply and I obliged him:

> I have no intention of engaging in any controversy with Mr. Casserly or with anybody else about my views with respect to gag rules by public boards or bodies, or the ban of *Citizen Paine,* or my membership in or representation of the National Lawyers Guild.
>
> I have taken a stand on matters that I regard as being in the public interest and will continue to do so, from time to time, as the occasion arises and as my conscience dictates. I presume when I do, there will be those who will disagree with me and will express their criticism in varied forms. I have no wish to prevent them and will always uphold their right to do so, and I hope in this respect I shall not be found wanting, particularly in those "times that try men's souls."
>
> My views are, in my judgement, conceived in good faith, and dictated by good conscience. I cannot, nor do I wish to, control any construction which anybody may seek to place on my views.

There was not much Dr. Curran could do with that reply except to report it to appropriate bodies.*

*Years later, in 1974, when I came to be the president of the City Council, my help was invoked by some fifteen of the teachers' heirs. Even though the Feinberg Law had been unconstitutional, some of those who lost their positions because of its harshness had failed to file a claim for appropriate compensation for the wrong done to them.

After much exchange of letters between myself and the Board of Education and the corporation counsel's office, the matter was ended satisfactorily and compensation was eventually paid to those who had filed a claim and to those who had failed to do so within the proper time limitations.

The main instrumentality in spreading hysteria and hate was the House Un-American Activities Committee, which had come into being in 1938 under the chairmanship of Martin Dies of Texas and flourished in the postwar period.

Francis Walter of Pennsylvania became the new chairman of H.U.A.C. in 1949. One of his victims was Martin Popper, a colleague of mine in the National Lawyers Guild. Popper represented clients in Poland and Czechoslovakia and had visited them behind the Iron Curtain. By that time H.U.A.C. was expanding its activities to include an investigation into the issuance of passports to persons who traveled outside the United States. "Are you now, or have you ever been, a Communist or member of the Communist party?" was the question posed. Popper said the question was improper. He said the First Amendment guaranteed him freedom to belong to any political party he might choose, and he refused to plead the Fifth Amendment. As a consequence he was indicted for contempt of Congress.

The ensuing trial took place in the United States District Court in the District of Columbia before Judge John J. Sirica.* Leonard Boudin and I conducted the defense. We knew that jurisdiction over passport legislation was vested in another committee and that H.U.A.C. had no right to inquire into that area. We needed someone to prove it. James Roosevelt was the only representative who would come forward and give testimony about it. But it was the devil's own job to get permission from the congressional bureaucracy for Roosevelt to testify.

*During this case Sirica was a tense and nervous man, frightened by the atmosphere of the times. He brushed aside, with obvious impatience, the profound legal arguments addressed to the legal and constitutional shortcomings of the government's case. His behavior on the Watergate case came as a great surprise to Boudin, Popper and me. He was about the last judge in the federal court we would have expected to proceed against Richard Nixon with such courage, courage he had signally failed to display in the Popper case. His past history may have been the reason the Nixon administration saw to it that the case was tried before him.

Finally we called Chairman Walter to the stand. He was a very hostile witness. The Establishment regarded it as an act of downright effrontery. The jury, made up of frightened government employees, all of whom were themselves subject to surveillance, took less than an hour to reach a guilty verdict. The appeals court set it aside. The indictment was permitted to die a natural death. There was no compensation to Popper for the harassment conducted against him by the Congress of the United States and the Department of Justice.

Hollywood writers, producers, actors and actresses were among the first to be hauled before the H.U.A.C. "Are you a Communist? Have you ever been a member of the Communist party?" were the classic questions. Some of those called had opposed Franco or joined anti-Fascist groups or had permitted their names to be used on advertisements protesting restrictions on constitutional rights. Others had attended dinners honoring colleagues labeled as Communists. Still others had shown sympathy for the constitutional rights of Communists. Failure to answer the questions and involve colleagues resulted in loss of employment. Hollywood producers were compelled to establish a blacklist, and many of the most talented writers and performers became unemployable. There had not been a single shred of evidence produced that showed that they had used their art for political ends.

Some of the victims expressed their opposition to H.U.A.C. in unequivocal language. Lillian Hellman, one of my most prestigious clients, was one who did so. Responding to her subpoena, she wrote:

> I do not like subversion or disloyalty in any form and if I had ever seen any I would have considered it my duty to have reported it to the proper authorities. But to hurt innocent people whom I knew many years ago in order to save myself is, to me, inhuman and indecent and dishonorable. I cannot and will not cut my conscience to fit this year's fashions, even though I long ago came to the

> conclusion that I was not a political person and could have no comfortable place in any political group.

She was later requested to appear but refused to testify.

Singer Paul Robeson was another who refused to be silenced by the witch-hunters. The hysterical Establishment was frightened that blacks would follow his leadership and he was haled before several investigating agencies. He testified that he was not a Communist, nor had he ever been one. It did not help, and soon his American concert tours were canceled, movie and stage opportunities lost. He chose to become an expatriate, an exile in the Soviet Union.

In 1949 a group of Robeson's friends had attempted to organize a concert for him, but right-wingers attacked with renewed vigor and the concert was canceled. His supporters planned a second concert, to be held outdoors about three miles from Peekskill, New York. Hooligans attacked, beating with sticks those who had attended. The police failed to halt the riot, and authorities in Westchester County never pressed charges against the culprits, many of them American Legionnaires. Ed Sullivan subsequently wrote in his newspaper column that the Robeson incident was regrettable, "mostly because it gives the likes of Paul O'Dwyer an opportunity for displaying his protest."

Against my instincts, but surrendering to what seemed to be good advice from a friend, I called Sullivan and asked to see him. He received me in his office at the Hotel Delmonico.

"You must be misinformed about what I stand for and what I believe in," I said. "Otherwise you would not have published that statement."

"It's nothing specific," he answered, "but I seem to connect you in my mind with headlines on issues on which I am much opposed."

There was a pause. "It's hard to talk against that," I said, getting up to leave.

Sullivan asked, "What would you suggest I write to set the record straight?"

"I'll leave it up to you," I answered.

Sullivan never did do anything to rectify what he had written, but my visit was not an entirely wasted effort. I learned something about him that helped me to deal with his attacks on Leon Bibb.

Bibb had been a performer on Sullivan's Sunday-night television show. He also had appeared at benefits, one of which was sponsored by a liberal group on Long Island, and the local American Legion had picketed his performance there. The Legion followed up its effort by protesting Bibb's periodic appearances on Sullivan's show. Bibb was ordered to appear before Sullivan to explain himself, and Harry Leventhal, Bibb's agent, called me for help. I knew that Bibb, who was black, would be ruined if Sullivan did not put him on the show, and I knew we had to come up with something unusual to get him back on. Sullivan had boasted that he had been helpful to black performers. I composed a letter to Sullivan for Bibb to sign:

> I am grateful to you for what you have done for Negro performers in America; so as far as my contract is concerned, forget it. I was brought up to think that Paul Robeson is a great person, a great human being and a champion of my people. I was influenced by him. I am not a Communist and I have never been a Communist. But I don't want you to be in any way embarrassed by my presence on your show. You have been too fine and too decent for us to forget that. What happens to me is not important.

Within hours after receiving the letter Sullivan sent for Bibb. The letter, we all believed, saved Bibb's professional life.

I was beginning to learn that to live and practice in that atmosphere a lawyer—especially a guild lawyer—had to use all the ingenuity and cunning at his command; otherwise his client would be just another lamb for the slaughter.

Moreover, by then the guild itself was being charged by H.U.A.C. and others with being an arm of the Communist party. I believed then that it was an unfounded charge and I still do, but the attorney general had established a "subversives list," and the guild was on it. The battle lines were drawn. In constitutional cases—trials of free speech and free assembly, particularly First, Fifth, Sixth and Fourteenth Amendment cases—the government argued, every time the Communist party took a stand, the Lawyers Guild followed suit.

We of the guild answered the charge simply by showing that the government's contention was not true: we and the party had taken different positions any number of times. Subsequently a federal court reviewed the decision of the attorney general and the guild was taken off the subversives list.

During the period of hysteria, lawyers were as frightened of H.U.A.C. as were the rest of us, and avoided taking sensitive cases. This was particularly true of cases brought under the Smith Act. To remedy the situation, which cast shame on the whole judicial system, Sylvester Ryan, the presiding judge of the United States District Court for the Southern District of New York, made an appointment with leaders of the local bar associations. He called the chairman of the state bar association, officials of the New York County Lawyers Association, and me, as the representative of the Lawyers Guild. Judge Ryan explained that defendants coming before the courts to be tried for alleged Communist affiliations had complained that they could not get lawyers to defend them. "I want to make sure," he said, "that this charge shall have no substance, and I want you to go to your organizations and get lawyers who will come forward and defend any of these defendants now or in the future in court. It would be a sorry day," he concluded "if the views of citizens, no matter how radical, would prevent them from getting adequate representation in our courts."

The Bar Association of the City of New York scanned their membership and found no one who would defend "Communists." The state bar association scanned their membership and found one lawyer. I found eight, who, however, required exorbitant fees to offset an expected loss of income.

A number of lawyers who had represented liberals continued to do so, but their views were well known and both lawyer and client received less than fair treatment before the Bar of Justice.

In addition to being grossly repressive, the Smith Act was retroactive, so that charges could be brought under it even though the alleged crime might have been committed twenty-five years previously. The constitutionality of this concept was tested in the Supreme Court, which found even those *ex post facto* provisions to be constitutional.

I argued that question in the Obermeier case in 1948. The government was attempting to deport Mike Obermeier, a labor leader who was general manager of Local 6, Hotel and Club Employees Union. The Immigration and Naturalization Service recommended that Obermeier be deported because, they claimed, he had lied about being a member of the Communist party. Following this recommendation, a federal grand jury in Brooklyn indicted him on three counts and charged him with having made false statements when he applied for his citizenship papers.

The government was successful in that case. Mike was convicted and deported to his homeland in Germany, even though during the war he had been a valuable member of the O.S.S., his son had fought in the U.S. Army, and his daughter had become an American college professor.

About the same time, I represented Arduilio Susi, an Italian immigrant, who was president of Chef's Local 89. In Italy young Susi had been associated with anti-Fascists. His uncle, a young senator, had been murdered by Mussolini's men. Many Italian Communists then were also anti-Fascists, and many times anti-Fascist forces coalesced. Susi's association with known Communists had recently got him into trouble here when he made application for his citizenship papers. The Department of

Naturalization did not want to move his application, and Sidney Elliott Cohn, the noted union lawyer, called me as his associate in the case. We decided to force the government's hand, and we pressed for a decision—an unheard-of maneuver in such cases, since it is customary, with civil rights cases, to let sleeping dogs lie. Our case came before Judge Leo Rayfael in the federal court in Brooklyn.

The government wanted a week's adjournment, but I wanted the hearing postponed only for a day. I asked to speak to Judge Rayfael in chambers. "Your Honor," I said, "the government wants to adjourn this case so that it will be heard by Judge Mortimer Byers, which will place me in the position of explaining to this octogenarian what an anti-Fascist is, and when I do that I will have placed both myself and my client in the position of belonging to some strange foreign cult. To Judge Byers," I continued, "that will seem like some sort of anti-American ideology, and Susi won't have a ghost of a chance of getting his citizenship. Now, you have every legal right to put this case before Judge Byers, but you don't have a moral one."

I didn't think I was making my point, so I continued. "And besides," I said, referring to his late father, "Judge Hyman Rayfael would agree with me, and if he were with us today, he would join me in this argument."

The following day the judge heard the case, dismissed the government's argument, and granted citizenship. We had a feeling we were not through with the government. It was a custom of the government prosecutors to scan forms that the "target" had filled out. In anti-Communist cases, if they could not have their way in a direct accusation, they pursued some collateral line. They convicted Earl Browder, onetime leader of the American Communist party, not of being an enemy of the country but of giving a fictitious name in a passport application. And so it went.

But much to our surprise, Susi's indictment never came, and he finished his working life as leader of Local 89. I could only assume that the government's informers were being used too often and were being held for more important game. In 1972 Susi's Marine captain son and I were present at ceremonies honoring Susi upon his retirement.

The hysteria that spread across the nation was, for the most part, an American phenomenon. While Europe was geographically much closer to the Communist threat, Europeans exhibited neither the panic nor the neuroses that were so common in the United States. I had occasion to notice the contrasting attitudes when I attended a convention of the International Association of Democratic Lawyers in Brussels in 1947. I was one of six American delegates at the meeting. All six of us were representatives of the National Lawyers Guild. The delegation included Bill Standard, a well-known maritime lawyer, Martin Popper, and a few younger men and women who wrote the position papers and speeches for us. Those in attendance came from every country in western Europe and from the U.S.S.R. and some of its satellite nations as well. The French representatives stayed together and aloof throughout the session. They had in their delegation Communist party and Catholic party members, who seemed to be able to stand together on the issues that were discussed. It was an eye-opener for me. I could not conceive of anything like that happening in the United States. The privilege of presiding at the convention was rotated among the national delegations, and when our time came, I was selected by the American group to conduct that session.

During the course of some ordinary discussion a Russian delegate departed from the protocol to denounce the exploiting colonial powers. A man named Jones, representing the British Labour party, concluded that the remarks were aimed at England, and indeed they were. The meeting took place during the last days of the Empire. India was not yet free. I gave the privilege of the floor to Jones, who presented his defense, such as it was. He then proceeded to indict the Russians for their treatment of the peasants in the Ukraine. The Russian demanded time for reply. I gave it to him. By that time Jones had made it clear that he believed he should be allowed to speak again. Popper and Standard made their way to the platform to suggest that the meeting was getting out of hand and that I ought to bring an end to the debate.

"It was your mistake," I said, "to select me for this job. Seldom has an Irishman been put in such an advantageous position. This Slav is hard put to explain away his country's conduct in the Ukraine, and that Saxon stands naked before the assemblage while his kinsmen still boast that 'the sun never sets in the King's Dominion' and on all of its slaves. You don't realize what poetic justice it is and how I am enjoying every moment of it."

When the session was over we were invited by our French colleagues to observe the trials of some wartime collaborators at the Palais de Justice in Paris, where Marie Antoinette was condemned to death. I don't know whether the defendants were guilty or not, but from what I observed, they had no better chance of acquittal than Marie had had.

After the session in Paris I returned again to Ireland. During the seven years I had been away (since 1939) family communication between Ireland and the United States had been extremely limited. I had acquired two additional brothers-in-law and now was greeted by a whole flock of nephews and nieces.

My sister Josephine had returned to Ireland, married John Byrne, a local shopkeeper, and started to raise a family. The three young Durkans thrived but showed no prowess on the athletic field, unlike their father. The oldest, Aidan was preparing to emigrate to New York, where he became the only teetotaler to make a career of brewing. Billy, the youngest, stayed home to study and eventually practice law. Frank, the third brother, came back with me to New York. He continued his education at Columbia University, and studied law, and in time became a partner in O'Dwyer and Bernstien.

My sister Linda had married Pat Flannelly, a schoolteacher in Mayo. Of the five children they eventually had, Adrian moderates an Irish radio program on an FM station in New York; Fintan is an accountant in Dublin; Betty teaches at the National University there; Enda is pursuing a career in hotel management in Ireland; and Irene is a schoolteacher and publisher of children's books.

Josephine and her husband had fallen on hard times. The war, with its rationing and lack of consumer goods, spelled disaster for small-town merchants, and conditions for the Byrnes went from bad to worse. Both parents were in indifferent health, and the family, including a daughter and three sons, emigrated to New York, where the children continued their education. Today Louis is a psychiatrist, Keneth a heating engineer, John a judge of the criminal court in New York and Linda Renner the wife of a dentist in Denver.

While their Irish cousins were heading toward careers in the professions, their American kin were destined to travel along parallel lines. Frank's son, Frank Jr., followed his father into the food-provision line and lives in San Diego, and my son Rory, after drifting awhile, wound up in Phoenix, where he married Kathie and entered the real estate business. Brian is a labor and trial lawyer, in practice with me, as is also his wife, Marianna. Billy, the eldest, graduated from Cork Medical School and is a physician in Albany, where he lives with his wife, Carole. Eileen, with her husband, Tom Hughes, who is also a colleague in O'Dwyer and Bernstien, is raising a family in New York. And Joan, my brother Jimmy's daughter, is a New York criminal court judge, like her cousin.

When I got to Ireland from Paris, however, the subject of the younger generations took second place to inquiries about things in New York. The oldest O'Dwyer, whom his parents had once hoped would be a priest, was by then mayor of New York. Kitty, his long-ailing wife, had died the year after Bill was elected.

That made him an eligible widower. Others may have been interested in how he wrestled with the problems of the world's largest city, but his sisters and nieces wanted to know what marital plans he might have and what his female companions were like. I elaborated on both. But the kind of woman I described elicited little approval from my sisters.

CHAPTER SEVEN

New Battles

EARLY IN my brother Bill's first term as mayor a few members of the American Labor party had suggested that I run for Congress from the Washington Heights–Inwood district in Manhattan. Eugene Connolly, the A.L.P. candidate in that district two years before, told me that if I could get the Democrats to support me he would line up the A.L.P. behind me. He said this combination would be tantamount to victory. On my return from Europe I pursued it further.

The district was primarily Democratic, but the party's candidate in 1946—Dan Flynn—had failed to satisfy Jewish voters living there that he was really opposed to the anti-Semitism then rampant in New York, and the voters had elected Republican Jacob Javits.

I went to the Democratic leaders and explained that I had been offered support from the A.L.P. Still smarting from the 1946 loss, they figured they had nothing to lose and seemed glad to have a willing candidate. I got the nomination from both parties.

My debut as a candidate for public office could not have come at a worse time, for red-baiting was at its peak, and all its techniques were practiced on me. Most of my campaign workers were friends and relatives, but I insisted that my brother not enter the campaign or endorse me. My supporters urged me to relent but I did not—a matter of pride and political independence; Bill's and my views were not the same.

I had little going for me with either the Democrats or the A.L.P. Henry Wallace had entered the presidential race as the Progressive party's candidate, and, in New York, the A.L.P. adopted him as their own. A.L.P. campaign workers were helping Vito Marcantonio, who had first claim on their loyalty, and the bulk of A.L.P. money was not wasted on candidates with Democratic backing. Moreover, Wallace's candidacy had placed me in the anomalous position of being on one line with Wallace and on another with President Truman. Furthermore, the President was also on the Liberal line with Javits, who nevertheless was supporting Republican presidential candidate Thomas Dewey. As a result of having constantly to explain to the voters that I was a Democrat, I was not able effectively to address the issues.

Each day the mail brought postcards from district Democrats asking for clarification of my party affiliation:

> Democrats demand to know if you're for Wallace or Truman or for communism or against it. Irish greatly agitated at two inconsistent roles. Better declare—great resentment and uprising against you—carrying water on both shoulders.
>
> Democratic captain

> Forty votes in our family in Congressional district always Democrat will go to Republican this year. Who the hell are you to accept American Labor Party endorsement—it is generally said that you are a Red—if so, a good Republican is better than a Communist pretending to be a Democrat. What a slashing you're in for.
>
> (No signature)

There were a few friendly communications, in particular one from Pete Smith in Brooklyn.

> I don't know you except by your recent actions which I like. I liked your acceptance of the A.L.P. designation. New blood is needed in the struggle for progress and in defense of liberty.

I paid little heed to these communications, but to any candidate under fire a friendly note is coveted, and it does bring indescribable comfort.

The campaign was not without violence, because feelings were running high, especially in Irish-dominated Inwood. My old enemies, the Christian Fronters and the Christian Mobilizers, scurried around causing mischief and creating havoc. After their almost nightly rampages we would have to call the glaziers to put in new windows at headquarters.

But I was not without friends in the Irish neighborhood, and old I.R.A. men and transport workers would hang around the meetings to shout at the hecklers and permit me to finish my speeches. And if the meeting was dull, I would take on a few hecklers myself. There is nothing better for livening interest than an exchange between the speaker and the hecklers. The Irish crowd in Inwood want to know how their compatriots stand up under abuse.

I was used to being red-baited. As early as 1945 I had received mail messages along these lines:

> I am not voting for your brother because I have it on substantial information that you are acting as a counselor for the Communist Party or the Communist organization in New York City.

Invariably I was asked to rebut the charges, and I developed an answer that I used frequently during the next decade:

> I have heard various rumors of the type you talk about, and, indeed, many others. I don't mind them, since I

> know it is the price one pays for taking a firm stand on matters controversial. I do not usually take the trouble to answer them, since a new rumor is aborning as the old one is disposed of, and the originators have more time at their disposal than I have.
>
> However, since you have written in the spirit of friendship, I will tell you there is no truth in the statement.

Once an accusation was made without proof, I knew it would do me no good to proclaim that I was not a Communist. But there were several occasions during the campaign when it was necessary to discuss the charge. At almost every meeting, during the question-and-answer period, a man holding a small slip of paper in his hand would stand. "Mr. O'Dwyer," he would read, "a question. Your brother, mayor of the city of New York, says 'the American Labor party is Communist-dominated.' Do you agree with that statement?"

I answered with a simple but resounding "No!" But it did not help me that Bill had made the charge, and even though I tried to ignore the questions, they persisted. On August 27 my nemesis, the Reverend Edward Lodge Curran, contacted me again, this time by telegram:

> YOUR BROTHER BILL O'DWYER MAYOR OF NEW YORK HAS CHARGED THE AMERICAN LABOR PARTY WITH BEING CONTROLLED BY COMMUNISTS. DO YOU STILL INTEND TO RUN FOR CONGRESS UNDER THE AMERICAN LABOR PARTY'S LABEL AND ENDORSEMENT?

Many of my Irish friends who were helping me in the campaign came to me shortly thereafter and said, "Look, Paul, we're your friends in Inwood, and we're constantly faced with questions of whether or not you are really a Communist. We know it's not true, but would you try to help us answer those questions?"

I told them that I really did not know what to answer. "You can tell the voters that I'm not a Communist," I said.

"We did, but it's no help," they countered. "That kind of answer begs the next question, 'How do you know?' That's where we're stumped. We'll have to give some evidence that you're not a Communist."

I thought about my friends and the dilemma and considered what kind of facts I had that might disprove the charge, and after a couple of days of thought I met the group and tried out my answer on them:

> I assume that the people believe that a Communist would not have his kids baptized or that he would not have them confirmed. Here are some facts: my kids were baptized Catholics, and the ones who are old enough are confirmed Catholics, and here are the churches where it happened.

I hated to have to give that kind of answer, but they were decent people and they were looking out for me among the Irish Catholic voters in the district who were beset by massive anti-left neuroses. I continued with more facts:

> Here are the names and telephone numbers of five priests whom I know well. Tell your questioners to call them if they need someone to vouch for my character.

My campaign workers were so impressed with the "ammunition" I had given them that they asked me to write it up so that they could distribute my notes to other workers. I did, and one devoted friend found my fact sheet so significant that he printed ten thousand copies and scattered them around the district. Javits' campaign workers picked up the leaflets, and the Republicans promptly accused me of running a racist campaign. I was being attacked by the Irish for being a Communist, the same label was applied to me by the Liberals, Christian Mobilizers and Catholic War Veterans, while in Jewish sections of the district I was accused of running a campaign catering to the very crypto-Nazis who were the most active workers against me.

These newest accusations called for an immediate clearing of the air, and I went to the office of the *Aufbau,* the German American paper read by the large refugee population in the area, and asked the editors to sponsor a forum so that I could explain my position and views to the refugees. They generously agreed.

The Javits campaign was well prepared for the meeting. They had blown up my note to ten times its original size and had plastered the poster on buildings throughout Jewish neighborhoods. But on the night of the forum I explained to the overflow crowd what exactly had caused me to distribute the notes to my workers and why I felt I had to defend myself against the unfounded charge. I pointed out the nature of the campaign and its inconsistencies. Interpreters came forward to volunteer and they repeated my position in German. I think the crowd was very much for me that evening, and I was invited to many synagogues in the ensuing weeks of the campaign.

My thoughts on communism were one thing, and my feelings about the rights of American Communists were another. I knew very well that if any citizen, no matter how unpopular his views, could not speak freely on street corners, I was living under a pretty bad system. Even that simple pronouncement made one suspect of being in sympathy with communism. At meetings I explained that under a Communist regime I would probably be one of the first to go to a concentration camp, for in every country where the Communists had taken over, liberals and intellectuals were the first to be put away. The reactionaries and moneyed class, I said, make deals with the Communists; it is the liberals who suffer.

What Communists do in Communist countries is one thing, I continued, and what we do in our country to dissenters is another. For this reason I wanted to fight for the right of a Communist to be a Communist in the United States if he felt like it. I judged the Constitution and the Bill of Rights on their own merits, but some Americans, it seemed to me, had the capacity to use the Constitution for themselves to the exclusion of those who might disagree with them. I tried to make these points to the crowds, and I don't know whether or not I was successful in convincing anyone, but I do know that most people listened, and this was half the battle and perhaps even the beginning of understanding.

There came a time, a month before election, when the smear tactics demanded a full-fledged answer. I called a press conference specifically to answer charges that my position as president of the National Lawyers Guild and my defense of labor leaders in court made me a Communist.

"Of course," I began, "I am not a Communist, nor am I a believer in Communist principles. I am a sincere believer in the Bill of Rights and the Constitution of the United States." I defended my presidency of the National Lawyers Guild and my right, which I would never surrender, to protect the constitutional right of any citizen without embracing the political philosophy of my client.

Leon Hershbaum, my close friend and colleague, was the campaign manager; and Chuck Meehan, well-known coach and athlete, was the campaign director. I was new to politics and did not realize that a popular sports figure would not add that much to my campaign, and as far as sports were concerned, a few of the things we did were a bit fraudulent. Chuck took me to the Polo Grounds to pose with Lou Little, and the newspaper photographers caught me discussing the finer points of football with Little. My knowledge of the game was meager, and anyway it did not matter. Sports fans feel that a politician is out of place at a sports event and an intrusion into their exclusive domain.

Although we faced tremendous opposition, there were some bright spots in the campaign. Actress Judy Holliday campaigned for me and raised campaign funds at cocktail parties. Folk singer Josh White sang "Strange Fruit" and other protest songs of the period at street-corner rallies, but sometimes I was forced to listen to Henry Wallace songs and remain silent. These were the mountain tunes of Dick Blakeslee and Woody Guthrie, and protest songs composed by Claiborne, Seeger, French and Harburg and written especially for the Progressive party.

There were some humorous moments also, and one incident in particular is worth repeating. My good friend Sean Keating, in order to show how grossly outrageous the rumormongers were, told an intimate gathering one night that "they have gone so far as to spread the rumor that Paul is keeping another woman and has a couple of kids by her." Hershbaum quickly pulled him aside and whispered, "Sean, how do we handle *that* rumor?"

"Ah, there's nothing to it," Sean rejoined, "I just made that story up."

"Sean," Leon entreated, "don't make it up. Already I believe it!"

Two other good friends, Fathers Sean Reid and Donal O'Callaghan, who had worked with me on problems of discrimination in Northern Ireland, sent me a donation with a note of explanation:

> When capitalists have such great difficulty in getting suckers to contribute to their campaign funds, how much greater is the difficulty when a member of the proletariat finds himself launched, not too gently, upon a political career? Realizing this we started a campaign among such intimate friends of yours as Peg Lynch, Mrs. O'Brien and some others of the inner circle of the Christian Front. Using the argument that New York would be a safer place without your pernicious influence and that a little bit more confusion cannot matter in Washington, we managed to extract a few Wall Street dollars to speed you on your way. When you get to Washington, we will use our influence to see that you are put on the Thomas Committee. Included in the check, but not dated, are a few prayers from Fr.

> Graham and Fr. Bradley. If you don't need them, give them to Oscar, but keep them away from Javits.

However, I needed more than prayers to win the election, and as the returns came in, I earned the distinction of being a congressman-elect for the shortest period on record—one hour. Soon after the polls closed I was declared the winner, and it was so announced on the radio and in the early editions of the papers. Congratulations poured into my headquarters from around the country, but I knew I had really lost to Javits. All the returns from Washington Heights were not in, and these were the areas where I knew I would come in second, because the Democratic captains there were working for my opponent. And when the ballots were counted, I lost by 1800 votes—out of 130,000.

Toward the end of that year the longshoremen in Brooklyn went out on a wildcat strike. Jimmy Longhi, a lawyer friend of mine, recalling a successful brewery strike that I had reluctantly led during the recent campaign, asked me to come in and talk to the longshoremen. He said that Joe Ryan, the tough West Side leader of the longshoremen, had tried to put a deal across that was being resisted by the Brooklyn Italians. Longhi explained that the latter had gone out on strike and were not going to accept the terms Ryan had negotiated for them.

Ryan had the habit of making his own deals. He was the elected head of the longshoremen's union, and the union itself was riddled with hoods. Many of the locals were headed by racketeers, and most of the members were exploited. As far as the shipping owners were concerned, they were doing better with Ryan, and they would rather put up with him than pay decent wages to the longshoremen.

I had had an earlier experience with Ryan, when I was in law school in 1927. The occasion was a membership meeting on wage negotiations. I was, and still am, a member of a checkers' local of the I.L.A., and was asked then to attend and vote. My friend Frank Bateman picked me up after class and we drove to the union hall in Chelsea. We were being called upon to ratify a contract, a fifty-cents-a-day wage increase, or two dollars and fifty cents a week more. Our local had voted a week earlier to reject the offer.

At the Chelsea meeting, however, we were in Ryan country, and when Ryan came to the rostrum, he told us that the other unions had agreed to their part in the contract. Of course they had; the other unions had never met. Our union was different—we were a democratic group and held regular meetings.

"If you fellas don't accept this contract," Ryan told us, "I'll charter another union this morning, and you'll be out." Ryan had an absolute power to suspend our union and charter a new one. Frank Bateman, sitting beside me, rose to complain. Three times he shouted "Mr. Chairman" and was ignored. A tough-looking hood came toward us, and when he got to where Frank was standing, he dropped a .45-caliber gun on the floor. As he stooped to pick up the gun his head came close to Bateman's and he growled, "Why the hell don't you shut up, and I mean right now!"

Frank and the rest of us got the message. Frank sat down, and that was the end of the dispute. The following day the contract was signed.

The years passed, and Ryan continued his iron rule. When Jimmy Longhi called me in 1948 he said he had called for two reasons: "You're the fella who ran for Congress who led the brewery strike, and, frankly, you're also the brother of the mayor."

I said that I really did not want to be known as the wildcat-strike expert, but he convinced me that my appearance at the hall might give some courage to the young Italian veterans who had returned from the war and who wanted assurance that their right to speak would be protected.

Jimmy Longhi, the poet-lawyer, now retired and living in

England, where he and his wife, Gabby, write and produce plays, knew the longshoremen, because his father had worked on the docks. He took it upon himself to try to democratize the Italian longshoremen's unions on Columbia Street, and, as a member of the A.L.P., he ran an unsuccessful campaign against John Rooney, the high-handed Brooklyn congressman.

The hall was packed when I arrived. I had learned my piece in English and Italian and told the men, "The days are gone when free speech is forbidden in Brooklyn. From this point on, there is going to be no more intimidation. I was a longshoreman, and I saw that gangster Johnny Spanish down at Garcia-Diaz pier pick out the longshoremen who were going to work and reject the ones he did not like. I saw his hard hat and his diamond stickpin and his pair of spats and his LaSalle car. Happily, his days are over and freedom of speech is the order of the day from now on—"

I was interrupted by a man standing at the back of the hall. "Excuse me, Mr. O'Dwyer," he said in a heavy Italian accent. "You say everybody have the right to speak. Can I come up to the microphone and tell what I know?" I told him that if he had something to say to come on up. He made his way through the crowd to the stage and took the microphone. "You know me," he said, "I'm Tony Anastasia."

He was my lesson in democracy. Tony spoke and spoke, and it was obvious that he wanted the men to go back to work.

When he finished, Jimmy Longhi took the mike, pointed to Tony, and in Italian said, "Tony, shame, shame. The spirit of Peter Panto is in this room tonight," referring to the young rebel longshoreman murdered by Tony's brother, Albert. I thought Jimmy was crazy to mention the Panto murder, and I feared that his life would not be worth a dime—and to make matters worse, Jimmy spoke in Italian, which everybody in the hall understood.

But Jimmy knew what he was doing. As an organizer for the A.L.P. he had talked with Tony Anastasia and convinced him after some long sessions that it would be good for Tony to keep himself "clean" and to do some good for his people. They sold Tony the liberal leanings of the A.L.P. Jimmy and his colleague Mitch Berrenson told Tony that everything would work out—and it did. Tony had come from a family that had in it one gangster and one priest. Maybe he was preconditioned by the priest's influence, and maybe the political philosophy of Longhi and Longhi's friend Mitch Berrenson was getting to him and he did develop a social awareness and social consciousness. By the time Tony died he had opened a medical clinic for longshoremen and also integrated the union, which held regular elections.

I became involved in yet another battle before the end of that year, one relating to discrimination in housing in the development of Stuyvesant Town, a project which allowed the insurance industry to fill its ample coffers while at the same time performing a useful public service. The Metropolitan Life Insurance Company had agreed to work with the city administration to wipe out a large slum area on the lower East Side and to replace the dilapidated tenements with a large apartment complex. The city had agreed to a tax abatement for twenty-five years. The idea was designed to provide much-needed new housing for its growing middle class.

The idea was conceived in the early forties, but the war had taken precedence and construction was postponed until the end of hostilities. When things returned to normal in New York, Metropolitan started construction, and the first tenants of Stuyvesant Town had moved into their apartments in 1947. The new complex was very desirable in many respects, and the Metropolitan made no secret of its intention to maintain it exclusively for Caucasians. And the law allowed them to exercise that right, even though black tax dollars were being used in maintaining a policy that excluded them.

Some people who had moved to Stuyvesant Town had formed a committee and had begun to invite blacks to visit them in their apartments. From that early effort to establish understanding with Metropolitan Life, they had developed into the Committee to End Discrimination in Stuyvesant Town. Paul Ross and Julius Cohen were leaders of the committee. Following their example, other groups had begun to demand the right of people to live wherever they could afford to.

When their initial leases expired, the members of the committee had been told to vacate. Apartments were difficult to come by. The tenants were paying a dear price for their principled position, because when they refused to move, the Metropolitan summoned them to court. They came to me to represent them.

We appeared before Judge George Genung, a Republican politician who had been elected from the "silk stocking" district of Manhattan. Everybody knew that the judge would be most unfriendly to the kind of radicalism the tenants were considered to be displaying. I knew our fate was sealed. Whatever doubts I might have had about getting a fair trial ended as I observed the attitude of the judge. I was never before so well treated; the judge was polite in the extreme. He deferred to me many times, which indicated to me that the decision had already been made and there was no chance of postponing eviction. The judge handed down an immediate decision granting the right of the landlord to dispossess. The tenants were without legal protection. Rent control did not control buildings erected after 1947. Discrimination laws in housing had not yet been enacted and my resort to the First Amendment was thin.

We appealed the decision nevertheless, on the grounds that it was a violation of First Amendment rights of free speech, in that my clients were being singled out for punishment because they had expressed their views and opinions. The Supreme Court then was not as sensitive to that issue as was the Warren court, which came later. We got nowhere on appeal, and that left the committee with an outstanding dispossess order.

The Lawyers Guild, of which I was still president, filed an amicus curiae brief with the state court of appeals. Our countersuit included not only the Stuyvesant Town Corporation and the Metropolitan Life Insurance Company but also the mayor of the city of New York, who had contracted with Metropolitan. It was a vain attempt to protect tenants from discrimination. The Metropolitan argued successfully that they had a perfect right to choose tenants in any fashion they pleased and that they were at liberty to discriminate if they so desired. Indeed, the law at that time was on their side. My attempt to make it a constitutional question was carried out in desperation and as a last resort.

I did not have much faith in the merits of these court maneuvers, and while we were waiting for the decision of the higher court, I asked for an appointment with the chairman of the board of the Metropolitan Life Insurance Company, Fred Eckert, who was then at least eighty-five years old. When the appointment was granted, I was sure the privilege was being extended to the brother of the mayor and not to the tenants' radical lawyer. It was a last personal appeal on behalf of tenants who would not be able to get other suitable apartments.

I arrived for the meeting on time and found that Eckert had assembled what seemed to be a quorum of the board of directors. The general counsel was sitting at his right, and Eckert pointed to an empty seat on his left. There was an awkward silence. "Mr. O'Dwyer, you asked for this meeting. Just what do you want?" asked the chairman.

I explained that I wanted to avoid having these tenants thrown out of their apartments and wished to present an alternative proposal. "The leases are up and you have not seen fit to renew them. I would like to suggest that you leave the tenants in their apartments as month-to-month tenants without a lease."

"Is that what you want? Is that what you have in mind? Is

there anything else you have to say?" was all Eckert could muster.

It was obvious that the directors of this powerful insurance company thought I was coming to them with a nefarious scheme—some trick—and they had to be ready with witnesses. "That is my proposal," I repeated. "I don't think these people deserve to be thrown out of their homes."

"We will consider what you have said and let you know in due time," said the chairman. And, as an afterthought, he added, "Mr. O'Dwyer, I want you to know that the Metropolitan Insurance Company does not promote policies of discrimination."

"What happened to my clients," I observed, "does not seem to jibe with what you have said, Mr. Eckert."

"The company is neither ahead of public attitudes nor behind them," he said.

"I would hope that a company like yours would not necessarily have to wait to be followers," I suggested.

"I'm sure that in the course of time what you've said will be properly considered. For the moment our decision will have to stand," he said. With that the chairman extended his hand. It was a gentle signal for me to leave. None of the directors nor the counsel said a word.

After some further agitation Metropolitan finally adopted the plan I had proposed. Many of the committee stayed in Stuyvesant Town and left in the normal course of events. Others found the atmosphere hostile and moved out when they got other accommodations.

It was not until introduction of the Brown-Isaacs Bill several years later that the City Council passed a law barring racial discrimination in public housing.

Other institutions practiced such discrimination as well. Most private schools, except parochial ones, were still segregated in 1948. I wrote a letter to the Columbia Grammar School, a private school around the corner from my residence, which my daughter Eileen attended, and inquired if any black students were enrolled there. The headmistress answered with a rather innocuous letter. "There are children here," she explained, "of Hungarian, French, Austrian, German and Russian extraction."

"That's impressive," I replied in a further communication, "but tell me, how many Negroes are enrolled?"

Her answer was that there were some Negroes on the waiting list and "when the time comes, they will be enrolled." I sent a letter some time later to inquire as to the status of those on the waiting list. Her reply was that "no Negro child is able to meet the tuition."

To counter the argument I wrote saying that I was sure some of the parents of the other students would join me in raising enough money to pay for a scholarship for at least a token Negro child.

The school stopped answering my letters, and as Eileen was soon to graduate, I'm sure they were simply playing for time. Eileen continued her education at the High School of Music and Art, an integrated public school with a fine reputation.

My family's reaction to my activities was supportive and, I think, somewhat proud. Our kids—William, Eileen, Brian and Rory—basked in the limelight of an uncle who was mayor of the city of New York and a father who was a candidate for Congress. We tried not to spoil them, and I think we succeeded. It required a lecture now and then to pull them down a peg.

Kathleen had been happy the first time I decided to run for public office. But I don't think she realized what politics entailed. Her opposition to my involvement came at a later date, when men seeking or holding office were assassinated. The red-baiting did not bother her. She had grown accustomed to it.

Nevertheless my new involvements forced some changes. I

worked long hours and was not home for dinner often. My clientele was working class, and it made little sense to tell prospective clients that if they wanted to see me they would have to take a day off from work with a loss of pay. If a client came in at 5 P.M., I might have to spend two or three hours going over his case, and I would then be late for dinner. As time went on, it was apparent that there were two things wrong with that arrangement. With the supper cold and everyone hungry and waiting, I would have a very cranky wife and kids when I got home, and it was self-defeating for me to follow this kind of rigid routine. Without any formal plan, an understanding came about. "Have your dinner and put mine in the oven," I told Kathleen, "and I'll be home later."

But this seemed an imposition on Kathleen. I did not want her to have to nurse my meal along, never knowing for sure when I would be home. It was much easier for her to cook one meal, eat with the children at a decent, normal hour, and be done with it. I began eating out during the week, and it made for a better life for us all. I tried to make up for my delinquency by dining out with Kathleen once a week and by spending almost every weekend with the family. That the children grew up whole and sound I owe largely to Kathleen.

I had never tasted alcohol until I was twenty-one years old, when, on my way back from the West Coast in 1928, I looked up an aunt who was living in Chicago. Her husband, Barney O'Rourke, was very proud of his home brew. I had never met my aunt before, but I had the feeling that it would be insulting if I did not sample Barney's brew. After that first drink it was easy. At the day's end, with or without a client, I might drop in on Tommy Ayers, who operated a speakeasy at Thirty-ninth Street and Third Avenue—the most popular "blind pig" in midtown, frequented by actresses and employees from CBS. They thought the Irish football players who came to see Tommy were cute and the Irish joint was quaint. The Filipino chef seemed out of place, but his food was good, and that made "this 'speak' different"—as the Passover question goes—"different from all other gin mills."

I always had heard that "whiskey was the Irishman's curse." But I soon found out that it wasn't whiskey in my case. At first my taste ran to beer. Later I went on to cocktails; and after that I went through an Italian-wine period; and still later, Jamaica rum. Even though I avoided whiskey, I began to recognize some signs that did not please me, that were indeed a bit frightening. After a couple of false starts, I gave up drinking entirely in 1959.

By the end of the 1948 election I felt that my political philosophy had taken shape, and I knew—even if reluctantly—that I was not capable of scoring the kind of success Bill had achieved. I had no capacity, like his, to enter a room filled with hostile people and walk out with everyone in agreement with my position. I knew that I could never get the diverse views of the Board of Estimate together, as Bill had done, and end up with their total support from the beginning to the end.

What excited me in politics was the liberalism fostered in the Roosevelt years. I had begun to think of politics as the only safeguard of what the political frauds called the American Way of Life. My defeat in the congressional race set me back, but I contented myself with aiding candidates I liked. I continued to build my law practice and to pursue a liberal course, and in turn to be pursued by red-baiters and others troubled by conflicts within themselves.

CHAPTER EIGHT

The Men Who Loved Freedom

I FIRST learned of the Irgun Zvai Le'umi and the American League for a Free Palestine through an advertisement in *The New York Times* in 1945 that outlined the Irgun's objectives and pointed the way for Americans to participate. Early Irgunists were followers of a famous Russian author and journalist named Vladimir Jabotinsky, who founded the "Zionist Revisionists," and their heirs in 1946 followed Menachem Begin, the eventual Israeli prime minister. The Irgun found fault with the more passive position of the Zionist organizations and believed that only by direct attack on the British in Palestine would the Jews ever achieve statehood.

In 1939, Mike Ben-Ami, a Palestinian Jew, set up the first organization here designed to favor the Zionist-Revisionist point of view. It was known as the American Committee for a Jewish State. In 1944, near the end of World War II, the American League for a Free Palestine came into existence. Declaring themselves to be an American committee, they wrote then:

> We, people of America, ourselves a free and mighty nation, born in a revolution against oppression and tyranny, have joined in an American League for a Free Palestine in answer to the call of the Hebrew Committee of National Liberation for help in the mortal struggle of the Hebrew people of Europe and Palestine for life and liberation.
>
> It is not the first time that oppressed and subjugated people of a foreign land have appealed to America for help, and whenever such a call reaches our shores, it echoes in our hearts and we respond with compassion and humanity. Free Czechoslovakia and Free Ireland are living examples of our response.
>
> Recognizing the validity of these demands of minimum human rights and human dignity for the Hebrew nation, the American League for a Free Palestine will dedicate itself to the full support of the committee in its endeavor to obtain for its people the rights of man while some will survive to enjoy them. Can we do less for a people than as the martyr of all nations? Can we do less when we fight for a better world based on right and justice? Can we do less for a people that gave us the Bible and the moral foundations for our civilization?

The American League for a Free Palestine had its headquarters at the old Hotel Astor. The organization had attracted all sorts of people. Stella and Larry Adler of the famous acting family were part of the group, as were importer Harry Selden, who spent a family fortune to keep the Irgun going. Ben Hecht, the playwright, Ham Fisher, the cartoonist, Ruth Chatterton, the actress, and Guy Gillette, the former United States senator, attended meetings. Author Louis Bromfield, Algernon D. Black of the Society for Ethical Culture, George Counts of Columbia University, Dave Haber of Yale, Fowler Harper, Francis Biddle and Victor House lent their names to the organization and came around frequently. So, from 1945, did I.

Because I was a non-Jew, my association with the committee was welcomed and I was used very frequently as a fund raiser in New York, Philadelphia, Hartford and other New England cities. My primary job was to extract money from people who had given previously to other Jewish charities. Our purpose was to get arms and ammunition and skilled manpower to Palestine so that the Irgun could conduct the fight against Britain. The fact that I had had waterfront experience helped in making arrangements when shipping was necessary. Before long I became a part of the over-all decision-making process.

Our activities were by no means confined to military affairs. We insisted on being heard in protest against our State Department. We demanded prompt U.S. recognition of the existing Jewish state and of its lawful authority over the territory under its control within the boundaries of Palestine as fixed by League of Nations mandate. Further, we demanded that:

1. The United States immediately lift the embargo on arms and munitions;
2. The United States exert its influence on any and all governments to remove blockades and any other impediments to the free flow of commerce and emigration to the Jewish State;
3. The United States bring the Jewish State and later the entire Middle East within the scope of foreign economic assistance;
4. The United States exert its influence to prevent the movement of any and all troops into Palestine and to stop other aggressive actions against the Jewish State;
5. Our government continue its present policy of not sending American military forces into Palestine;
6. The United States seek to implement these policies in conformity with the United Nations Charter, and where appropriate, seek action in the United Nations.

Ben Hecht became a foremost spokesman of the movement as well as its spiritual head, but he was totally unpredictable. On one occasion he and I were asked to attend a meeting on the east side of Manhattan, to persuade a rich Jewish merchant from the South to contribute funds. The merchant assailed us with accounts of his own extraordinary success, boasting that in the previous year he had given $40,000 to the United Jewish Appeal. At length he announced, rather patronizingly, that he planned to give us $5,000.

I was disappointed and Ben was enraged. But we were in no position to look disdainfully at the gift. Hecht's reaction nevertheless bordered on violence. "You're a cheap, rotten son of a bitch," he shouted, "you and your money. These young people out in the hills of Israel are fighting for your son and his son so that they may enjoy your ill-gotten gains!" The man pocketed his check and left.

Ben atoned by writing more plays for us, and they became the means to raise thousands of dollars for the Irgun. Fund-raisers were held all over the country. One especially moving and well-acted play was produced under the direction of Stella Adler. It was designed to raise a great deal of money in contributions from a packed house in Madison Square Garden. But the quality of the appeal for funds did not do justice to Hecht's masterpiece. Major Samuel Weizer from the British Army, who helped form the Jewish Legion, had been selected to make the pitch, and the choice was disastrous. He simply had no skill. Congressman Adam Clayton Powell, who was sitting beside me on the stage and who had become quite active in the committee, became impatient and whispered to me, "This guy's blowing it! Paul, I think this calls for a Baptist minister and an Irish revolutionary. You handle that microphone over there and I'll handle this one."

In unison we rose and in unison we took the microphones gently away from the major. We collected $75,000 from the crowd that night, May 13, 1948.

Several months earlier I had paid a visit to Ireland and had called on Mayor Robert Briscoe, the Jewish mayor of Dublin. Because he had been an I.R.A. man in 1919, I knew he would sympathize with the Irgun. For a variety of reasons Briscoe agreed to arrange for all the Irgun printing—literature and documents—to be done in Ireland. He had already arranged for volunteers to leave for Palestine from Ireland. The volunteers did not go to Israel directly; they went to France and left from the Port of Marseilles.

I was scheduled to go on to France for a conference at the Paris office of the Irgun, which was located in a hotel, but Briscoe had been told that the French police had closed it down. "I'd watch out if I were you," he said, "because the French may be on the lookout for visitors, and I advise you not to go to the hotel."

The French police and government had been favorably disposed to the Irgun and I couldn't believe they had given them a difficult time. I decided to visit the hotel anyway. But I took certain precautions. I did not take the elevator to the seventh floor, where the Irgun office was located, but instead walked up the back stairs. As I opened the landing door I heard the sound of typewriters and quickly followed it into the office. About twelve people were working, including Peter Bergson, who had been one of the Irgun's founders.

"When did you open up again, Peter?" I asked. "Briscoe told me the police shut you down."

"The mayor got his message twisted," Bergson answered. "The Sternists had a small office here and that was shut down, but I'm not sure the police did it."*

With the Paris office in the clear, I returned to New York with high hopes for success. Supported by the Jewish population of Palestine, backed by a well-oiled organization in Europe and America and headed by Menachem Begin in Jerusalem, the movement simply could not fail.

In November 1947 the United States voted in the United

*The Sternists were another, though much smaller, group of Israelis operating in the underground in Palestine.

Nations to support the partition of Palestine, but no sooner had the vote been taken than the State Department, unhappy with President Truman's position, set about undermining it. Furthermore, in March 1948, Warren Austin, the U.S. ambassador to the U.N., in direct contravention of the President's orders, declared that the United States had abandoned its support for an independent state and favored instead a U.N. trusteeship for Palestine. It seemed incredible at the time, but the story was later verified by Margaret Truman Daniel in her biography of her father.

As my brother was close to the President, a group of concerned citizens, including Edward Silver, the former district attorney and surrogate of Kings County; Nathaniel Kaplan, judge of the family court; and Maximilian Moss, the Board of Education's chairman, asked me to arrange a meeting with Bill. These men were not Irgunists; they were Zionists and had enjoyed a close working relationship with the President, and also with Bill. But the President had become frustrated by the duplicity of the State Department and irritated by the mounting pressures on him, and he had refused on three previous occasions to honor requests from the Zionist Organization of America to have a meeting with him.

I set up the requested meeting and the Z.O.A. representatives arranged for Rabbi Hillel Silver, a prominent Ohio Republican and nationally known Jewish leader, to attend. The meeting was regarded as critical; the Rabbi had received a special dispensation to travel on the Sabbath so he could be on hand.

Bill previously had called Gael Sullivan and Howard McGrath, the then and previous national chairmen of the Democratic party, to explain the deep concern of the New York Jewish community and the effect that the administration's inaction might have on the presidential election the following year. In the presence of the delegation Bill called the President. They exchanged pleasantries.

"Mr. President," Bill then said, "I recognize the fact that many agencies have called you, but I am calling as the leader of our party here in this city. I preside over the largest Jewish community in the world, and these, our citizens, are deeply concerned about the recent position taken by our country's representatives. I believe it would be unconscionable for us to withdraw support for partition. I know," he continued, "that next year I will have the utmost difficulty in getting cooperation here for a party that does not support the people of New York."

I know that Bill was hard pressed to make such a pointed argument, but the President, himself a master politician, respected it. "Bill," he replied, "you may tell our constituents my position remains unchanged."

He was as good as his word. On May 14, 1948, Israel declared itself an independent state, and ten minutes later the United States, speaking through the President, became the first nation to recognize it.

The ensuing Arab-Israeli war had marked repercussions in New York. The American and British governments declared an embargo on arms to Israel, and the F.B.I. and other government agencies moved in to crack down on arms smugglers here. The New York City Police Department was called in to cooperate. Some members of the Jewish community talked to me about the situation and I suggested we take it up with the mayor. In the meantime, however, an incident occurred that brought the matter to a head.

Nahum Bernstein was an active participant in Jewish affairs here and was deeply involved in getting necessary supplies to the Haganah. While the United States government had taken an unconscionable position on military aid to Israel, many Americans cooperated with those engaged in shipping armaments to the young nation struggling for its existence. The following account, supplied in 1977 by Mr. Bernstein at my request, was typical of the cooperation afforded the Israelis by their American friends:

My name is Nahum Amber Bernstein. I am a lawyer associated with the firm of Bernstein, Seawell & Kove, 233 Broadway, New York, New York 10007.

During 1947, I was approached by Rudolf Sonnenborn, now of the Regency Hotel, 277 Park Avenue, New York, New York 10017. Mr. Sonnenborn knew of my interest in Zionism and my service in the Office of Strategic Services during World War II. In the Office of Strategic Services I was chief of the Department of Police Methods and taught thousands of personnel in the Office of Strategic Services: Wire tapping, bugging, surveillance, safe cracking and other police methods. Mr. Sonnenborn told me that a member of the Haganah was here from Palestine. He was with the British Jewish Brigade and his name was Shlomo Rabinowitz [later known as Shlomo Shamir, head of the Israeli Air Force, after the state was created]. I was introduced to Mr. Rabinowitz who told me that he had been a colonel in the Jewish Brigade under British command. Mr. Rabinowitz asked me whether I could set up a school in New York City to train young men and women of the Haganah in the same way young men had been trained in the O.S.S. I told him I thought I could do so by recruiting my staff of experts whom I had known during my service in the O.S.S. In the latter part of 1947, I set up such a school in the Young Israel Building located on 14th Street in the City of New York and we held classes at night training some 30 to 50 young men and women sent over from Israel by the Haganah. We had classes in secret cipher, wire tapping, bugging, safe cracking, surveillance and other police methods, including a most advanced reporting technique. The classes of instruction were held under the cover of Bible classes and the students wore yarmulkas. When they graduated after five or six weeks of training, they were as proficient in police methods as any of the graduates of the O.S.S. whom we had trained.

The details of the school project are contained in a book entitled *The Pledge* by Leonard Slater, published by Simon & Schuster and later in paperback by Pocket Books.

While the school project was proceeding, we were also engaged in collecting strategic material for the Haganah in preparation for the inevitable war that would surely develop once the British had completed their avowed withdrawal from Palestine. These materials included plastic explosives, Waring blenders for the destruction of secret documents in the event of a hasty attack by the enemy, and huge caches of small arms which we collected from former United States service men. One day late in 1947, a shipment of such strategic materials was being loaded on a ship in the port of Jersey City, New Jersey, when the rope loading cage broke open and caused a huge case of strategic materials to be dropped on the pier. The case was broken and the materials were visible. The ship officials called in the FBI and the FBI called in the New York City police as well as the New Jersey police, and the place was swarming with agents of the FBI, the customs authorities, the New Jersey and the New York police.

Fortunately, before the break we were deeply concerned with having our materials destined for the Haganah go through the strike lines because there was a strike going on in Jersey City at the time. I have verified that the actual break at the Jersey City dock occurred on January 7, 1948, and 77 crates were seized and moved from their mooring in Raritan Bay to the Naval Munitions Depot at Earle, New Jersey.

My law partner was Edward S. Silver, who was District Attorney of Kings County (Brooklyn, New York). He was later appointed Surrogate of Kings County. Mr. Silver was a very good friend of Mayor William O'Dwyer. I contacted Ed Silver and told him prior to January 7th that there was a strike at the docks in Jersey City and that we had a shipment destined for the Haganah which we wanted to clear through the picket lines. I suggested that he speak to Mayor Bill O'Dwyer and explain that the shipment of the 77 crates was a shipment of emergency medical supplies for the Hadassah Hospital in Jerusalem. Ed Silver took me to Mayor O'Dwyer's office at City Hall and told Mayor O'Dwyer of our problem. Mayor O'Dwyer said that he would immediately call the police commissioner and give him the numbers of our trucks and direct the police commissioner to arrange with the New Jersey authorities for the free passage of our trucks through the picket lines.

When the break occurred, my partner Ed Silver ran over to Mayor O'Dwyer's office at City Hall and explained the great difficulty we were having. Mayor O'Dwyer said that he understood the problem extremely well because he had experienced similar worries during the period when secret supplies were shipped to the Irish Liberation Army in Dublin. Then Bill O'Dwyer in our presence called the police commissioner of the City of New York and asked him why so many New York policemen were being engaged in an investigation on a Jersey City dock when there are more important crimes to be concerned with in New York City. He instructed the police commissioner to withdraw all the New York police personnel working on the case.

With the New York contingent of police totally withdrawn from the case, the small group of FBI agents and New Jersey police had little to go by and no arrests were made.

A few days later, I testified before a Congressional Committee and explained that we were merely trying to collect and deliver emergency supplies for Jewish American projects who might be isolated in Israel if the Arabs were to attack.

If it had not been for Mayor Bill O'Dwyer's intercession, I am convinced that many of our key people might have been indicted and sent to jail, and our important projects for the Haganah would have been badly damaged.

But some arrests were made in New York nevertheless. Among the people I had met while working with the league was Esther Antin Untermeyer, a Detroit attorney and former judge, who had been married to the poet Louis Untermeyer. They had a son, Joseph, who was then nineteen and had joined his mother in the cause. One day Esther called me at my office.

"Something very serious has happened," she said. "Our son Joseph has been locked up and is now in the Twentieth Street Station House for possession of arms which were on the way to Israel. I am beside myself with guilt because it was my involvement that got him into this mess. I'm sure they are giving him the third degree now."

I told Esther that I did not think this was the case but that I would call the station house and find out what was going on.

I placed the call and asked for the detectives' room. As luck would have it, Dave Mullee answered. He had been born five miles from Bohola and I knew him well.

"Is that you, David?"

"Yes, it is," he replied, "who's this?"

"This is Paul O'Dwyer, David. Do you have a young man there named Joseph Untermeyer?"

"Indeed we do," he answered.

"David, is he in difficulty?"

"I wouldn't think so," the detective answered.

"Would it be all right for his mother, who's very much concerned about him, to come and see him?"

"Of course she can," he said.

"David," I asked, "what will be the charges?"

"He will be charged with a violation of 1897 of the Penal Law"—which, I knew, dealt with the possession of dangerous weapons. "Paul," my friend continued, "don't be concerned. He's a good boy."

"David, what kind of stuff did they have?"

"It's beautiful," the detective whispered excitedly. "If we had only had it in 1919, Paul, the situation in Ireland would be different today."

I called Esther and told her the news and said that Joseph would be arraigned the next morning and that I would be there to represent him.

Joseph and two other youths had been apprehended in a loft building on the west side of Manhattan by Mullee and another policeman as the lads were packing merchandise for Israel—old clothes wrapped around new rifles. The police had discovered the cache by sheer accident. A man riding in the freight elevator had bumped against one of the sacks and discovered the arms. Assuming they were destined for gangsters, he called the Tenth Precinct.

To establish possession of those guns as required under the law, however, was another matter, and Mullee said the boys had made no admission. When we came before Judge Frederick Strong of the magistrate's court for the hearing, I presented three defenses on behalf of the two clients I represented:

> These guns were in transit to Israel and were bound to the people who were fighting for their liberty. Any attempt to stifle the people of another country from gaining their liberty would be against public policy in the United States, and therefore, no court could declare it a crime—to help people gain their freedom!
>
> There was no exclusive possession shown, that the guns were in a loft and the boys' presence in that same loft did not constitute possession. This was not the kind of case where the police could claim the defendants had been captured with guns in their pockets.
>
> There was no admission that might be construed to be proof of ownership or possession.

In a motion to dismiss the charges I argued:

> Now, if Your Honor pleases, with respect to my motion to dismiss, we must necessarily have to comment on two items of the officer's testimony. The first has to do with the cause, and inasmuch as it is brought in here, we have to make some comment about it. That is a situation which calls for the indictment of somebody, but not these two defendants. The indictment of Glubb and Abdullah and Bevin, and perhaps even some people here in our own country would be more likely.
>
> Yesterday, in Jerusalem, Abdullah rode into that Holy City. He rode in because American money was made available. Eight million dollars was made available so that England could make arms and ammunition available to

Abdullah and to Glubb and to Bevin and to the Mufti. And so, if you were to go into that feature of it, not these two defendants, but the ones I have named stand convicted of mass murder before the court of public opinion of the world. Now, we get down to the technical question before Your Honor. I had to comment on the other because of the fact that it is part of the people's testimony here and it should not go unanswered before any tribunal where free men love their liberty.

Insofar as they are concerned, these two defendants, were it to be shown that they were actually engaged in the business of sending arms and ammunition to the defenseless citizens of Palestine, that, indeed, sir, in my opinion, would be a worthwhile act. While it is true that our government may take on the position of neutrality and the people of the United States have taken on the position of a sympathetic approach to the problems of the United Nations and the problems of Palestine, it is quite apparent that the position of the people is at variance with that of our government. It has been said that we are neutral, but we cannot possibly be neutral while we supply eight million dollars to England, who in turn buys arms to send into Palestine and performs mass murder. Consequently, it is our money that actually permitted and caused the Mufti and Abdullah to go into Palestine and perform mass murder, aided and abetted by Glubb and Bevin. To get down to the actual fact of possession and if we go into a technical argument, I do not want it to appear either before this court or outside of it, that I am depending upon a technicality, and so, consequently, I have made the previous statement.

But, actually, inasmuch as I will not go into the question with respect to the defendant whom I do not represent—he is ably represented here—I think what applies to one applies to the other two. This is a situation where we are dealing with the Sullivan Law, which had in the beginning the purpose of keeping guns out of the hands of gangsters. People who wanted to commit crimes were to be the victims of this law, not men who wanted to see that honest men—men who love freedom—are protected in their homes and in their hillsides. The Sullivan Law has no application in this case. Section 1897, under any circumstances, should not be applied to a situation of this kind.

After a brief recess the magistrate announced:

> I follow your eloquence, Mr. O'Dwyer, insofar as our country's origins are concerned, and I recognize what our position might have been in 1776, but since that time things have changed considerably. I doubt very much that your defense—which might have been all right then in Boston or even in New York—can stand you in good stead today.
>
> I will not hear you on your argument that the guns were in shipment, and I don't think I have to pass on either of your second points. I will take up the question of exclusive possession, and find that there was none and that none was proved.

Thereafter I became a stakeholder for the Haganah. They had made arrangements to buy bazookas from American gangsters and ship the arms to Israel. Four representatives came to the office one day—an ex-cop named Harris, who was the 5-percent man, a rabbi, and two very bright young men from the Haganah. They came unannounced and explained to me that they had made a deal for the bazookas for $60,000. The bazookas were needed, they said, so that the Israelis could pierce the Arab tanks that were crossing the borders of Israel. They all agreed, they said, that I was the person to hold the money until the guns were delivered.

Several days later, while I was engaged in the trial of a case in the Supreme Court in New York City, a young lawyer stopped at the counsel table and dropped a manila envelope on the other papers I had been using. "Paul," he whispered, "there's sixty thousand dollars in negotiable securities—bearer—bonds in that envelope."

"Are you out of your mind?" I said. "Don't you know that the gangsters are probably watching me to find out when I get the cash? You mean I have to carry this envelope from here to Wall Street?"

"What the hell am I going to do with it?" he pleaded. "All I was supposed to do was deliver it to you."

"Look," I entreated, "take it down to 130 William Street to the office of Sean Keating and tell him to mark it 'Israel.' He'll know what to do with it, and just to make sure, I'll call him before you get there."

"Can he be trusted?" the lawyer asked.

"He would no more part with that money than Chaim Weizmann would," I answered. "He's a member of the league, but besides that, he served time in Ireland."

The money was duly delivered to Keating and remained in his office safe until the bazookas were delivered to the Haganah.

In December 1948 I and a number of others honored Menachem Begin at a dinner in New York. Even after victory had been achieved, controversy still surrounded the Irgun. My good friend Harvey Rosen, secretary of the Fire Department, sent me a letter he had received from our mutual friend Harry Avrutin, field director of the American Trade Union Council of the National Committee for Labor Palestine:

> I was exceedingly shocked when I picked up today's *New York Times* and found Paul O'Dwyer's name listed as a member of the reception committee for Mr. Menachem Begin.
>
> I recall that you contacted me and asked me to aid him in his campaign for Congress. Knowing Mr. O'Dwyer's convictions and activities, it is indeed surprising to find him on a reception committee for Begin. Mr. Begin is the leader of a dissident group in Israel known as Irgun, is head of the most reactionary anti-labor elements in Israel.
>
> I have already been informed that Philip Murray of the CIO and a number of others have disavowed and refused to associate with the reception and have denied any relationship with the so-called reception committee.

> Knowing your interest in Mr. O'Dwyer, I am sure that you will contact him on the matter and ask him to make a public exodus from the committee.

Rosen was an officeholder in my brother's administration. He also was a trade-union leader, and he had obviously been given the job of getting me off the committee as part of the larger task of isolating Begin when he came here. Harvey asked me for an answer. I obliged:

> The Irgunists are good boys, and they did a very intelligent job of chasing the British out of Israel. If Israel were to wait for freedom to come from the conference table, Harvey Rosen would be getting Social Security before the matter would come up for the second reading. To ask me to turn my back on the Irgunists would be like asking me to denounce the Irish Republican Army. I have been not merely a name on an ad, I have been working actively to help them and support them for a number of years.

Not all the letters and comments were adverse. Following a speech I gave at Carnegie Hall, a letter from Sigmund Zauberman arrived. His entire family, including his eighty-eight-year-old mother, had perished in Hitler's gas chambers. He wrote:

> Your address last night at Carnegie Hall impressed me so much that I am firmly convinced that you are to be the one mentioned by the Prophet Isaiah who, in the future, is going to be the judge among nations. I am 66 years of age, but have not heard until this day a non-Jew speaking with the ardor coming from such a warm, true heart, as you did about matters of Jewish concern. Every word of yours was balm and delight to my wounds that have not yet been healed, and Lord knows whether they ever will heal.

Within a few months of Israel's independence I became chairman of Supplies for Palestine, Inc. Our purpose was to help the veterans of resistance and their heirs. Many of the freedom fighters had left widows and children, and many of them were in need and did not fit into army relief programs. The United Jewish Appeal sent their funds to the majority party in Israel, but there were bureaucratic difficulties attached to giving assistance to the victims who had been part of an illegal army and an illegal movement. We believed that our compatriots also deserved the opportunity to rehabilitate themselves so that they too could find their place in the new nation of Israel.

Thereafter, however, I withdrew from involvement in the internal politics of Israel. The battle was won, and much as I admired the daring Irgunists and the courage of their leader, I did not share their philosophy. My interest was in Israel and not in a particular political party.

CHAPTER NINE

The Quiet Fifties

THE YEAR 1951 was a poor one for the O'Dwyers. My brother Bill, in failing health after an easy reelection campaign, had resigned as mayor in 1950 to become President Truman's ambassador to Mexico. Thereafter the Kefauver Senate investigating subcommittee, inquiring into the relationship of government and organized crime, had come to New York. The committee's investigation was highly publicized, and the former mayor and his administration were raked over the coals. The results were devastating, and in one year's time Bill's reputation sank from an all-time high to an all-time low.

It was impossible to counteract the campaign of abuse. I tried at first, but found myself losing my case, because no one was interested in the defense. The media had a story and made no effort to separate rumor from fact, assuming that Bill's official absence from the country made him fair game.

Federal investigators invaded my brother Frank's vegetable farm in California and started digging it up with shovels. They went to nearby towns in search of bills of sale for cement, in which, presumably, they expected to find ill-gotten gains from New York encased. Then they leaked an account of their activities to the press.

Frank detested politics and always had. He had been a California resident for fifteen years and was away from the scene. He wanted to sue, and it was months before I could persuade him that the litigation would never end. He was especially bitter that his wife and son had been made to suffer.

As for me, I more or less dropped out of public life for a while. My law practice had suffered for lack of attention during five rather exciting years, and the business of providing for a family of four children and a few nephews and nieces, who had become all but stepchildren of Kathleen and me, was pressing.

Our children suffered at school, no doubt, but Kathleen and I had counseled them during the halcyon days not to let their uncle's prestige give them ideas, and accordingly, we advised them that, as fate works both ways, they were not responsible for the older generation's problems. My withdrawal from politics, moreover, afforded me a chance to attend to their needs, which I had long neglected.

My gregarious instincts meanwhile had found an outlet again in the affairs of Ireland. In January 1950 I was invited to an executive meeting of the American League for an Undivided Ireland. The group met regularly at the Irish American Historical Society building on Fifth Avenue. Its chairman was Richard Dalton, who had been active in the organization for more than forty years. The purpose of the league was to urge congressional hearings regarding the partition of Ireland and to publicize the tyranny visited upon the Catholic minority in the six-county area of Ulster.

The executive committee consisted of fairly elderly citizens, all of them my seniors by at least twenty-five years. With more than the usual solemnity they asked me to become a member of the executive board, but more important, they wanted me to be their national coordinator. They informed me that Congressman John Fogarty of Rhode Island had, at their request, presented what had become known as the Fogarty Resolution to the House of Representatives. The resolution had, with boring regularity, been filed, and with equal regularity, ignored. The resolution condemned Britain's role in Ireland and called for a plebiscite by all the people of Ireland as to the fate of Erin. Since a majority of the people could be counted on to opt for a thirty-two-county Irish republic, it was a resolution in the best Irish revolutionary tradition. Resolutions of similar import had been introduced in the Senate by Herbert Lehman, and later by a young man from Massachusetts answering to the name of John Fitzgerald Kennedy. The Senate resolutions fared no better than their companion in the House.

Finally, after many attempts, the league decided to mount a nationwide campaign in support of the Fogarty Resolution. The elderly members considered themselves the link to carry forward the *Cliab Solus* ("Sword of Light") from one generation to the next. With great solemnity they told me of their work and their plans. It was their belief that the attempt to achieve complete freedom for Ireland would begin again soon, but as their lives were coming to a close, they might not be around or vigorous enough to play a role, and they wanted to ensure that someone would be there to take over.

In the spectrum of American politics they stood mostly to the right, and they and I were miles apart. My orientation, moreover, was very public. Only a year earlier I had completed my tenure as president of the National Lawyers Guild, which was still, at the time of our meeting, designated by the attorney general as a Communist front.

"You must recognize," I said, "that I have taken certain positions that have made me controversial. I have been chairman of the National Lawyers Guild, and have taken strong positions concerning various matters of civil rights and civil liberties, and the chances are I will be taking those positions again.

"You know," I continued, "I have been severely criticized and condemned by Dr. Edward Lodge Curran, the *Brooklyn Tablet* [the Catholic newspaper sponsored by the diocese of Brooklyn] and a large assortment of Catholic leaders, both lay and clergy, as well as by right-wingers of many persuasions. I would not be surprised if it were disclosed any day now that I am suspected by the House Un-American Activities Committee."

Richard Dalton spoke for the group. "Devoy had not attended church in years," he said. "Parnell was no plaster saint and Pagan O'Leary was never nominated for Knight of St. Gregory." They all laughed. "Besides," said Charlie Rice, "as far as we know, you do not have as many illegitimate children as the Emancipator" (referring to Daniel O'Connell, the Catholic Emancipator). "And you can't be as anticlerical or as irreverent as Wolfe Tone," added Connie Neenan, the youngest. "We know your position on Ireland, and you're not likely to wilt under pressure," concluded Ed Egan, "and that's all that matters."

It was impossible to reject the offer, and besides, most Irish Americans had long regarded me with suspicion and/or derision, and I was elated to discover that I was still trusted by those I most revered.

My responsibilities as national coordinator for the league took me to Los Angeles for speaking engagements and press conferences about the situation in Ireland. Among the people I met there and who assisted me was Michael Collins, who had been the owner of the Tuxedo Ballroom, where we held the first meeting of the American Friends of Irish Neutrality, and who had since moved from New York to California. Through Michael I met Harry McDermott, the *shames* (sexton) in charge of the Jewish Center of Wiltshire Boulevard, whose spiritual leader was the revered Rabbi Magnin.

Harry had the job of maintaining the premises and had hired greenhorn kids from Ireland to work for the center. But the rabbi and the board of directors told Harry he must give preference to refugees from Europe.

Harry thought it was the right thing to do and did so. But after a while the premises began to deteriorate. The board complained and Harry was called on the carpet. He explained that many of the maintenance staff at the center had held jobs of importance in Germany and they lacked the desire or capacity to work as porters and cleaners. Thereupon the rabbi told Harry to go back to the Hibernian Hall and hire whomever he wanted.

(A few months later, back in New York, I had occasion to contact Harry McDermott again. My friend Phil Reiner had moved to the West Coast and his mother and brother were visiting him there during the High Holy Days. They wanted in the worst way to get into Rabbi Magnin's synagogue for services. Phil had called me and said, "Look, my relatives are here and I can't get them into Rabbi Magnin's synagogue. Can you help?" I called Harry long distance and told him I needed tickets for services. "They're terribly hard to come by," he said, "but let me see what I can do." He called me back and reported, "Your friends are fixed up." When I told Phil the news he couldn't get over the fact that he had had to go to an Irishman in New York, who in turn went to an Irish *shames* in California to get his tickets for Jewish services in Los Angeles.)

From Los Angeles I went to San Francisco for another press conference, and I contacted a number of Irish organizations there, ranging from the Gaelic Athletic Association to the Knights of the Red Branch. I was, in a sense, the national needler to get the older organizations moving and to keep alive the spirit in the United States so that when the day of reckoning came they would be there to help the people of Belfast and Derry.

I visited groups in Cleveland, Toledo, Cincinnati, Buffalo and Syracuse, and paid calls on my friends in Jersey City, Boston and Philadelphia. I reported my findings to the board of directors of the league. They felt that the time was ripe to begin holding congressional hearings on the Fogarty Resolution. People came from all over the country to testify in Washington. Still the resolution remained locked in committee. But on March 29, 1950, the foreign-aid bill was passed, with an amended proviso that its benefits would not be available to countries answering to certain descriptions. The prohibition, by its language, excluded aid to Great Britain. The victory was a temporary one, but it did establish that there was in Congress a significant bloc disposed to help Ireland attain freedom. Besides, the newspaper accounts pointed out that there was a serious denial of civil liberties to the Catholic minority in Northern Ireland.

Sir Basil Brooke, prime minister of the Stormont government in Belfast, came here on a tour to counteract our activities. We hired a newspaperman to dog his footsteps. Bill Peer briefed the press and supplied them with a list of questions. Brooke's predecessor had proclaimed his government to be "a Protestant government for a Protestant people" and had complained that too many Catholics were being hired in Belfast. His party excluded Catholics from its ranks. Armed with these facts, the media here discredited the emissary, who shortly ended his stay and went to Canada. Although not officially welcomed in New York, Brooke was welcomed by Governor Adlai Stevenson in Illinois, which did not help Stevenson when he ran for President two years later.

Despite the league's success and my own, however, my earlier civil liberties activities did on occasion get in the way. The league organizer in Cleveland, my good friend James McCoy, wrote to me on September 5, 1950, telling me that "some people here have been raising questions about your views in light of the comments you made after the riot in Union Square Park." After customary indignation, I adopted the customary unindignant reply:

> There was nothing much to the New York incident. A group of people, presumably leftist and Communist, made an application to have a "peace rally" at Union Square. The Police Commissioner denied the permit and Bill O'Dwyer backed up his Police Commissioner. On the day of the proposed rally, several thousand people showed up and began to walk around the square. The police broke up these groups and from what I gather may have, on occasion, used more force than was necessary. However, that's a controversial question and I would not pass judgment on it lightly.
>
> The main question that concerned us in the National Lawyers Guild was whether or not a permit should have been granted, and it was to that question that we addressed our attention.
>
> My own view is that I believe a permit should have been granted. My thought is that you don't prove you are a believer in democracy by acting like Russians, and a denial of free speech is something that smacks of totalitarianism. I am against it abroad and I am against it here. The question of free speech, however, comes up usually with organizations that are unpopular. Nobody really wants to deny a Democrat or a Republican the right to talk, and it is tested only when a radical speaks. He is the one with whom we are generally in violent disagreement.
>
> Many people have misconstrued my belief in civil rights as an endorsement of the views of radicals. I think my political views are rather old-fashioned. I take seriously all the provisions of the Constitution, and when the Declaration of Independence speaks of the equality of man, I think that Americans should take it literally, and I mean all men—that includes black men and white men, Jews and Mormons, and Protestants and Catholics and Moslems.
>
> When I was in my early teens I saw the then totalitarians going through a quiet countryside killing, slaughtering and plundering an innocent people. They didn't call them

> Reds and they didn't call them Nazis; they called them Black and Tans, and they left a lasting impression and if somebody raises an eyebrow now at some of the things that I say, I can't help it.
>
> At the last convention of the Guild, held in New York last May, we passed unanimously a resolution calling for the end of a divided Ireland. This was heartily endorsed by Surrogate Pat O'Brien of Detroit, who is one of our prominent members.

Jimmy McCoy was able to use my letter to assuage the ill feelings in Cleveland, and I was able to speak there many more times for the cause of Irish freedom.

In 1951 there did not seem to be much hope of Congressman Fogarty's bringing his resolution up for a vote again, so we organized a letter-writing campaign and succeeded in getting enough congressmen to sign a petition to bring the resolution to a vote on September 27. New York *Daily News* reporter Ruth Montgomery had some fun with the outcome of that vote:

> *Unify Irish? Think of Virginia, suh!*
>
> Washington, D.C., Sept. 27 — Catcalls and derisive laughter today climaxed an abortive attempt in the House of Representatives to demand an end to the partition of Ireland.
>
> Dubbed the Second Irish Rebellion, the House resolution failed on a roll call vote of 139–206 after Representative Howard W. Smith (D.–Va.) playfully threatened to "amend the resolution to end the unlawful partition of West Virginia and Virginia."
>
> "We're a-stickin' our long nose into somebody else's business," Smith drawled, "but if we're a-gonna start a war with the Irish, let's start it first with West Virginia."
>
> *How 'bout that coal, suh?*
>
> "You all," he continued with a wave of his hand at his Yankee colleagues, "unlawfully split West Virginia off

from my state 100 years ago, so let's have a plebiscite of Virginia folks—not West Virginia, mind you—to regain these coal mines and riches we need so badly."

The Irish resolution, sponsored by Representative John Fogarty (D.–R.I.) would have "expressed the sense of the House" that all 32 counties in partitioned Ireland—not just the six Northern Counties concerned—should vote to end partition.

What the British could say!

But Representative John Vorys (R.–Ohio) claimed that this move would "impose minority rule—just what we're against at home—on the non-Catholic peoples of Northern Ireland."

Chairman James P. Richards (D.–S.C.) of the Foreign Affairs Committee warned that if the House passed "this silly measure," the British House of Commons would probably pass one telling us to "mind our own business." He added that Britain might also "order us" to give statehood to Hawaii and Alaska.

But Smith of Virginia had the last say. "There's only one reason why we're a-actin' on this today," he snorted. "That's because we've already got our fingers in everybody else's business in the world except Ireland's so some of you think we oughta get into this mess, too."

Even though we failed to pass the resolution, and even though some members of the press made fun of the serious efforts we made, we succeeded in bringing attention to the fact that discrimination was rampant in Ireland and the Stormont government was persecuting the Catholic minority. We argued that the Stormont government was sowing seeds of violence that would flower in later years. The purpose of the campaign had been to raise the consciousness level of Irish Americans about the situation in the homeland and to try to change it. At the end of the campaign there was little change in conditions in

Ireland, but we had succeeded in keeping the issue alive in the United States.*

For the next several years I devoted myself to my law practice—largely estate planning, court litigation of all kinds, and, to be sure, civil rights cases. Oscar Bernstien was an indefatigable worker, and we worked together as energetically as at any time in the forty years of O'Dwyer and Bernstien.

I became fascinated with show business clients. Common sense told me they were not good professional risks, but I enjoyed their company and wanted to represent them. Some sought me out; I sought out others; and ultimately O'Dwyer and Bernstien acquired enough writers and performers to put a thriving law practice in financial jeopardy. I sought such clients generally in the early evening, sometimes stretching over into the early morning.

It was on one of those evenings, somewhere between Harvey Rosen's El Borracho and Sherman Billingsley's Stork Club, that I met Ella Logan. When she stayed in New York, Ella put up at the Hotel Meurice on West Fifty-eighth Street for the reason that in the small, dark and intimate Chez Vito Room at the back of the ground floor Vito had collected the best Gypsy fiddlers in all Romany land, and the music invariably suited Ella's mood.

Ella became my friend and client soon after *Finian's Rainbow* came to town. The star of the show was this pixie girl from Scotland or Ireland—nobody was quite sure whence she hailed—a born thespian, with a wry wit and the most beautiful voice I have ever heard. As Sharon she seemed to have stepped out of mythical Glocca Morra, and her song struck a responsive chord in millions of Americans. Her career was launched, and her tremendous talent took her throughout the world.

*On March 8, 1979, at a press conference in Washington, D.C., in answer to a reporter's question Nobel Peace Prize–winner Sean McBride said that the present change in attitudes in England and Ireland is due to activities in the United States.

Ella fell in love with and married producer Freddie Finklehoffe, an Orthodox Jew and Sabbath observer. She became Orthodox and kept a kosher house and did all the things required of a Jewish wife. If there was any restriction on gambling in the Hebraic codes, Freddie did not know about it, for he loved the horses and loved to gamble and he spent all of their money. Ultimately his gambling took precedence over everything else and the marriage shattered.

Ella had interrupted her career to marry Freddie and had difficulty after the divorce putting it back together again. She went on the road, a euphemism for torture. At one point she called me and asked me to meet with Billy Rose, the greatest showman of his day, to discuss with him the possibility of reviving *Finian's Rainbow* on Broadway. I was told to indicate my interest, of course, in her being the star of the show again.

When I broached the subject with Rose, he shrugged his shoulders, and said, "Well, there's a lot that's left to the imagination in putting on shows, and while it does strain mine somewhat to think of Ella at this point in her life again being a little girl right off the boat from Ireland, I suppose we could talk about it."

I never dared tell Ella (who was then about forty years old) what Billy had said.

While she was on the road she wrote to me regularly—sometimes long stories, often filled with humorous complaints. Never had I a more engaging client. When the London office of the Music Corporation of America, acting as her agent, booked her into Newcastle on Tyne, they promised that someone would be there ahead of her to plug her Monday-night opening in the press. But it so happened that she was scheduled to open during the Jewish High Holy Days, and Mr. Payne of M.C.A. wired her saying that, due to the Holy Days, he would not arrive until later in the week. She wrote to report to me how she had handled the affair.

I shot back a wire saying, "Don't you have a 'goy' or Reform Jew in the office?"

I don't need to tell you, Paul, later in the week, as you know, was too late. Monday is the day to state your case, as critics only come to the first show. Well, the holiday was over on Monday at sundown, so on Tuesday, Mr. Norman Payne came—but the stretching of the remains, may she rest in peace, was over by that time, and he was as helpful to me as Whittaker Chambers was to Alger Hiss.

Ella chided me from time to time for neglecting her.

A fine bloody friend you are, but I will forgive you because you are an immigrant and because you are a dear friend of that famous poet and scholar Sam Slitz [an uncouth mutual acquaintance] and because you don't know any better and because you have raised a fine family and never swear.

A few weeks later she mailed me a letter from my brother Bill, her new lover, had sent her from a hotel in Mexico: "And now my Laggin Love," he wrote, "with the night in her hair, who am I to make a greater bid for your patient attention?" In the margin she had penned, "He's a descriptive bastard, ain't he?"

In France she took up the cause of Maurice Chevalier, whom she loved, and she wrote me:

A few years ago, an American performer living in France sent a letter to the State Department denouncing Maurice as a red, etc., etc. But I think Maurice had a very good point there when he said to me, "Ella, I am still the most popular performer in France, especially with the workingman. It is obvious that if I was ever pro-Communist, they would grab the chance to publicize it and say Maurice has chosen to be with us."

Ella went on for pages telling me what I should do to help Chevalier:

> Tell him that he must place his case in professional hands. You see, they have attempted to film the Chevalier story here in the U.S., but the deal got cold when he was refused a visa. So make it plain to him that he should put this matter in professional hands and the less he has to do with it, the better. The courts should be closed soon, so write or phone. Don't leave me with a bad impression of you, otherwise you will find that Fuller never made a bigger brush as [sic] the one I will give you when I come to New York.

When she was in town Ella performed at my campaign rallies, belting out a song she had made famous, "Follow the Fella who Follows the Star." Not too many followed the fella, but everyone loved Ella.

Toward the end of her life Ella sold her home in Beverly Hills, and the sale paid off all her debts and took care of the bequests she had made to close friends and relatives. She outlined some instructions that she wanted carried out after her death: "Don't waste time on mourning, but make certain that there's whiskey enough for everybody. I wish only the most inexpensive of burials, but *not* inexpensive booze for any friends who might attend to cheer me on my way."

A few months later she died of cancer.

The rewards of representing the artists of America were not of the financial kind, and in the practice of law, Mammon too must be served. During my "leave of absence" from politics from 1951 to 1958, I became increasingly involved in a variety of cases dealing with general litigation and certain aspects of the business world. On the advice of a business associate, I decided to become involved in banking. The immediate reason for my adventure into this most exclusive calling was the result of a trip to the Emigrant Savings Bank to get a mortgage loan to help buy the future Irish Institute building on West Forty-eighth Street. I was disappointed; the bank refused to grant our request for a mortgage loan of $25,000 on a $55,000 building.

My antagonism was particularly aroused because the Emigrant Savings Bank had begun life as the Irish Emigrant Savings Bank, and Irish emigrants had enriched it to a point at which it had over one billion dollars on deposit. Moreover, the rejection of the application was a personal slight, as I had offered to go as guarantor on the bond and have some of the people who were on the board of directors of the institute do likewise. Accordingly, I looked into the history of savings banks and found that their original purpose was a very good and eleemosynary one: to promote a program to train the immigrant class to put away a few dollars so their savings would help them in need.

I sought the advice of experts in the field—my friends Tom Shanahan, president of the Federation Bank and Trust Company, a comparatively young and thriving institution, and Tom Quinn, founder and president of the Inter-County Title Company. I told them I was thinking of forming a new savings bank. They thought the idea was worth exploring, and Shanahan put me in touch with his brother Pat, who was anxious to come aboard.

They made arrangements to have me meet state banking officials. The idea of new banking institutions did not appeal to the officials. They had very negative feelings about our plan and talked much about the difficulties it would entail. I was not encouraged, but I decided to keep trying.

I wrote to Joseph Kennedy and outlined our plan. I explained that, on the basis of the history of savings banks and savings-and-loan associations in New York, there was little financial risk involved. (The originators of a savings institution do not buy stock; the money is placed on deposit and is kept there until the banking officials say it is safe to withdraw it.) A month later I received a reply saying that, although he felt honored to be asked, he had withdrawn from all directorships "ever since Jack has been elected" (to the Senate).

Other replies, although more availing, committed small sums, and I realized that it would take years to make the bank a success. I decided instead to become a director of the Union Mutual Savings and Loan Association, where I acquired a working knowledge of banking practices. New York banks had not yet broken down the racial barriers in their hiring practices, and they were on the threshold of the redlining policies which came to public attention two decades later.

CHAPTER TEN

Reform

When my brother Bill resigned as mayor in 1950 to become Truman's ambassador to Mexico, he was succeeded by Vincent Impellitteri, the president of the City Council, who, under the city charter, became mayor until the next election, which took place in November of that same year. At that time if Impellitteri expected to get the nomination of the Democratic party, he was the only one in New York who believed he would, and, in fact, he was ignored by the five county bosses, who chose Judge Ferdinand Pecora instead. To everyone's amazement, Impellitteri, running as an Independent, won. He served the remainder of Bill's term, without distinction, and was then successfully challenged in the Democratic primary by Robert Wagner, Jr., who won in November 1953.

Wagner was reelected in 1957, and in his second term sought to gain control of the fractious Democratic party. He encouraged insurgents to challenge existing leaders for the county leadership posts and thereby precipitated an internal power struggle.

By 1961, when the next election rolled around, the still-divided party bosses were forced into the position of selecting a candidate other than Wagner. On the other hand, the satellite Liberal party (which had received 25 percent of the City Hall patronage) chose Wagner.*

I believe Wagner did not really make up his mind to seek a third term until he discovered that the bosses had met and secretly decided to do him in, when a stubborn streak was awakened in him. In the meantime the Democratic Reform Movement, of which I was a founder, had grown, and while Wagner never recognized or encouraged Reform, he was aware that the Reformers had materially weakened the old-line leadership. That and the fact that I had worked in Wagner's two previous campaigns made for more than a marriage of convenience so far as we were concerned.

The Wagner success in the subsequent election (he was opposed by the Democratic state controller, Arthur Levitt) was due in great measure to disillusionment of New York City Democrats with their leaders. Reform Democrats provided Wagner's margin of victory.

The Reform Movement could hardly have been called a youth movement: Senator Lehman was near eighty, Mrs. Roosevelt seventy-five, Tom Finletter sixty, and I fifty-one when we organized the founding committee after the Democratic debacle of 1958, when the entire slate of statewide candidates, save Levitt, went down to defeat. At the club level, however, the young people were taking over, and a group of them met with me in my district. They found it difficult to understand me and questioned my motives in joining the movement. I had been out front on civil rights issues before

*For several years Alex Rose was in fact the Liberal party. Alex was the head of the hatters' union, but men began to discard hats and the union membership dwindled, giving Alex all the time necessary to manipulate his party.

most of them were born, but they knew nothing of my activities and were quick to conclude—without inquiry—that my name and association with Bill O'Dwyer and Bob Wagner made it unlikely that I would be anything but an old-line regular Democrat in outlook and commitment. Even though I was stereotyped, I forgave their ignorance and agreed to help reform politics on the West Side of Manhattan.

I joined the newly formed F.D.R.–Woodrow Wilson Club, made up of members of two rival clubs and filled with energetic, youthful and extremely ambitious young men and women. Denis Mahon was the Democratic "boss" of the district, and had been for more than thirty-five years, and he had never before been challenged in a primary. His captains had grown old and fat and lazy. Because they had never had a primary fight, they had become complacent and had lost contact with the voters.

In addition, it was clear that, in the middle-class districts at least, Mahon and others like him had come to the end of their power. Mahon was tall and impressive. He was the Commissioner of Records, by virtue of a political appointment. He lived an austere life in the neighborhood and held court at the clubhouse on Ninety-sixth Street and Columbus Avenue every Monday and Thursday night, according to tradition. He believed in rewarding those who worked in the club and in the party, those who were at the clubhouse to handle various personal problems of the constituents. No discussions, ideological or otherwise, ever took place in the club. It was a service organization. Mahon expressed no opinions either for or against the liberal, progressive or conservative position. His success as a leader was judged by the number of jobs he was able to acquire for club members from the Tammany patronage machine. He had many commissioners and judges to his credit, and, in the fashion of the time, they were grateful to the "boss." No taint of scandal clung to his selections and the only criticism was with the absence of democracy in their preferment.

A generation before Mahon, district leaders had always hailed newcomers to the neighborhood, but in Mahon's time the newcomers had been blacks and Puerto Ricans. Not only were they not welcomed but they were discouraged by conduct that could be described as insulting. Thus, until the new residents could constitute at least 50 percent of the voters, they had no hope of electing a black or Puerto Rican as an officeholder. Moreover, since they were not around when patronage was being dispensed, they missed out on those rewards too. It was Mahon's attitude toward these minorities that convinced me to join the Reform effort to oust him. I was affected by the Reform demand for more democracy in the clubhouse, but it was not my overriding motive.

By 1960 the Reform Movement had scored minor local successes and had moved on to a more ambitious program. The West Side Assembly District, taking in parts of Harlem and the area around Columbia University, had a new Reform district leader named William Fitts Ryan, and a nonconformist assemblyman named Dan Kelly, who had played a lonely role in Albany exposing Republicans and pricking the consciences of his Democratic colleagues. Part of their election district covered a congressional district on Manhattan's West Side, and in that district James Scheuer sought to get the Reform endorsement against the incumbent Congressman Ludwig Teller. Dan Kelly and I sought the same support for the same office.

Soon after I expressed my interest in the congressional race I was interviewed by a small group of young people on my qualifications for office. It was an extremely awkward session. I bridled at their questions. I knew that most of them were young children when I was fighting in the beleaguered remnant of the postwar liberal community, and I resented what I felt was their patronizing attitude toward me. Their revolt seemed insipid. It carried them no further than the edges of the precinct and stopped abruptly at the street where the ghetto began.

John Kennedy had begun to make his bid for the presidency

then, and suspicion regarding Irish Catholics was coming to the fore again. It seemed clear that the latent anti-Catholic sentiment that had routed Al Smith in 1928 was still present in the land. It was whispered here and openly stated there that Kennedy would not support government-sponsored birth-control programs, because they would be against his faith. In an interview I too was asked by some young New York liberals for my views on birth control. "Would the fact that you are a Catholic affect your judgment in this and similar situations?" My temper was at boiling point, but I uneasily restrained my feelings.

"I'm sure that in this and every position I take, the beliefs taught in early childhood do play a part," I responded testily. I could not refrain from lecturing them. "The total man," I continued, "is a product of a variety of forces that have affected his thinking, his living and his being and that are tempered by his weaknesses and strengths." They asked no more questions. They reported that I had failed the test, although in truth no one had ever put the question to me. They never did understand that my irritation sprang from their attempts to stereotype me.

Despite my misgivings, I went ahead. By 1960, Bill Ryan was the secure leader of the northern end of the congressional district, and Denis Mahon had been replaced by Hedi Piel. I pressed my effort to get to Congress.

The battle lines were drawn, and the night came for the club's vote. Jim Scheuer, who lived on Twenty-third Street, far away from the district, challenged me for the nomination in my own club. Word of the contest got around and those who had been with me in many a civil rights battle came to the club and began to work up support and to explain to the newcomers about the struggles in which I had been involved. I won the first round. The next night, however, there were a recount and a revote. I was literally counted out, and Scheuer won.

He won, I think, because I was the victim again of baiting. A young Irish American woman who had been a member of the evaluation committee was somewhat incensed at the turn of the discussion in committee and decided to publicly state what had been the committee's reasoning. Number one: I was ineligible because I was Bill O'Dwyer's brother; and number two: I had a long history of left-wing leanings and affiliations. The members of the committee stood accused. They did not deny the charge. They remained silent. They waited for me to attack. I never did. I permitted them to suffer from the exposure.

By the second night everyone had caught on to the fact that if a candidate wanted the support of the club he had to go through a procedure called "pulling"—an operation consisting of telephoning friends to bring their friends to the meeting and vote for the candidate. It did not matter that the friends or friends of friends were not residents of the district or even residents of the county. Indeed, even in those early days of Reform, candidates paid membership dues in return for votes. It became an accepted practice. It provoked no word of protest from those who had just thrown the rascals out of office. Anyway, I did not want to go forward without the enthusiastic support of the club, and I made no further effort to get the nomination. As for Reformers, they had created their own habits, and we were destined to live with them for ten years.

Our congressional district was predominantly Jewish, and some of the club members believed that a Jewish candidate would have a much better chance of winning the nomination and would fare better against the then congressman, Ludwig Teller, a well-respected man. I opposed this reasoning, and I thought that if our candidate had the support of Mrs. Roosevelt and Senator Lehman, and if he was right with the issues, he would stand an equal chance with the liberal Jewish voter.

The candidates now narrowed down to Dan Kelly and James Scheuer. Mike Nisselson, president of the Federation Bank, who was a friend of Scheuer's and mine, asked me to meet with them for lunch in the hope that I could give his candidate a word of advice. We met at the Lotus Club.

"There are only two of you in the race at this moment, and if you can resolve the situation quickly, you will avoid a third candidate's coming in," I said. "Why don't you make a sporting proposition to Dan Kelly, and if you want me to intervene, I will. You can toss a coin. You've got a fifty-percent chance of winning, and if there's an understanding that the loser of the toss will support the winner, the Reform candidate has a good chance of beating Teller." Scheuer was cold to the idea and Nisselson was annoyed with him.

Soon after my conversation with Scheuer another Reform meeting was called. What I had warned Scheuer would happen did in fact take place. Another candidate entered the race—Bill Ryan. He represented a large area, only half of which was in the congressional district. "All of my workers will be available to me in a primary," he said, "and none of my club's captains will be available if I do not win." Kelly failed to get support, and Scheuer and Ryan were the final contestants.

I supported Ryan at the meeting and said, "It is not a question of Scheuer or Ryan. It is a question of who can win for Reform in this first contest—and Bill Ryan has enough campaign workers to cover the whole district."

I campaigned for Ryan, especially in the Hell's Kitchen area, where from 1902 the McManus family had been Democratic leaders. It was no place for a Reformer.

On primary day I stopped at one of the McManus polling places. A young Jewish student from outside the district had been assigned as a poll watcher for Ryan. Truly, he was miscast, but Reformer Ryan had been unable to get anyone from the district to protect his interest there. Soon a longshoreman came in to vote. He showed the effects of alcohol as he announced his name and address. The youthful poll watcher stepped forward. "I want to challenge this man," he said, explaining that he could not find his name on the registration list.

"You want to challenge me?" said the voter belligerently.

The law student responded, "Yes, because you are not living at the address you say you are."

"Look," the voter shouted, "I live in that house. My grandfather and father before me were born in that house. We have lived in that house for three generations. But you said that you challenge me, then come outside!" The voter removed his coat. A challenge had a single meaning in Hell's Kitchen.

I went over to the student and said, "Look, he thinks you want to fight him."

"I don't want to fight him," the kid replied.

"You said you challenged me," the longshoreman continued. "What are you talking about? Come on, weasel! Come outside and fight!"

I approached the longshoreman and quietly told him that "challenging" someone was a phrase used in a polling place. "It has nothing to do with fighting," I said. "And besides, this fellow couldn't fight you. He's in no shape. Take a look at him; you'd take him in a wink."

I calmed the longshoreman and told the kid to withdraw the challenge. "If we need to challenge the voter later," I advised, "we've got his name and address."

Next to come in to vote was an elderly nun, robed heavily in the habit of that day. As she approached the desk the law student already had his hand up to challenge her. Before we had a second confrontation I intervened. "Hold it! Hold it!" I interjected. "You're surely not going to challenge a nun in a Hell's Kitchen polling place. We're going to have hell to pay in this place if you stick around much longer. Go on your way in peace and I'll take over."

Minutes after his departure the district leader, my friend Gene McManus, came in to check things out. He spotted me and yelled, "Paul, what the hell are you doing in my district?"

Gene, like all district bosses, felt his district was his barony, his private domain, and he wanted to know why I was intruding in his establishment. "Gene," I replied, "there's a new day and it should not be difficult for you to observe the rules. The rules require a club to be open to everybody. But if you have control of a club, the members will vote the way you want them to vote. You can be Reform and still have your way."

"Paul," he answered, "we've got Reform with the primary. The primary means that fourteen thousand voters in the district have the right to come in and elect me, and anybody who wants to run against me can try to corral the fourteen thousand votes. On primary day, if he beats me, I'm no longer the leader. I'm not anybody's messenger. The way you're telling me, after I get elected I've got to go back again after winning and have two hundred club members tell me what to do and who to select for a job or for a candidate."

He used such bold logic that I could not really argue with him, but I protested, "But you and you alone make decisions, Gene."

"That's what I was elected to do," he countered. "I'm the leader."

"But, Gene, you have your special squad to bring the vote out that you can rely on."

"Reformers," he spat out, "are going to have captains. Somebody's got to bring out the vote. These bastards aren't going to come out by themselves. Somebody pulls them out; otherwise they're going to watch T.V., and the whole thing will break down. Besides, are you telling me the Reformers will bring out the vote that opposes them?"

"Well," I said, "what about discussion of the issues, Gene?"

"What issues? Paul, tell me what issues I was against? Was I against Workmen's Compensation? Was I ever against Widow's Pension? Was I against Social Security?" McManus continued to run down the whole list of issues supported by the Socialist party in the 1920s, which later became the progressive measures adopted during Roosevelt's time. Gene was right; he had supported these issues and so had all of his assemblymen, senators and congressmen. I don't think I won the argument.

Bill Ryan won the primary and went on to become the first Reform Democratic congressman, and he set the standards for others to come. While he was still a candidate he and I had worked out his labor position, which was as aggressive as it was refreshing. Ryan also led the fight to admit mainland China to the United Nations, and galvanized the opposition to the House Un-American Activities Committee and nuclear-weapons testing. He began to speak out on the issues and was the first congressman to raise his voice against United States involvement in Vietnam. An early environmentalist, Bill more than anyone else was responsible for Gateway National Park, preserving the wilderness shoreline area facing the Atlantic Ocean from New Jersey to Long Island. His death in 1972 left a void not easily filled.

While the Reformers were gathering behind Ryan in 1960 the West Side delegation to the National Democratic Convention was being selected. There were no primaries then, and the selection process was in the hands of local leaders and the leaders of the state Democratic organization. I could not hope to be selected by the state leaders since I had played a leadership role with the Reformers, but in my own club my name was presented with my consent. At an interview I indicated that I would support Adlai Stevenson, Hubert Humphrey, or John Fitzgerald Kennedy. Of all the nominees for delegate I was the only one to put Kennedy on a par with the other two contenders.

Stevenson, the hero of the liberals and progressives, provided a focus for the need for reform within the party because of the shabby treatment he had received from New York Democratic leaders when he was the Democratic candidate for President in 1956. Stevenson's defeat then was blamed in part on the old guard, whose clubhouses remained closed and unlit at night throughout the campaign. On the other hand, many remembered Humphrey for his persistent civil rights position, and labor unions supported him for his advocacy of their cause.

The club's committee read out the names of the presidential candidates and the persons the club could support as delegates. When my name came up, Leonard Plato, my sponsor, whispered to me, "Why did you have to mention Kennedy's name? He's no favorite here, and because you mentioned his name, you'll get second billing."

I was not chosen by either faction of the party that year to be a delegate and I did not attend the convention. Kennedy won the designation, but he was less than the darling of the liberal West Side.

After Kennedy won the nomination I became one of the cochairmen of the campaign in New York State. We were appointed by Robert Kennedy, who came to New York to straighten out the wrangling between Democrats. Bobby's reputation as "ruthless" was not well known at the time, but New York Democrats came to know how he had earned it. Altogether, it was obvious that the senator from Massachusetts had a long way to go in order to win the support of liberals here. Appointing liberals to key campaign roles helped, but it was not enough, so John Kennedy met with Mrs. Roosevelt soon after he was nominated and won her support. He then convinced Arthur Schlesinger, Jr., and other intellectuals from Ivy League schools to join his campaign. These gestures went a long way toward curbing suspicion and hostility, and with a step at a time, the candidate disarmed the intellectuals, who finally agreed to support his campaign. But it took the sight of Richard Nixon on television and the memory of the good men and women he had destroyed to move the liberals in the direction of their checkbooks.

It became obvious, however, that Cardinal Spellman favored Richard Nixon over Kennedy. The Al Smith dinner held each year is sponsored by the Catholic Archdiocese (commonly referred to as the Power House). Its purpose is charitable and its politics are conservative and the roster of those in attendance includes leaders of industry, banking and politics. It is the place to be for any ambitious candidate. In 1960 Nixon and Kennedy were there together, ostensibly in the interest of Catholic Charities, but really to advance their candidacies or perhaps not to jeopardize their chances by being marked absent. The moneyed Irish Catholics at the dinner gave polite applause to Kennedy, but they came to their feet for Nixon, and the cardinal achieved the next to impossible: he mispronounced Kennedy's name.

My role as cochairman of the Kennedy-Johnson campaign in New York did not involve me in any policy decisions. I did some speaking on behalf of the team, and I had the task of bringing the Reformers out to campaign and exhibit as much enthusiasm as they could muster for the ticket. After the election Kennedy asked me to chair local committees in support of Medicare and voter registration, both of which I did.

By 1962 the Reformers controlled about 60 out of 1200 votes at the state Democratic convention, which was called to nominate candidates for governor, lieutenant governor, attorney general and United States senator. Although it seemed a futile exercise, I agreed to carry the Reform banner and seek the Democratic nomination to oppose Jacob Javits for the Senate seat. The Reformers supported me enthusiastically, even though we knew no Democrat was going to win. We felt it was necessary to move Javits away from vacillating positions he had taken on many issues important to the liberal community.

The Kennedys were boosting the candidacy of prominent New York attorney James Donovan, who had brought about the exchange of a Russian spy named Rudolf Abel for the United States U-2 pilot Francis Gary Powers. Donovan was then attempting to duplicate his exchange-of-prisoners feat by negotiating the release of Cuban expatriate invaders taken at the Bay of Pigs. If Donovan could lead the Bay of Pigs prisoners out of Cuba and back to the United States, he would put an end to an episode that continued to be a source of embarrassment to the President.

From the Reform point of view it was considered important for somebody to make the race who would keep the liberal issues of the day before the public. The regular organization did not quarrel much with Javits' positions anyway, and they were ready to accept blindly whomever the Kennedys supported.

For the first time in half a century there was a floor fight for the office of U.S. senator, at the Syracuse meeting. For the first time, too, the Reformers caucused, declared for a candidate, and held together.

I had been able also to get the support of blacks from Harlem and Brooklyn, and the support of the few Puerto Rican delegates who attended. State Senator James R. Watson, from Harlem, a family friend of long standing, nominated me, along with a young man named Erickson from Long Island whom I did not know but who thought well of my candidacy. John O'Connor Conway, Democratic county chairman of Oswego County in northern New York, whose club I had once visited, seconded my nomination. Several delegates from the regular ranks in Manhattan came over after the nomination and said they would support me. The Reform delegation, made up of young people, took to the floor. Walkie-talkies were used for the first time as the young people began to canvass the upstate delegations, which up to that time had not been specifically instructed how to vote and had no special interest in the outcome.

For the first time the upstaters were made to feel important. Never before had anybody asked them for a vote; they were used to being told that so-and-so was the party's candidate. They had never expected to be consulted ahead of time and they never were. I was placed by my floor manager in a strategic place on the floor. Soon the floor manager would get a request from a young man or woman for my presence at the Chemung County delegation or any one of the other fifty-six upstate county delegations. The floor representatives reported that if I would stop by, I was assured of that county's vote or a substantial part of it. From the few Reform delegates we started with, a boomlet began to take shape. We had taken the city bosses by surprise.

Then I had to confront my old friends in the Kings County delegation (Brooklyn). I had heard them just announce their votes for governor and lieutenant governor. By the time it came to vote for senator, there had been a day's delay and an intermission, and three-quarters of their delegates had gone home. I walked over to the leadership, John J. Lynch, Aaron Jacoby, and the chairman of their law committee, Harold Fisher. We got to the issue immediately. Donovan was from Brooklyn, although he was not active in politics.

"I want to warn you," I said, "if you attempt to give all of your votes to Donovan, I'm going to call you on it, because your delegates aren't here."

Monroe Goldwater, the octogenarian parliamentarian of the party, was summoned from the stage. "Paul, why are you making trouble?" he asked.

"Monroe," I replied, "I just want a fair count." I knew that heavy pressure was being put on the black delegation from Brooklyn to vote against me and to support the organization candidate.

"Harold Fisher takes the position that delegates can be chosen now to fill the vacancies of those who have left," he argued.

"They can't fill the vacancies with delegates from other counties. They must be residents of Kings County and have the delegate's proxy addressed to them personally, and I, as a candidate, have the right to examine them," I countered, by no means as sure of myself as I pretended to be.

In the meantime one of the leaders from Forest Hills came

over and told me that "they're out to cheat you in Queens. We all got instructions. But I'm going to bolt for you."

I approached the Queens chairman, Andy Mulrain. "Andy," I said, "how many votes do you have for me? If you tell me you've got a whole delegation for Donovan, I can tell you that I know you don't, and you don't have half the delegation present." Andy had been my brother's commissioner of sanitation and also my friend—before and since—but on that day he was "organization" all the way and I knew it. However, faced with possible trouble, Andy caucused his delegation, counted heads and consulted with his district leaders. Soon he was back to me. "How about two for one?" he asked, and my first deal with the old guard was consummated. The Reformers were overjoyed, and now they went to work with renewed vigor.

But the stumbling block was still Kings County. They wanted to deliver their entire block of votes in tribute to their leaders. Two of them—Lynch, seasoned and competent and my friend except when party discipline was at stake, and Jacoby, an old-line spellbinder—were determined that there would be no defections and that they would deliver their total vote for Donovan.

In the meantime, though, support for me from the upstate counties was taking shape. One of the bandwagon joiners was a fellow I had worked with in the Irgun, who had moved upstate and become active in the Democratic party. Since nobody in his hometown cared about going to the state convention, he attended and got several members of his delegation to vote for me. Others had known my brother, and still others were Irish Americans who either did not know or did not care about my views but knew I was active in Irish causes. Donovan was also Irish, but there were essential differences. He had not been associated with things Irish in their minds. In the out-of-the-way places the Democratic party was still in the hands of Irish Americans who had been Democrats since their forebears settled there as workers in the construction of the Erie Canal and the railroads.

My steamroller was moving, and the convention leadership began to panic. Billy McKeon, the state chairman and a native of Auburn, an upstate community, was summoned. He left his post on the platform to try to persuade our young people and prevail on all the upstate counties to hold fast for Donovan. McKeon was spotted by the young delegates and he was followed everywhere he went.

"Have O'Dwyer get over to Tompkins County," were the orders coming through the walkie-talkie to the floor manager. "There're a couple of votes wavering."

Because the kids had displayed such a great amount of enthusiasm, some of the upstate delegations began to relish the discomfort of the big-city bosses. Somebody came up to me and commented, "How can they be bad? They're really doing some campaigning, and no one has ever asked for my vote before. It's great!"

We began to pick up more steam, and at that point many others were regimented to help McKeon to go over to the upstate delegations. Peter Crotty, my friend and county leader in Erie, was enjoying the scene. We had much in common. Peter was the first county leader to extend himself on behalf of black constituents. He was amicably disposed to my candidacy, and he felt the party was fussing about nothing, since no one was going to defeat Javits anyway. His philosophy was: if the young people wanted to make a fight on Javits, they should be permitted to do so.

"There're some anti-Crotty votes in Erie," Peter advised me in good humor, "so get them first, because if you get help from me first, you're likely not to get them. You can count on twenty-eight votes from me."

I went back to Brooklyn and got into a showdown with the delegation leadership. None of the Reformers could deal with them, because Reform hadn't made any headway yet in Brooklyn.

Monroe Goldwater came over to me. "Look, Paul, they're entitled to do what they want to do in Kings County," he said—and that was the official pronouncement from the party.

"All right, Monroe," I replied, "I have sixty kids on the floor with walkie-talkies. They have given me a count, and you don't have a quorum, and you don't have a convention if I call for a quorum vote."

"Paul," he pleaded, "you wouldn't do that, would you?"

"Don't count on it, Monroe," I said.

"You know, don't you, Paul, that if you call a quorum, that means we don't have a convention, and there's not enough time under the rules to call another meeting before election time. If you do what you say you will, the Democratic party won't have a candidate for attorney general or senator. We would be a laughingstock for long and many a day. And you would be blamed for it," he threatened.

"I'd be glad to convey that warning to my delegation here," I said, "but I rather think they would be unimpressed. They have little concern for your discomfort. The people who are forcing the quorum call are your friends in Kings County. I would suggest, Monroe, you tell them of the predicament in which the state committee finds itself."

Monroe told the leaders what I was prepared to do. They went onto the platform to take a count, with Billy McKeon holding up the business of the convention while they deliberated. After a careful survey they decided they had enough votes to protect Donovan, and when they came back to the floor Monroe Goldwater walked over to me and whispered, "Will you take thirty-five votes from Kings County?"

"If each one were free to vote, I would get forty-two," I answered.

"Okay," he said, "forty-two it is."

The organization had enough surplus votes to beat me even with the extra votes out of Kings County. The heavy hand of the machine began to come down hard on the delegates. The vote was taken, and Donovan was nominated. But I got some support in each of the upstate counties, except in Albany. Mayor Erastus Corning, Leo Quinn and Congressman O'Brien could not return to Albany if any chink in the Democratic armor were displayed at the convention.

The end result was a defeat for the insurgents, but the kids on the floor got experience at a statewide meeting that was to prove invaluable in future years.

Despite my discomfort with the Reform Movement's limitations, Reform did open the doors of the political organizations for me and for others who otherwise would have had little opportunity to break in. In 1963 my new local Reform district leader, Hedi Piel, suggested that I become a candidate for one of the two new posts of councilman-at-large for Manhattan. She argued that I could make it and that I was the only Reform candidate who could. A few Reform Democrats had been successful in district elections, but in a Manhattan-wide race they had limited appeal. The Reform Movement was made up at that time mostly of the young Jewish and white Protestant middle class. Blacks and Puerto Ricans attended meetings but found the language strange. It had nothing to do with hunger or rats or child mortality. They could not get enthusiastic about reform of the Democratic party. The white ethnics—the Jewish poor, the Italians, Irish and Greeks and most of the others of European descent—were suspicious of the very word "reform." It had been thoughtlessly chosen. To Orthodox Jews it meant a departure from or a rejection of the basic tenets. And reformation to the Irish meant Henry VIII, Cromwell and the Famine. In short, although Manhattan was the Reform stronghold, Reformers were outnumbered even there.

But Hedi saw no disadvantage in that. "In the black and Puerto Rican areas you'll win easily, and you'll hold your own among the labor-oriented in the old-guard districts," she said. I was not anxious to take another rebuff at the party councils or in the primaries, and I wasn't sure that being councilman was what I wanted. "It's the only game in town," was the way Hedi put it.

I thought I should ask Mayor Wagner's advice before I made any move. My brother had appointed him to the prestigious post of chairman of the City Planning Commission. It had started him up the political ladder, and I had supported him against the party bosses in 1953 and again when the same bosses sought to unseat him in 1961. Wagner listened and encouraged me to enter the race.

Soon thereafter I had a meeting with some friends at my home and they too encouraged me to make the try. I notified the Reform officials that I would be a candidate.

There were several steps that had to be taken. The Reform organization had set up its own complicated and weighty nominating machinery. It was so democratic that it was well-nigh unworkable. There were fifteen candidates, who traveled from club to club. At no time was a meeting called in Harlem or in the "barrio" (Spanish Harlem) or in the old ethnic areas. Finally the day of reckoning came. Reform delegates met to select their candidate. The meeting commenced at 10 A.M. and lasted all day. The wrangling over the rules took a couple of hours. At length the first vote was tallied. The low candidate was eliminated. The fight for the votes of the fallen one went into high gear and our floor campaign lost no advantage. Finally, at five in the afternoon, two candidates remained—Eugenia Flatow, a very intelligent and capable member of Bill Ryan's club on the West Side, and me.

The Lexington Democratic Club, in the "silk stocking" district, was the oldest of the Reform clubs. Its members were also the most experienced, most prestigious, most powerful and best heeled. They maneuvered so that on the last ballot they held the deciding block of votes—uncommitted. They did not like either Flatow or me. They proposed a compromise candidate from the Lexington Club, who had not gone through the tortuous route we had endured. Flatow's manager and mine promptly rejected the demeaning suggestion and they were required to make the choice between us. My views were in no measure to their liking. But Bill Ryan was an aggressive leader and mildly radical. The well-to-do members of the Lexington Club saw Ryan as a disturbing force, and the Riverside Club, which was his vehicle, was supporting Flatow. They decided Genie Flatow was less acceptable and threw their votes to me. I won as the lesser of two evils.

After months of prattling about ideology, the final Reform decision centered on rivalry for power between an East Side respected establishment and West Side upstarts.

The County Executive of Manhattan Island was a comparatively small group, known as Tammany Hall. Before Reform each district club had an Indian name. The local assembly-district leaders constituted the County Executive, and they met to bestow the Democratic nomination for high office on the willing and the faithful. Old-guard leaders greatly outnumbered Reform representatives. Each was suspicious of the other and neither was anxious to support any candidate who found favor with the other. When my name was put forward by Reform members, many old-timers refrained from voting. Only a signal from Mayor Wagner would send them in the right direction.

Senator Joseph Zaretzki, then the minority leader of the state senate and a district leader, was a good friend of mine. When his time to vote came, he announced that he had spoken to Mayor Wagner and the mayor had told him he would like to have O'Dwyer as the nominee. Many of the leaders who had abstained from voting then followed Zaretzki's lead, and I became the candidate of Tammany Hall, with the least amount of enthusiasm ever recorded for one.

My designation by both wings of the party spelled immediate

trouble for me. Reformers demanded that I support every Reform candidate running for office against any old-guard nominee. To do so would have meant repudiating some of the very leaders to whom I owed the nomination. There was a clash. I said that I thought it would be immoral for me to accept the vote that gave me the nomination and then immediately seek to dethrone the giver as unworthy. I told the Reform leaders that they should not have nominated me at the Executive meeting if they wished me to take that course of action. One-third of my own club refused to participate further in the campaign, and the adventure was on the rocks before we were fully under sail.

A nomination under such conditions was bound to entail opposition in the primary. It took no time at all for a rival to develop—not one, but two.

Robert Blaikie, an alert maverick Democratic leader, announced his candidacy and the same day commenced a court action to abolish the office as unconstitutional. The second candidate, John Young, was much more aggressive, personal and direct. "The issue is whether New York should have another O'Dwyer in City Hall," he said. The man who made that the theme of his campaign had come out of Harlem politics and had been Congressman Adam Clayton Powell's press secretary. The press asked for my reaction. "The question is really addressed to the people," I said, "and I assume they will answer." The press dropped it. Blaikie condemned the attack, and kept on condemning it—too much I thought.

It was apparent that nothing was going to be easy for me. If I wanted this position, I was going to have to fight for it on every street corner in Manhattan.

When Blaikie came into the race some of the old-line Democratic leaders decided that they were not going to support me any further in the primary. In this predicament I realized I could not totally rely on anyone but my own friends.

Edward Costikyan had come from the periphery of the

Reform Movement. But when he came to power, Reformers had not supported him. From a study of my relationship with the county leader I realized I had come into the campaign with a double disability—the conflict between Reformers and the mayor and that between Reformers and the county leaders. Under those circumstances neutrality was as much as I could hope for from Costikyan. It was not easy for him to do it, but he maintained a hands-off approach during the primary campaign.

Among those to whom I appealed in my distress was J. Raymond Jones. In 1963 he was the political boss of all Harlem. He came to my assistance to help keep the leaders from supporting either of my opponents. Jones was a remarkable man. Born in the Virgin Islands when they were Danish possessions, he had come to New York as a young man. The Democratic party in New York was still segregated when he joined it, and Harlem's black residents were then, for the most part, Republican—a throwback to Lincoln's day. Jones had learned his politics from the Irish political bosses who had preceded him. With Jones taking an active role, black citizens of Harlem had abandoned the Republican party and joined forces with the New York Democratic machine. Jones became the first black man to be a member of the mayor's cabinet and the first to be leader of Tammany Hall. By 1963 his power extended to the national scene: he was a close confidant of Lyndon B. Johnon.

Having Jones as an ally was helpful to me in yet another way. I was concerned about John Young. He was spending money and his posters were up everywhere.

The primary meant untiring efforts by my family, friends and political adherents. There were many in my campaign who did not at all approve of my views. I knew that if I lost this test I was finished in politics, and it took all the energy we could muster to remain afloat. Then several things happened to turn the tide in my favor. Blaikie began to attack the Reform Movement and the Reformers returned to the fold. Jones and my civil rights friends in Harlem turned openly on Young, and Senator Zaretzki came into the campaign enthusiastically. The final results were decisive. I had won Harlem against a black candidate and I carried all the ethnic areas. The Reform districts came through with a comfortable majority.

I faced three opponents in the November election: Amos Basil, the Liberal party candidate; Richard Aldrich, the Republican; and Robert Parrish, the Socialist. Only two of us could be elected, and in the end Aldrich and I won.

The following February the mayor's budget message was presented to the Council. It was a daunting document, but we were forced to muddle through it, each one pretending to know its contents, each acting like a certified public accountant. Fortunately my law associate Bernie Richland, who had worked for the city's law department, was available to give me assistance. And thus I became aware of certain practices that produced shock waves a decade later.

The message had been put together by the most skilled bureaucrats, deliberately designed, it appeared, to confuse all but the initiated. Throughout, it was rigged against the possibility of the Council's understanding it, and the pressure of time worked to ensure a vote of approval. I was told that it would be an act of irresponsibility to vote "no"; if the Council were to do so, there would be no pay for the Police and Fire departments. "Hogwash," Richland had said, so the first year I voted against the report of the Council Finance Committee. The next year I saw that the administration had borrowed money to balance the budget, and that, I had been led to believe, was illegal, so again I cast my vote against the budget. But the vote meant nothing. By an overwhelming margin the budget was approved by the Council, many of whom entertained hopes of being appointed to the bench by the mayor.

Moreover, all of my bills died in committee. But most of them were reintroduced later and became law after I had left the Council. My only success was with the minimum-wage law, which the labor unions convinced the mayor to approve.

In 1965 my two-year term as councilman-at-large came to an end. The people had answered John Young. They did not mind an O'Dwyer back at City Hall. We never mentioned it, but I knew Bill was happy about my election, and particularly because the issue was raised and buried. He died in the middle of my term.

I did not wish to remain in the Council and in 1965 sought to join with a mayoral candidate as a candidate for president of the City Council. Neither Paul Screvane nor Abraham Beame, the two Democratic mayoral candidates, found me acceptable. So I made a decision to become a candidate for mayor myself and proceeded to qualify. As a candidate I knew I would be entitled to join in television and radio debates, and I believed I would make a better impression than my opponents in any discussion about the city's problems. But when Bill Ryan entered the field, the unthinkable happened: the Democratic candidates so splintered the vote that in November a Republican, John Lindsay, edged out Beame and seized the prize.

CHAPTER ELEVEN

Civil Rights Struggle

PRESIDENT KENNEDY'S plan to register as voters large numbers of citizens in the lower economic brackets ran into a snag in the nineteen states in which a literacy law was in effect. Regrettably, New York was among them. There the literacy test as it applied to Puerto Ricans was particularly unfair. The percentage of those voting in Puerto Rico was much higher than our national average, but in the Puerto Rican neighborhoods of our town registration was as low as 15 percent. New York's literacy law had been enacted during the period of hysteria immediately following World War I.

Even before my activity in the President's registration drive, I had been involved with the literacy/voting-rights problem. During the La Guardia administration I had represented a group of teachers charged with overassisting their literacy-test students, elderly Jewish citizens on the lower East Side, to pass the test. Apparently the teachers had filled in the test papers themselves. A complaint was filed, and William Herlands, a wheelhorse in the Republican party and La Guardia's commissioner of investigations, hauled the teachers before him for a mayoral inquiry. I represented them at the hearings. I urged them to invoke the Fifth Amendment if they were questioned. They did so, and a stalemate resulted.

During the intervening years I often had thought of the unfairness of the literacy requirements and how shameful it was that New York should be lined up with eighteen reactionary states. Finally I decided to attack the restrictions in court by representing a Puerto Rican woman, Marta Cardona, who was well versed in Spanish but who knew no English. I started that action in 1963.

Mrs. Cardona's husband was a waiter. They had both been born, raised and educated in Puerto Rico in schools maintained by the American government in which all subjects, including American history, were taught in the Spanish language.

Previous cases challenging the constitutionality of the literacy law had not fared well. But times had changed and there were new judges on the court of appeals. I called the late "Marcie" O'Rourke, then the commissioner of elections, and asked him to convene the board to hear my request to give the literacy test to Mrs. Cardona in Spanish. The commissioners, by a vote of three to one, promptly rejected my application.

I then went into the state Supreme Court and raised the constitutional question.

Because I planned to take the case to the U.S. Supreme Court, I laid careful groundwork and established that American flags flew over the schools in Puerto Rico and that schoolchildren there learned the history of the United States in Spanish. Their teachers' salaries, I pointed out to the court, were paid by tax money from the national treasury, and the schools were government establishments. I argued that the state of New York could not override a Puerto Rican's right to take the voter literacy test in Spanish.

My adversaries in a previous attack on the literacy test two years earlier (Comacho) were Louis Lefkowitz, the state attorney general, whose obligation it was to defend the statute in the kind of test I was forcing, and the corporation counsel of the city, who was there to uphold the decision of the Board of Elections. But much to my chagrin, I was opposed also by Burke Marshall's office in Washington—the Civil Rights Division of the U.S. Department of Justice. Ironically, the very branch of government charged with protecting the rights of citizens was actively supporting the wholly irrational and disabling statute.

At that time I went to Washington to challenge Marshall in a personal interview. It got me nowhere, so I took my case to the National Democratic Club, where John Bailey of Connecticut, the chairman of the Democratic National Committee, was holding court. "Besides being unconstitutional and unfair," I argued, "the literacy test is politically stupid. Here are 750,000 Puerto Ricans, 90 percent of them potential Democrats, and the Kennedy administration is actively engaged in barring them from voting. Their votes," I continued, "could make the difference between a Republican governor and a Democratic one." Bailey agreed and promised to give it attention. "You can help," I pressed, "if you can get the President to tell his brother what the facts of life are." Bailey's promise of immediate redress was never fulfilled.

I relied on the testimony of the editor of *El Diario* (a New York Spanish-language daily) and other experts who had traced the history of Puerto Rico and America's relationship with the island from 1898, when, with annexation, the effort to Americanize the Puerto Ricans began. The effort failed. Puerto Rican children were not learning their lessons in English, because they had no idea what was being said to them, and at home their parents could not help them. Following a Columbia University study in 1933, the United States abandoned the effort. Thereafter it had promoted Spanish as the primary language in the Puerto Rican schools.

When I initiated the Cardona case in 1963 I relied on the

evidence I had previously presented to the court in the Comacho case. The facts stood undisputed. But New York judges were not sympathetic to my argument and ruled against Mrs. Cardona. I appealed to the appellate division and lost again. I went then to the state court of appeals in Albany, where for the first time three judges found merit in my contention. Four others—the majority—disagreed. This was the first sign of hope I had experienced in the courts, and I was off and running to the United States Supreme Court.

In the meantime President Kennedy had been murdered, and Robert Kennedy, no longer U.S. Attorney General, had become the junior senator from New York. As the legislative representative of this massive bloc of voters and potential voters, he had become totally committed to my position.

I had informed Senator Kennedy of my challenge to the literacy test, and on the Monday of the hearing in the court of appeals his office called and asked me to send the briefs and records to Washington to be used for a speech he was making on the Senate floor two days later. On Wednesday, using the arguments pressed unsuccessfully in New York, the senator offered the "American Flag Amendment to the Voting Rights Bill," and it was passed. It substituted the mother tongue for English in all cases in which the mother tongue was the language used in schools over which the American flag flew. It applied to citizens of Louisiana, New Mexico and Puerto Rico and to American Indians. The "American Flag Amendment" was challenged by two citizens, John P. and Christine Morgan. It came up for argument before the Supreme Court the same day the Cardona case was being heard.

Opposing me again was the attorney general of New York, Louis Lefkowitz, and once more, to my chagrin, the New York City corporation counsel joined him. This time, however, the Department of Justice was on our side. Technically it was there to argue for the constitutionality of the "American Flag Amendment," but we were both in the same boat. The Supreme

Court upheld the constitutionality of the amendment, and in the Cardona case the high court reversed the decision of the New York court of appeals.

Justice Tom Clark, a close friend of my brother's, had a note delivered to my counsel table. It read: "Bill would have been very proud of you today." I looked to the bench and we exchanged glances, and the stiffness of the occasion seemed to wilt.

The National Association for the Advancement of Colored People meanwhile had been conducting a vigorous campaign for voters' rights throughout the South, and Medgar Evers, the leader of the fight in Mississippi, had been murdered. The day after the killing a group of students from Tougaloo College (an all-black institution) prepared to march through a residential part of Jackson to protest the slaying. A crowd gathered, and the police were called. Soon paddy wagons and trucks moved in to haul the arrested students to a compound. Lois Chaffee, a teacher at the college, was observing the scene from a nearby porch when the police moved in, forcing some of the students to "escape" to the same porch. When the police too reached the porch, swinging billy sticks and rifle butts indiscriminately, she cried to them to stop—and was arrested and charged with inciting to riot.

In her own defense, against a reduced charge of disorderly conduct, Lois alleged that the police were beating the students when she intervened. She was not only convicted of disorderly conduct but indicted for making a "false charge" against the police.

Carl Rachlin, the attorney for most of the civil rights defendants in the South at that time, called me in New York and asked me to take the case for "the movement." He explained the details and I readily agreed. I flew to Jackson as soon as I had prepared my brief.

There were only two black lawyers in Mississippi at that time, and I was obliged by law to bring in one as my associate if I could. (No white lawyer in Mississippi would take a civil rights case.) I spoke to both black lawyers and both refused.

Rachlin and I then met with the prosecution and indicated to them that I would commence an action in the federal court there against the state of Mississippi and the city of Jackson for violating the civil rights of Lois Chaffee. The threat amused them.

The Civil Rights Act of 1964 had not yet been enacted, and Federal Judge Sidney Mize, who tried the case, was in no way sympathetic. He exhibited no hostility, but every ruling was adverse. If he knew any constitutional law, it was not evident. At length the state's attorney raised the question of my standing. "What about that, Mr. O'Dwyer?" the judge inquired.

I explained that I had tried to get a local lawyer to act as local counsel on behalf of Lois Chaffee but had met with no success. Carl Rachlin, sitting next to me at the counsel table, leaned over and whispered, "Now watch the black lawyer make a liar out of you."

Sure enough, the judge asked the black lawyer, Jesse Brown, about my comments. He addressed Brown by his first name, as was the custom then in the South for whites speaking to blacks. "Now, Jesse," he said, "you've appeared before me in the past in civil rights cases." Brown replied in the affirmative. The judge then asked Brown if he had ever had any trouble representing a client. Brown answered that he never had.

"Mr. O'Dwyer indicates," the judge pressed, "that you would not take the case."

"Well, that's not quite right, Judge," was the answer.

There it was, the direct confrontation; and the judge was faced with a dilemma. Either I was lying or Brown was lying. I am sure that the judge would have liked to make me the liar, but he would have had to take the word of a black man against a white man to do so. The judge went on, "Now, Mr. O'Dwyer, Jesse says he will take the case. He's a lawyer here, and I don't want to break the rules; the rules are clear. A case in this court must be pleaded by a Mississippi lawyer. Others may then join the counsel table."

After the judge had dismissed us for the day Brown and I continued our discussion, but I was still unable to convince him to take the case. I flew back to New York and wrote a letter to the judge saying that I would obey the rules of the court up to a point, "but when the rights of my client are jeopardized by your rules, I'm afraid that the rights of my client will come first. I am ready to appear in court for her and to protect her rights, and it will be up to you to decide that I can't."

A few days later the judge called on the telephone to tell me that he had talked to Jesse and that Jesse was prepared to take the case—which was true enough. Jesse Brown was prepared to take the case for one thousand dollars, which I had to pay him in order for him to lend his name, even though all I got for the money was the use of his name on court papers.

In the course of preparing the case for trial on the merits, I went to Tougaloo College and interviewed numerous witnesses who had been brutalized when they sought to register to vote. The next day only one, a minister named Houston, appeared in court to testify. After his appearance, because he was the only one to whom I could direct my anger, I railed against the witnesses who had failed to appear.

"You know, you bring me down here to try the case. I have prepared the evidence and am able to prove by the testimony of witnesses that there was intimidation, but the witnesses don't show up in court."

Houston explained patiently. "Paul, you must understand that to a black man in the South this federal courthouse is an instrument of tyranny. You may have faith that something will come out of this case, but they have none. You can't get them in here, because they don't believe justice will be done. It never has been!"

Various officials took the witness stand. I sought to establish their racial attitudes. Judge Mize ruled the subject was not relevant. I attempted to show what they had said during previous campaigns for election. The judge excluded any reference to the witnesses' prior statements. I moved on to other subjects. The mayor of Jackson was the most loquacious of the witnesses. He said there was no racial problem in the South except what was imported by radical societies from the North. He singled out the N.A.A.C.P. as an example. In contrast to Judge Mize, the mayor appeared hostile and antagonistic.

The mayor finished his testimony and was excused. On his way out of the courtroom he paused at my table. I expected to be told off as another northern agitator, but the South is full of surprises to a visiting Yankee. He put a hand on my shoulder. "Your brother was very good to me when I, as mayor of this town, visited New York City," he said. "If there is anything I can do to make your stay pleasant, please let me know."

Southern hospitality and good manners, however, were a poor substitute for justice, and I appealed from Judge Mize's decision dismissing the complaint. Meanwhile I had bought time for Lois Chaffee, and she remained free on bail. I took the case to the Circuit Court of Appeals in Atlanta. By then it was November 1965.

The circuit court ruled against us also, but we were able to keep Lois out of jail pending further appeals. About two years later I got a telephone call from the prosecutor's office in Jackson and was told that I could dispose of the Chaffee case with the payment of a five-hundred-dollar fine. I told my caller I would get back to him, and I phoned Rachlin and Lois. I asked her if it offended her in any way to accept a conviction of a lesser charge than the original one. The new charge, "interfering with police," delighted Lois and she said it was the one charge to which she would gladly plead guilty. We accepted the offer, because we did not want to risk a trial in that environment lest Lois end up spending several years in a Mississippi prison.

I first heard of the Mississippi Freedom Democratic party in early 1963 when I responded to a letter asking for volunteers to go to Mississippi to work on behalf of their candidates. The M.F.D.P. was an early attempt to open up the all-white Democratic party in Mississippi to full participation by the black population.

I arrived in Mississippi and met Eleanor Holmes, a black law-school graduate not yet admitted to practice, who was in charge of the election project. (She is now a high federal government official.) She assigned me to work for Victoria Gray, the M.F.D.P. candidate for Congress from the southernmost part of the state. My job was to go to campaign meetings and speak about civil rights to the black audiences. Our purpose was to show them what might happen if blacks did vote.

The M.F.D.P. was fed up with the status quo. The official Democratic organization was then a white-supremacist party, and it did not even attempt to attract token blacks into its ranks. Whenever blacks tried to register to vote, they were frustrated in their efforts. So it was a foregone conclusion that the M.F.D.P. would not be successful at the polls that time. But the party was making its voice heard, and the people began to listen.

When I returned to New York I was determined that I would do all that I could for this fledgling political party in Mississippi. The politics of participation needed all the help it could get, and I encouraged Reform clubs in New York City to "adopt" a sister club in Mississippi.

In 1964 I was selected a delegate-at-large to the Democratic National Convention, and I represented the Reform element of our party in Atlantic City. It was at this convention that the M.F.D.P. made its first appeal for national recognition. Knowing that the group would be in trouble if they entered the American political scene without a constitution and bylaws, I drafted a constitution partly based on that of New York's Democratic party.

The M.F.D.P. challenged the right of the delegates of the regular Democratic party in Mississippi to be seated at the convention on the grounds that they were not democratically chosen or representative of the vast majority of Mississippi Democrats. That challenge took place before the convention got under way in a dramatic confrontation before the Credentials Committee.

I enlisted in the floor fight to secure seats for the M.F.D.P. delegates, and I took the issue first to the New York delegation to see to it that the white Mississippi delegation, gaining their seats through murder, fire-bombing and the like, were not seated. We proposed that in their place the delegates of the M.F.D.P. be seated.

I sought out New York State Democratic Chairman William McKeon. "I want to raise the Mississippi question before our delegation," I said, "and I also want to nominate Eleanor Clark French as national committeewoman."

Billy told me that if I agreed to hold off on Mississippi until after New York had elected its national committeeman and committeewoman, he would call a special meeting in the afternoon on my proposal. I agreed. In the meantime the state leaders, who did not want any sign of division, convinced Mrs. French not to permit her name to be put in nomination, so that Edna Kelly could be reelected. Mrs. Kelly represented a Brooklyn congressional district in which the population was overwhelmingly black. She had little in common with most of her constituents, and she became anathema to them. To have her as the female representing the state of New York on the national committee was a further slight to the black population, and I thought she ought to go. We had no hope that year of electing a black woman and had to wait until 1968 before Representative Shirley Chisholm became the national committeewoman from New York.

New York had two representatives on the Credentials Committee, by which the Mississippi question would be decided:

Jack English, from Nassau County, a Kennedy intimate, and Joyce Austin, from New York, an intimate of mine. Joyce knew my views were firm, and she fully approved of the efforts I was making. Lyndon Johnson, however, did not want the issue of the M.F.D.P. raised on the floor of the convention, and Hubert Humphrey was there to put out any fires. It was common knowledge and everywhere accepted that if the issue came up openly on the floor, Humphrey could forget about the vice-presidency.

The M.F.D.P. retained Joseph Rauh, executive director of Americans for Democratic Action, to represent them at the hearings conducted by the Credentials Committee, which were televised and which showed graphically that the white establishment, through violence and threats of violence, had prevented blacks from participating in Mississippi's public or party affairs.

I went back to McKeon. I did not need to remind him of his promise. With the old guard, breaking one's word—even to a Reformer—was forbidden. With the nomination of Ellie French out of the way, Edna Kelly had been reelected. The incumbent Carmine DeSapio had lost his local leadership, and like an old Eskimo whose time to be left on the ice had come, he accepted his fate gracefully and with dignity.

"What will you be looking for?" McKeon asked with some impatience.

"I want a resolution directing our two delegates to the Credentials Committee to vote to seat the Freedom Democratic party," I told him.

"You have your work cut out for you," he said.

"The state committee has already expressed itself along those lines," I argued.

"The state committee cannot bind the elected delegates," he reminded me, and of course he was correct.

The supporters of the M.F.D.P. used another tactic. We sought out Credentials Committee delegates from other states; the younger advocates made the first approach, and the older ones came in later to show that the plan could work. The convention rules favored us. We needed only 10 percent of the Credentials Committee, or eleven votes, to bring out a minority report on the convention floor. It seemed easy, but the 1964 convention was a controlled convention, and the party leaders did not want it otherwise. Getting 10 percent to favor democracy in our party proved to be an insurmountable task. There was even less hope of democracy in the other party, where no one would even raise the question.

The only real business of the convention as far as the leaders were concerned was to wait for Lyndon Johnson to tell us who would be his vice-presidential candidate. After he made his choice known, our function was to affirm it.

At the convention's beginning I was practically alone in the credentials fight; few of the New York delegation had enough interest to get involved either way and the rest took their cue from the leadership. Later, however, a few other delegates from New York joined the battle. Between the morning and the afternoon meetings of the New York State delegation, Edward Costikyan, leader of New York County (Manhattan), called a meeting of his delegates. To his amazement and mine, we found that there were some serious questions as to how far we should go in instructing our delegates. So I was not surprised that, at the afternoon session where the issue was presented, all the big guns of the party were in attendance. Mayor Wagner was presiding, and he was flanked by Averell Harriman and Monroe Goldwater, the venerable law chairman of the state committee. I moved that our two delegates go instructed to vote to seat the M.F.D.P., and the issue was joined.

A few hours before the caucus met I had gone back to the church where the Freedom Democratic party was headquartered. Its delegates were there in faded clothes and patched blue jeans, and all their enthusiasm was intact. Some had hitchhiked and others had traveled to Atlantic City in old jalopies to participate in this great convention. They wanted to be part of our country and they were willing to join the very organizations that had oppressed them.

At the delegation meeting later I tried to explain the Mississippi Freedom Democratic party members to New Yorkers: "It seems to me," I began, "that these people truly stand in the shoes of those who came to conventions at the beginning of our Revolution. They too have come out of jails and marches. And they have come, as our political forefathers must have come, with a message from the Tom Paines and the Sam Adamses, and they have come to demand of Jefferson's party that we keep faith with its pledges. Besides," I continued, "the Mississippi Freedom Democratic party has met all the requirements of the law, the law of the state of Mississippi, while those who are seated in their place have qualified by violence, arson, threats, discrimination, bigotry, tyranny, and every form of intimidation imaginable. If the regular delegates from Mississippi do not have blood on their hands, they have come sponsored by those who have.

"They come with the sponsorship and approval of apostles of hate," I concluded, "and their presence here is a stench in the nostrils of those who created our tradition. These Americans who come here to remind us of our obligations to liberty and equality should be seated or this party had better change its name and live forever condemned by its proven hypocrisy!"

My appeal brought many New York delegates to their feet. But my feelings of exhilaration died aborning when the frustraters rose to speak one at a time. They readily acknowledged the virtue of the Freedom delegates and the justice of my plea, and of course they proclaimed themselves to be on my side. But "wisdom" and "caution" were required, they said, in dealing with these century-old problems and customs. Finally a plea "not to tie the hands" of our representatives won the battle. Walking from the hall, Averell Harriman, who was Johnson's agent, became quite abusive. He shook his finger in my face and said, "It is all right for you to be taking this position. You have no regard for the President of the United States or what problems he faces, and you don't care."

"If Harry Truman could have risked his election in 1948 by virtue of his position," I responded, "there's no reason why Lyndon Johnson can't do it in 1964 when he is assured of election. Let me remind you that Truman won without the South and without New York. Besides, Averell, if you had shown half of this enthusiasm for anything when you were governor, you would have been reelected!" On that note respective supporters led us in opposite directions.

(It is difficult to understand why Johnson did not want the issue brought out on the floor. His civil rights position as President was near perfect and was the best of any President since the Civil War. Had I known then that he was going to be as good on civil rights as he was to become, I probably would not have taken quite so vigorous a stand. On the other hand, there is no way of knowing if some of the things we were doing did not push him toward his firmer positions. Johnson was the kind of leader who did not make moves unless he knew he had consensus.)

While the debate was raging in the New York delegation, Governor Lawrence of Pennsylvania, the chairman of the Credentials Committee, announced that he was proposing a compromise on the challenge to the delegates of the old party of Mississippi and the application of the delegates of the M.F.D.P. His plan was to seat the old-guard white delegates and allow two at-large delegates of the F.D.P. to be the guests of the convention. Governor Lawrence's proposal was adopted by the Credentials Committee, and we could not get even eleven delegates to vote for a contrary minority report.

Joyce Austin and I left the third meeting of the New York State delegation to get the reaction of the F.D.P. to the compromise. They voted against it, and I reported this news back. "These delegates did not come to Atlantic City," I said, "to ride in the back of the bus."

The Freedom delegates had a falling out with Al Lowenstein, Joseph Rauh, Martin Luther King, and others, all of whom felt that a significant and advantageous compromise had been hammered out and that the F.D.P. had won an important victory. I would have been inclined to agree with them had I not listened to the F.D.P. delegates. They had won a point, but there was little solace for those who had worked to seat the entire Freedom delegation when it was explained that their two delegates-at-large had no vote. Several of us gave up our floor passes to the F.D.P. so that more of their members could sit on the convention floor. The regular Mississippi delegation was so enraged by the proceedings and so frustrated by being challenged at their own party's national convention that they boycotted the convention and would not take their seats on the floor. The convention leadership was forced to bring in a group of convention marshals to try to occupy the empty seats. However, whenever a Mississippi seat was vacated after that, it was filled immediately by an F.D.P. delegate.

Out of our agitation and as part of Governor Lawrence's compromise plan came a firm determination that the 1968 convention would have new faces and new rules for the selection of delegates. Black Mississippians would never again be kept waiting outside the convention hall.

Three years passed before I went to Mississippi again. In the early spring of 1967 I went to Sunflower County to lend a hand in a special election. In 1964 there were 25,000 blacks registered in Mississippi; by the end of 1967 there were 200,000. For the first time in a hundred years there was a possibility of electing blacks in the Delta.

At the invitation of Fannie Lou Hamer, the most powerful black politician to come out of the Delta, Manhattan Borough President Percy Sutton, Harlem Congressman Charles Rangel, Anita Chubb and I arrived in the town of Sunflower a week before the election to give the workers the "benefit" of our experience in political battles in a northern city. These neophyte election workers were preparing to make Sunflower a significant political adventure.

There were no hotels in Sunflower, so I was assigned to stay in the home of a Mrs. King. She had had fifteen children, and fourteen were now living in northern cities. I noticed that the window of Mrs. King's living room was boarded up. She explained that the Ku Klux Klan or the White Citizens' Council or hoodlums from both organizations had thrown tear-gas bombs into the house and had also set fire to it, front and rear at the same time. She had incurred their wrath, she said, during the summers of 1964 and 1965 when northern freedom riders were put up in her house. Happily the fires had been put out, but Mrs. King had not had the money to put in a new pane of glass.

On the day of our arrival in Sunflower the northern experts and the southern activists addressed a large gathering in the church, and after the meeting we got down to business and talked to the leaders about the election. The election was for mayor and five town councilmen. There were seven black candidates for the five vacancies, which meant that none of the blacks had a chance. Our job was to convince everyone to run only five candidates. We talked one candidate into withdrawing from the race and then went after the last holdout, a minister of one of the out-of-the-way churches in the county. He was a large, obese man who knew nothing about politics and had had little or no education. He took up a position in the center of the room and stood on a stool. In all of his decisions, he said, he was influenced by the Good Book. Charlie Rangel had made an impassioned plea to the minister to withdraw, arguing that he was doing violence to the cause of black representation in Sunflower, but the minister held his Bible aloft and quoted passages that in no way seemed relevant. Percy Sutton took up the cudgels, recalling in the mildest tones what his and Charlie's experience had been in Harlem politics. Sutton suggested that the New York example equally applied to Sunflower. He reasoned that obviously a man in the minister's position who withdrew from the race could only gain stature in the public eye. The minister would then have a greater reputation for being a man of justice and honor, and since he was a wise, practical politician, and since blacks were on the march in Mississippi, there would undoubtedly be a need for a man of his leadership capacity in the not too distant future.

The minister did not seem to realize the mischief he was causing by splitting the black vote. But some in the room suggested that he was in debt to a few business institutions in the town, and was, they reasoned, in no position to advance the cause of black representation.

In desperation Sutton made a final bid. "A sacrifice such as you, Reverend, are called upon to make today," he said, "would definitely mean a Harlem parade in your honor like the one we arranged for Martin Luther King when he visited Harlem." The minister showed no sign of being moved, and my two companions threw up their arms. In the face of the failure of my two comrades, Sutton and Rangel, I decided to try my luck. "I represent a number of people in the north," I said, "who have great hopes for Mississippi. Many people say that the blacks themselves are at fault for their failure to get along among themselves." I stated further, "Many people, black and white, up north spent money in order to get the voting rights for blacks, and they are looking to this election to decide whether or not their money was wisely spent."

My argument was not subtle and it made no greater impression than the arguments put forward by my colleagues. We sought some other area where we might score. After a while we discovered that the minister's wife was very much against the position her husband was taking. We worked on her until late into the night. She too failed to get the candidate to budge. By midnight we stood as we had at noon: six black candidates and five white candidates for five positions.

We bade our hosts good-night and as a parting shot, we asked the minister to think over the things we had said. He said he did not think there was anything to think over. We had, it would seem, only convinced him how important he was and how necessary it was for him to represent the people.

The following morning he appeared at headquarters and spoke to Percy, Rangel and me. He said that he had failed to understand fully the implications that were involved, and he had not known that the federal government was interested in the outcome of the Sunflower election until I had spoken last night. He had obviously confused me with some sort of government official. He had felt that my talk about money had had something to do with federal funding, then just beginning to come to the South. In any event, he said, this revelation had caused him to make up his mind. He was determined to withdraw from the race. We took his signature on his declination of candidacy. Our first mission was accomplished.

I had received my full share of kidding from Charlie and Percy. They insisted on calling me "Mr. Paul" part of the time and proclaimed that I was the leader of the expedition. Then they would say jokingly that it was their hope that while in the South I would beat the bushes to check for danger, and then if none existed, I would give them the signal to come along. I would be Sutton and Rangel's "white hunter," in contrast to the jungle expeditions where the black guide beat the bushes and took all the risks for "massa."

I noticed that when Percy told this story to black audiences both in the North and in the South he got quite a laugh. In my case, it amused the listeners that the roles were reversed. After the incident with the minister, however, I was able to turn the tables on Charlie and Percy. I could point out that their powers of persuasion were obviously limited to the New York City region. It was equally plain, I reasoned, that I had a wider appeal, since it was my intrusion that had persuaded the stout minister to withdraw his candidacy.

But the Sunflower adventure was not successful at the polls.

The caucus had selected a young man to spearhead the drive, and his candidacy was resented by many for personality reasons. Every black vote was needed, and every black vote was not forthcoming. The election, however, was a proving ground, and men and women who had never previously known anything about politics became experts. My two subsequent efforts in campaigns in Mississippi—late in 1967 and in 1969, when I assisted Charles Evers, the brother of Medgar, in the contest for mayor of Fayette—were successful.

From 1964 to 1966 events in Mississippi generated an atmosphere of hope, and the Civil Rights acts of 1964 and 1965 gave long-awaited guarantees that the Constitution finally would be honored. During the same period, on the other hand, certain events in Kentucky produced only frustration and despair. I had occasion to go to the federal courts again, to defend eight Kentucky men charged with attempting to blow up a bridge leading into a struck coal mine.

The defendants in Mississippi and Kentucky differed in the color of their skin, but they had in common a fundamentalist Christian religion, a dearth of education, and desperation born of poverty and exploitation. The blacks, with hope, resorted to the ballot. The white Kentuckians, without hope, resorted to violence. Davy Crockett, Sam Houston, Jim Bowie, and Andy Jackson were their heroes and affirmative action was part of their creed. Before I arrived in the courthouse in Jackson, Kentucky, to defend the striking miners, they had blown up twelve power plants and seventeen railroad bridges, which were being used by scabs to get coal out of struck mines. Management's abrupt withdrawal of hospital benefits to them and their families had brought them into direct conflict with the law; the result brought I. Philip Sipser and me to Appalachia to defend them.

Two young men, Stanley Aronowitz and Hamish Sinclair, had been studying the conditions in the Kentucky coal region and appealed for our help. They reported that there was only one Kentucky lawyer, Dan Jack Coombs, who would take on these cases, and he could no longer handle the volume of unrepresented miners in need of aid. Coombs welcomed our entry on the scene.

The background was simple. In the days of United Mine Workers Union leader John L. Lewis, miners and management had got along well, and the fifty cents a ton put away for the miners' hospitalization had been a great boon to them and their families. But when the day of automation came and strip mining began, the owners not only laid off five hundred miners in Hazard alone but also seized the opportunity to renegotiate the contracts. The parent U.M.W., wracked with corruption and crippled by dissension, virtually abandoned its wards. They were supplanted by scabs paid $6.00 a day, replacing men previously paid $25 a day, union scale.

The five hundred chose Berman Gibson, one of their number, to lead them. Called "the pickets," they roamed the countryside, attempting to make it unprofitable for the mineowners to operate, and unhealthy for the scabs. In their undisciplined way they tried to restore the status quo ante, with little respect for the law and order that had ignored them.

When eight were arrested, the United Mine Workers Union refused to provide a lawyer for their defense, lest this link put the union in jeopardy of another management suit. Neither would the union contribute money for a lawyer or for a bail fund. Dan Jack Coombs was in sympathy with the miners' predicament but was swamped with work and could not manage alone.

We met first in New York, with a group Aronowitz and Sinclair called the Committee of Miners. Gibson and several other defendants were among them. We were extremely impressed, especially by Berman Gibson. Whatever their crime, the circumstances of their arrest made it clear that they were being railroaded through the courts without regard either for proper procedure or constitutional guarantees. It was an uneven contest—the mineowners, sheriff, railroad police, state police and F.B.I. on one side and eight impoverished miners on the other.

After several procedural skirmishes in the federal courts in Jackson, Kentucky, and Cincinnati, all of which we lost, the prosecution asked that the case be transferred for trial to Lexington, the only place in Kentucky where, according to the prosecution, the government of the United States could get a fair trial. The court in Cincinnati granted the request. Our clients would stand trial in the lush horse country rather than on their native heath. "The Constitution provides that a citizen shall not be required to travel long distances from his home in order to answer criminal charges," I objected. But it was a losing battle. We knew we had a hard fight ahead.

The defendants were no Berrigans or Ellsbergs, nor were they chic radicals with ideological complaints. There were no northern, eastern or western cocktail parties to raise money for their defense. They were nameless poor whites, and although there were more provisions of the Constitution violated in their case than in the Harrisburg and Catonsville cases rolled into one, no civil rights organization appeared in their behalf.* Sipser and I were serving without fee and we paid our own travel and living expenses, but there was an urgent need for money for stenographic minutes. As a last resort, Sipser appealed to Jimmy Hoffa, whom he had once represented.

*The federal appeals court, in affirming the convictions, pointed out that four defendants, those who had confessed, were convicted, while the other four, who had not confessed, were acquitted. The appeals court found that the convictions had been based "upon the defendants' own confessions." However, it brushed aside the appellants' contention that they had been tricked into making the confessions. Sixteen years later, M. Wesley Swearingen, one of the F.B.I. agents participating in the case and referred to in the court's opinion, told Justice Department lawyers investigating corruption in the bureau that evidence in the case had been fabricated and the defendants tricked into signing the confessions. Three of the four convicted were illiterate.

Jimmy came through with a check for $5,000, which kept us afloat for a while.

The trial was a caricature of Appalachian life. The sheriff, himself a mineowner, testified for the prosecution, notwithstanding the fact that he had previously shot one of the defendants in a shootout on the main street of Jackson, in which the sheriff also was wounded. Moreover, the F.B.I. conducted a personal vendetta, bred of rage against moonshiners, and there was no doubt that the bureau had violated the defendants' rights several times. The judge chided the agents for their questionable zeal—the appearance of fairness had to be observed—but in fact His Honor's behavior left little question where his sympathies lay. When the jury, to our astonishment, acquitted four of the eight, the judge retaliated by imposing harsh sentences on the others.

We took the case to the Circuit Court of Appeals. The four convictions had been based on signed confessions by illiterate defendants. Furthermore, the defendants had been held for countless hours without benefit of counsel and had been subjected to grueling examination by some of the fastest-talking F.B.I. agents in the field. The whole case boiled down to the question of the constitutional rights of criminal defendants.

Sipser and I prevailed on Leonard Boudin, the country's foremost constitutional lawyer, to write the brief on appeal, and the appeals court agreed that the constitutional rights of the defendants had been violated. But as the events complained of had taken place before the law in the landmark Miranda case had been laid down, the court ruled that the convictions must stand. On this kind of tortured logic the defendants were condemned. The court, however, as if struck by conscience, recommended that the sentencing judge take the Miranda case into account on an application to review the sentence.

The sentencing judge was from Tennessee. We pointed out to him how incongruous it was to have guilt or innocence determined by the sole element of time. The argument took place the day after Thanksgiving in 1967, one year after the Miranda decision. The judge's ruling was a halfway attempt to obey the Constitution. He reduced the sentences for all. What interested him most, however, was not the constitutional protection he was sworn to uphold but the fact that Herbert Stacy, one of the defendants, had become a preacher while awaiting his sentence. The court reduced his sentence by two-thirds on that account, and reduced the terms of the others somewhat less. All of the defendants were back in their native hollows within ten months, to renew the fight against the mineowners.

CHAPTER TWELVE

Movers and Shakers: The Politics of Peace

We are the music-makers,
  And we are the dreamers of dreams,
Wandering by lone sea-breakers,
  And sitting by desolate streams;
World-losers and world-forsakers,
  On whom the pale moon gleams:
Yet we are the movers and shakers
  Of the world forever, it seems.

ARTHUR WILLIAM EDGAR O'SHAUGHNESSY

IN THE early 1960s only a handful of Americans questioned United States involvement in Southeast Asia. The story of the Montagnards, who had earlier in history fled before the Vietnamese and taken refuge in the hills, was a familiar one to me, and I sympathized with them and their neighbors more than did most of my countrymen. The evils of colonialism had been practiced again, by the Japanese and the French, on an unoffending people. The Vietminh's gallant fight and final victory over the French at Dien Bien Phu should have made the Vietnamese our allies, but in the cold war we found ourselves for some unexplainable reason helping the beleaguered French, the latter-day equivalent of the British of 1776.

No one has credited Eisenhower with being a great President, yet he resisted the urging of John Foster Dulles, who was bent on making war against the Vietnamese. Eisenhower did agree to give nonmilitary aid to South Vietnam, but that was as far as he would go. On the other hand, he either did not know or could not comprehend the full extent of the mischief Dulles was doing by means of a series of treaties in Asia that were to act as justification for our involvement in war after Dulles was gone.

By 1964, however, the war had become the paramount issue in our presidential campaign, and when the victorious peace candidate thereafter joined in, the people took to the streets—at first just a few, but later millions. Lyndon Johnson defeated hawk Barry Goldwater, scoring a landslide victory. Early in 1965 it was clear that President Johnson had broken his promise to the people and was pouring thousands of soldiers into Vietnam.

By 1965 many Democrats were alarmed by the growing dissension in their ranks, and leading Democrats looked with great disfavor on suggestions of Reform Democrats that President Johnson be denied renomination in 1968. My own club, the F.D.R–Woodrow Wilson Democratic Club, resolved by vote at the end of 1965 to deny Johnson its support unless he stopped the war. We constituted an insignificant fraction of the whole Democratic party, but our example inspired similar action by other clubs. We had no idea how powerful the movement would become. It was born out of pure frustration.

By August 1966, as the State Democratic Convention met in Syracuse geared to nominate a candidate for governor, our group, mainly from Manhattan, could muster less than 10 percent of the delegates in support of a peace plank. But we prepared to bring the matter before the convention. The state leadership, anxious to avoid a floor fight, sought out the Reform caucus in a spirit of compromise. Led by former Governor Averell Harriman (who first made us aware that President Johnson was conscious of our activities and was annoyed by them), they proposed that the convention go on record as opposing the war, but that the President be referred to as "a man of peace." It was a meaningless platitude, and I argued against the compromise. But Harriman's accusations of "treason," which we believed he was communicating from the President, intimidated most of the Reformers, who accepted the language. Our first attempt at a showdown failed then and there.

Thereafter we turned our attention to the election of 1968. From the latter part of 1966 to early 1967, at the urging of Phil Sipser, I invited representatives of antiwar groups to meet at my law office weekly for lunch. As a result of the exchange of ideas, a strategy evolved: we simply had no choice but to oppose the President in his bid for reelection, which meant a fight in the primaries. We resolved to run our own candidates for seats at the national convention and to take our fight to the convention floor. (New York law recently had been amended to open the primaries to dissenters like ourselves.)

Sooner than we expected a movement emerged. The vast majority of its supporters were entering politics for the first time. Their strength was their singleness of purpose, their weakness their intolerance of the party they hoped to conquer and whose leadership they despised.

Such groups as Concerned Individuals Against the War, Concerned Democrats, and Independent Democrats mushroomed in clubhouses throughout the state—and country—and shortly merged in the Coalition for a Democratic Alternative (C.D.A.), which title remained with us until November 1968. Sarah Kovner, a young Reform Democrat in the city, agreed to become the executive secretary of the coalition and began to coordinate efforts throughout the state.

In the fall of 1967 Allard K. Lowenstein and other peace activists from New York and California organized a meeting in Chicago for the purpose of formalizing our efforts on a national scale. No important party figure attended, and while the media covered the proceedings, they were generally "put down." Almost all commentators agreed we were not going anywhere and had little chance of getting off the ground.

Our need was apparent to us from the start: to find a formidable candidate to oppose Johnson. The logical contender was Robert Kennedy, and at that time I was all for him. But Kennedy's advisers held him back. They misjudged the mood of the country and the intensity of the antiwar feeling, especially among intellectuals and Protestant clergymen.

In May, Senator Eugene McCarthy of Minnesota had asked James Wechsler, the editor of the *New York Post,* to try to persuade Kennedy to run. McCarthy pledged his immediate and full support if Kennedy would do so. But Wechsler's effort only hardened Kennedy's refusal. McCarthy then decided to present his own name as a candidate. He did so in the capital about a week before our Chicago meeting, which he addressed, but without generating much enthusiasm. (We were not prepared for the measured tone of McCarthy's protest.)

After McCarthy spoke, the conferees split up into state caucuses. Most of us from New York were dubious. I, however, was not. I had not met McCarthy before, but I admired his reserve (exactly what put others off), especially as it in no way diminished his obvious resolve. Here was a man who had decided to take on a most unenviable job. He had everything to lose and, as of that moment, nothing to gain—not even a place in history. He had been in campaigns before and knew the power of the Johnson machine and what it could do to any future ambition he might have. He could not expect any help from his colleagues in the Senate, and least of all from Kennedy. Yet he was willing to make the fight, and for quiet courage, if for nothing else, I thought he deserved our support.

I said so, but most of the other delegates did not agree. They fell back on the excuse that they had no authority from their respective groups back home to confer their endorsement on McCarthy. I did not want the press to carry the report that McCarthy had only minimal support, and I proposed that we agree to recommend McCarthy's candidacy to our respective organizations at the local level. The delegates were sticklers for democracy, and that resolution passed unanimously.

After the Chicago meeting, columnist Mary McGrory asked me where we were at, and I told her that I thought most of the delegates were Kennedy supporters. "If Kennedy had said the same thing today that McCarthy said, this crowd would have been wildly enthusiastic. Besides, they are not sure McCarthy means to go all the way." "They don't know McCarthy," she said. "What you have done has made him a real candidate, and nothing will make him change from that position."

None of us had measured the man, nor did we even suspect his capacity to electrify the nation with his quiet sanity. We were not fully to realize it for several months.

Things changed immediately after McCarthy came to New York on January 6, 1968, to address a meeting of the peace coalition and Democratic clubs supporting him. McCarthy spoke in the same quiet way he had spoken at the Chicago meeting, but by this time people were becoming more accustomed to his manner, and the New York caucus endorsed him. Thereafter the antiwar Democrats formed a permanent structure, which eventually provided delegate candidates from almost all New York's congressional districts.

At the January coalition meeting the executive committee, of which I was a member, voted to sponsor its own candidate for U.S. senator, to run against Jacob Javits. Our strategy was to have a statewide candidate committed to McCarthy who would carry the banner in each district election for delegates to the national convention, thereby enhancing our chances of returning an impressive number of delegates to the convention.

Al Lowenstein was generally regarded as the man best suited, and all of us were content that he be the candidate. However, Al procrastinated. His close ties to Kennedy made it difficult for him to reach a decision that would displease the senator. While Kennedy was not yet a candidate, he was a force to be reckoned with in New York politics. Furthermore, he did not want any candidate for the Senate who was not considered a Kennedy supporter exclusively, and we were equally determined that our candidate should be seen as being totally committed to McCarthy.

Late in January the executive board met with Lowenstein and urged him to be our candidate. He could not give us an answer, and we postponed our decision several more times. Finally we set March 11 as our deadline for action.

A few days before that date I got a call from the Senate. It was Bob Kennedy, urging me to postpone the meeting. I told him that although there was a sense of urgency about coming to a decision, we could wait another week, during which there would be ample opportunity for all views to be presented before the decision was reached.

The question was mooted. Within a few days McCarthy scored his stunning upset in the New Hampshire primary, and a day later Kennedy announced his candidacy. He entered the field to the utter dismay and confusion of the McCarthy forces, however much they might otherwise have welcomed his opposition to Johnson.

On March 16 some 120 delegates of the coalition met in Albany. Notwithstanding repeated calls to me from both Kennedy and his brother-in-law Stephen Smith, we agreed to nominate our own candidate for the Senate. When it became obvious that Lowenstein could make no commitment for the Senate race, I yielded to Phil Sipser's repeated entreaties and consented to run.

Lowenstein was in attendance in Albany. I believe he was opposed to my candidacy, and he was not alone in his view. A number of delegates had come to the meeting to express the same feeling. They were almost all supporters of Senator Kennedy, and they knew that our efforts must adversely affect his candidacy. They spoke vaguely of unity without defining their terms, and they were accompanied by a busload of Manhattan followers. They held out the possibility that Manhattan Borough President Percy Sutton would be the candidate of the regular Democratic organization. The arguments, pro and con, lasted at least two hours. At length a motion to select a Senate candidate came to a vote, and passed, 78-73, with the Kennedy forces in strenuous opposition.

West Side leader Alex Rosenberg then put the question to me directly. "Paul, if you get the C.D.A. nomination here, will you nonetheless support Sutton if he enters the race?"

I answered, "I can give you my word now that if Sutton consents to be a candidate, my nomination will be undone immediately, and you won't have to do it. I will."

With that, the Rosenberg faction swung its support to me. The floor shortly was thrown open for nominations. Allard Lowenstein's name was entered and he declined. My name was entered and I accepted. No other candidate came forward. And thus, in an atmosphere of bitterest division and discussion, did I become a candidate for the United States Senate.

By the time Robert Kennedy declared for the presidency he enjoyed my genuine affection and respect. The tragedy of the assassination had brought out wonderful qualities in him. But I had committed myself to Senator McCarthy, and I felt that if I were then to abandon him because a more powerful candidate had entered the race, I would be setting a very poor example for the young, who by then had engulfed us. I couldn't do it.

A few days after my nomination Steve Smith called again and asked to meet me. Over lunch he indicated what I gathered was Kennedy's real irritation. In a word, it was Resnick. Congressman Joseph Resnick, a wealthy upstate representative and acknowledged Kennedy hater, had just entered the race as a pro-Johnson candidate for the Senate. Nassau County Executive Eugene Nickerson, a Kennedy supporter, had lately received the nomination of the regular Democratic organization. Inasmuch as Resnick had been alternating anti-Kennedy and prowar pronouncements, the Kennedy forces wanted him defeated. Smith believed that two doves and one hawk running against each other in the primary would give the edge to Resnick. Smith therefore wanted me to withdraw from the race in favor of Nickerson.

Again I refused. I said that if any of us had any real chance of defeating Javits in the fall, "your argument might be viable. But," I continued, "inasmuch as we are all functioning to elect as many delegates as we can [O'Dwyer for McCarthy, Nickerson for Kennedy and Resnick for Humphrey], then I'm not listening to that argument."

Thereafter I moved into the McCarthy headquarters on Columbus Circle and began circulating petitions to get on the ballot, which I shortly did.

McCarthy spent little time campaigning in New York State; our primary was the last in the nation, and McCarthy, Kennedy and Humphrey were slugging it out in such states as Indiana and Oregon. California was next, and everyone agreed that whoever won California and New York would be in the best position to capture the Democratic nomination.

And then, in his moment of triumph, Robert Kennedy was gunned down in Los Angeles. The tragedy brought campaigning to a standstill. Political headquarters closed down all over the state. Some of us wondered if there was any point in going on. Martin Luther King had been murdered in April. As Tom Wicker of *The New York Times* observed, you can't have democracy by assassination.

The contest was now between McCarthy and Humphrey, with George Wallace in the wings, and on June 23, three weeks after Bobby Kennedy was shot, McCarthy won half of the convention delegates and I won the Senate primary. Undoubtedly a last-minute swing of Kennedy support to McCarthy helped, but I had expected all along that we would win a large number of delegates for McCarthy. On the single but overriding issue of the war the people were with us, and I'd felt it from Montauk to Buffalo.

On primary night we were headquartered at the Commodore

Hotel. *The New York Times,* located three blocks away, had not sent a reporter because almost to a man the media were forecasting Gene Nickerson, the regular organization candidate, as the winner. Indeed both CBS and NBC were about to project the election of Nickerson to their audiences when some unexplained figures began coming in from Harlem, Bedford Stuyvesant and other black neighborhoods. Gabe Pressman, the ace commentator for NBC, called to tell me, "Something is happening here. We were ready to declare Nickerson the winner, but we're withdrawing the projection." At 1 A.M. Nickerson conceded defeat and appeared onstage at the Commodore to offer congratulations. A few minutes later John Burns, the chairman of the State Democratic party, paid the customary visit.

My own people were surprised at the victory, but McCarthy was not. During the first part of June I had promised him that if I lost the primary I would be available to stump the country for him after it. "Well," he answered, "thank you, but I don't think that's going to be possible; you're going to win." Of course it could have been his way of discouraging any barnstorming by me on his behalf.

As the Senate candidate I was chosen to lead the McCarthy delegates to the national convention, and accordingly, I took steps to assure that the regular Democratic organization in New York assigned us half of the at-large delegates. The organization refused in an acrimonious state-convention meeting at the Commodore, and by prearrangement, as soon as the vote was recorded, I rose from my place on the dais to leave. All of the peace delegates left with me. The press reported our defiance, and the wire services carried the story throughout the country. A few days later I got a call from Joe Duffey, the chairman of the McCarthy forces in Connecticut. Apparently the Connecticut delegates were facing the same sort of problem. Joe asked me to join them at a meeting with the Connecticut regulars in Hartford the next weekend.

When I got there I found Joe at loggerheads with John Bailey, the chairman of both the Connecticut and national parties. Bailey was not about to surrender any more delegates to McCarthy than he had to, but on the basis of popular support, the rebellious Democrats were entitled to more. There was only one way the McCarthy delegates could show their anger, and so they too, at a given signal, walked out. The cards were stacked against us, but the politics of peace overrode all other concerns.

I left for Chicago with Kathleen and our sons Brian and Rory a day before the opening of the national convention. Neither Brian nor Rory had taken a very active part in the campaign and Rory particularly seemed disenchanted. But the events in Chicago changed all that for both of them.

From the first day the atmosphere in Chicago was one of despair for the antiwar forces; it was transparently clear that Lyndon Johnson was directing the convention from his Texas home. The Kennedy delegates, in order to keep their forces intact, had lined up behind George McGovern. Most of their leaders, however, would not accept the substitution and fell in with Humphrey. I addressed the convention on two subjects—the war and civil rights. It seemed an exercise in futility.

Richard Daley dominated the proceedings. No seats were available to the wives of the delegates, although Daley's political supporters were given front balcony seats, whence they could display banners in praise of their benefactor. Security was airtight. The police in charge had no knowledge of what was expected of them, and accordingly turned their frustration on the enraged delegates. At one point I saw Alex Rosenberg, my New York coordinator, being bodily pulled from the hall by policemen. Richard Newhouse, a Brooklyn clergyman, and I seized Rosenberg and linked our arms around him. We were all dragged outside. Later, news reached us that the Chicago police had gone berserk in the streets, beating people indiscriminately and young people particularly.

In desperation we turned to Edward Kennedy, who was not present, as our last hope of unity. I appealed to McCarthy to release his delegates for a Kennedy draft, and at length he magnanimously agreed.

The "Draft Teddy" movement failed because the power of Johnson was everywhere. It was Johnson's convention: his "peace" plank, his credentials victories, his vice-president catapulted into the nomination. It was in every way a fitting tribute to the architect of the most disastrous policy in the history of the land. And it assured that no Democrat could be elected President that year.

The subsequent election was regarded then as a defeat for the politics of peace. But it clearly was responsible for putting a stop to the war. Nixon knew perfectly well that what had happened to Johnson would happen to him unless he withdrew our troops, and he acted accordingly.

But in November of 1968 what was to happen could not be foreseen. What was apparent was the devastating effect of the election on the antiwar Democratic machine. After the Chicago convention I was the lone surviving standard-bearer of the antiwar movement in New York, and with my defeat by Javits in November, the coalition clubs and organizations began to disappear. A few weeks after the election Eleanor Clark French invited me and more than a hundred other leaders of the coalition to her home to meet. So great was our disillusionment that only eight appeared, and even among the eight there was little enthusiasm for continuing the effort for a contest that was four years off. Nixon was President-elect, and that had created its own shock effect.

Prior to 1967 I had held the Senate in awe. Coming close to that brotherhood and, more especially, watching its vacillations and lack of principle and commitment during 1967 and 1968 gave me the feeling that I could indeed do better than most of its members. Also, having had the dry run on Javits, I felt that in 1970 I would have a fair chance of taking the state against

Republican Charles Goodell, who had been appointed by Governor Rockefeller to fill out Bobby Kennedy's unexpired term. But to get into that contest I would have to win the Democratic primary, and to do so I needed a statewide organization to support me.

With this in mind, I agreed at Ellie French's to be temporary chairman of the moribund C.D.A. Thereafter I called several meetings, and in January 1969 we met to authorize Arnold Weiss to prepare a constitution. I subsequently visited most of the remnants of clubs that had been active in the previous year and urged them to join the new coalition. I enlisted the help of many others. I placed the organizing on Long Island in the hands of McCarthy delegate and insurance executive Don Schaffer. The suburban counties of Westchester, Rockland and Putnam were organized by my 1968 campaign manager, lawyer Phil Sipser. Linda Fisher, who had worked on my campaign in Albany, organized the remainder of the upstate counties. We finally sent out the call for a delegate assembly to meet in early February 1969.

Our efforts proved successful. About 400 delegates met at the Henry Hudson Hotel in Manhattan and conducted the first reading of a proposed charter. I agreed to continue serving as temporary chairman until a permanent one was elected. Organizations from Buffalo, Syracuse, Rochester, Binghamton and Albany, as well as from the suburbs and New York City, were now a revitalized coalition representing about 20,000 hard-core Democratic activists who were determined to be an issue-oriented body committed to peace and social justice. We named it the New Democratic Coalition.

After an equivocal role ending in a lukewarm endorsement of John Lindsay in the 1969 mayoral race, the N.D.C. turned its attention to the statewide election of 1970. Because I was going to be a candidate for the Senate, I resigned as chairman and began to scout around for support, among the N.D.C. clubs and elsewhere. In January and February, N.D.C.-sponsored meetings around the state provided the candidates with an opportunity to meet political leaders and the media.

In March the N.D.C. held its delegate assembly. I was nominated for senator, but Congressman Richard Ottinger of Westchester and Benjamin Rosenthal of Queens, as well as Congressman Max McCarthy of Buffalo and former Kennedy aide Ted Sorensen showed remarkable strength. Gene Nickerson, the Nassau County executive, received the N.D.C. approval for governor over Howard Samuels of Off-Track Betting. Basil Paterson, the black state senator from Harlem, became the N.D.C. candidate for lieutenant governor and Bobby Kennedy's former speech writer, Adam Walinsky, was endorsed for attorney general. As a silent rebuke to incumbent Arthur Levitt, who was running for reelection, N.D.C. did not endorse a candidate for state comptroller. It has been our custom in New York to reelect our bookkeepers on state and local levels. Nobody understands the job, and any attempt to find fault usually bogs down during a recital of stale and boring statistics. All the comptroller needs to do is issue a statement periodically showing he is minding the store and people will return him to office. Such was the case with Levitt.

In 1970 the state committee met in convention at Grossinger's, the Catskill resort, to select the organization candidates. Ted Sorensen won the party designation for the Senate seat by garnering 50 percent of the vote; I received 25 percent—most of which came from N.D.C. delegates—which qualified me for the primary. Dick Ottinger and Max McCarthy were determined to stay in the race, and each collected signatures necessary to qualify him. Arthur Goldberg, the former ambassador to the United Nations, was nominated for governor and provoked a storm by asserting his right to determine who would be his running mate, a tactical error that foreshadowed an extremely inept campaign.

Unity was not to be that year. Basil Paterson, a black lawyer of uncanny wit and skill and N.D.C.'s candidate, was nominated by the convention for lieutenant governor. Adam Walinsky, in his first attempt at electoral politics, became the official candidate for attorney general. And Arthur Levitt, the state's long-time comptroller, was redesignated for that office. Thus the official slate contained not a single Italian or Irishman.

In the race for Senate there were three announced candidates at the end of the convention: Sorensen, Ottinger and I. Max McCarthy had announced that he would not seek the nomination. Within days, however, he changed his mind and decided to run. It is difficult to understand why. He enjoyed little prominence, and it had always been difficult for an upstate congressman to convince voters of New York City that he was a viable candidate. McCarthy proved to be no exception.

On the other hand, Dan O'Connell, Albany County's venerable Democratic chairman, told me that McCarthy would do me harm—by splitting the ethnic Irish Catholic vote. The old man's assessment proved once again to be right. Max McCarthy did take votes away from me, enough to make the difference in the primary. Ottinger, at great expense to himself, won the nomination, and in the embroiled November election of that year he and all the other Democratic candidates save Arthur Levitt went down to defeat.

The 1970 primary gave me a clear picture of where my constituency was. Notwithstanding Ottinger's expenditure of more than $2 million in the primary, I came in second in the four-man contest on the statewide count; but among the New York City dwellers I had come in first. In 1968 I had also carried New York City. It did not take any special insight to conclude that if I confined myself to New York City I would improve my chances of success. In Jewish and liberal areas I scored heavily, and the black and Puerto Rican areas gave me a strong vote of confidence.

I looked forward next to taking part in the 1972 campaign to oust Richard Nixon, whose efforts to extract us from Vietnam had become genocidal, but out in Harrisburg, Pennsylvania, the

Berrigan-McAlister case meanwhile landed in federal court. That grand court battle prevented me from being at home when the Democratic party put its 1972 convention delegates together. Being absent from the noisy, disorganized scene at Miami when George McGovern was nominated was helpful to me in 1973; I could not be blamed for the debacle that ended in such a landslide victory for Nixon the previous year. As I appeared before the members of my party the next year, 1973, my sins of questionable loyalty were comparatively old, and time had dulled the hostility of the conservative Democrats to me and to my candidacy.

CHAPTER THIRTEEN

Protest: Harrisburg and Fort Worth

ON NOVEMBER 28, 1970, headlines across the nation announced that the F.B.I. had broken an antiwar conspiracy involving Catholic nuns and priests who had plotted to blow up important office buildings in Washington, D.C., and who had embarked on a separate adventure to kidnap a high government official (later identified as presidential adviser Henry Kissinger). J. Edgar Hoover, who made the accusation, characterized the schemers as the "Catholic left." He described the plan as a bizarre plot. Spectacular arrests followed, and among those charged was Sister Elizabeth McAlister, who taught the history of art at Marymount, a college founded a century before to provide an education for the daughters of rich Catholics. Also accused was Father Philip Berrigan, a Josephite priest, whose mission had been among the poorest people in Baltimore. He had reportedly masterminded the plot from his cell in Lewisburg Prison, where he was serving a sentence for having publicly burned draft cards—government property. In quick succession, the F.B.I. rounded up Father Neil

McLaughlin and Father Joseph Wenderoth, who belonged to the Josephite order; Anthony Scoblick, a former priest; Mary Cain Scoblick, his wife, a former nun; and Eqbal Ahmad, a native of Pakistan. They made up what became known as the Harrisburg Seven.

The spectacular charges were contained in a speech Hoover made before the Appropriations Committee of the Senate during an appearance in support of his application for an additional $14 million to deal with this new threat to the nation's security. To make sure the story got wide coverage, Hoover distributed copies of his statement to the press before he testified.

The details of the charges were not supplied until much later. And to most observers the story would scarcely have been believed were its author anyone other than J. Edgar Hoover.

During the months that followed, the press periodically was given pieces of the story, which finally began to take shape. It seems that one summer's afternoon at a beach house on the Connecticut shore, Eqbal Ahmad, a Pakistani professor of revolution at various universities, stopped by to pay a visit to two vacationing Marymount nuns—Sister Elizabeth McAlister and Sister Jogues Egan, who had been the college president. During the course of the afternoon the Vietnam war was discussed.

Daniel Berrigan, a Jesuit and brother of Philip, who had been in hiding, had been captured shortly before and was then serving a sentence for his part in the burning of draft cards and other government records. The conversation drifted into a discussion of Vietnam and the disgrace of having so prominent a member of the academic world as Henry Kissinger advising the President on the prosecution of the war. A plan to turn him around was introduced into the conversation. To do this it was thought necessary to remove him from his environment and place him in the custody of scholars committed to ending our nation's involvement in the war. It was hoped that if Kissinger were kept secreted by this group and other academicians for about a week, he would publicly acknowledge that his acts in advising the President to continue the war were highly immoral.

The second part of the accusation, dealing with a plot to blow up the air-conditioning system in government buildings in Washington, was not without foundation. Earlier, when Phil Berrigan was at large, he had nurtured a hope of so disrupting the system that the bureaucracy would never forget it and the incident would provide a signal to protesters here and abroad that the peace movement was virile and determined. Moreover, Berrigan and Father Wenderoth had gone on a mission of exploration through the principal arteries of the Washington catacombs. They wore khaki overalls usually worn by engineers, and armed with pencil, paper and clipboard, entered the underground. There they encountered some workmen, who apparently supposed them to be efficiency experts. Encouraged by the success of their masquerade, the clergymen made their way to the main office of the system. Explaining their mission—to effect certain economies in the system—they asked for and received a complete set of blueprints, which neither of them could read. Thereafter they concluded that the undertaking could not be accomplished without risking injury to people, and the idea, if not then abandoned, was shelved until it was brought back to life in Lewisburg by Boyd Douglas, a young F.B.I. informer.

The grand jury that indicted the clerics on January 12, 1971, sat in the federal courthouse in Harrisburg, Pennsylvania. The jurors were drawn from eleven surrounding countries, whose residents were among the most conservative in the country. Totally submissive to government authority, adherents of fundamentalist religions, and deeply committed to a literal interpretation of the Bible, they constituted ideal jurors from the prosecution's standpoint. The area was one of the last strongholds of the Ku Klux Klan, which the year before had applied for permission to parade in sheets in the town of York, twelve miles to the south. It was no coincidence that the prosecution was conducted in Harrisburg rather than in Boston or New York, either of which city had equal claim to jurisdiction. The government proceeded on the theory that Father Philip Berrigan had, in his cell in Lewisburg Prison, conspired with others to interfere with the prosecution of the Vietnam war. Choosing Harrisburg as the site of the trial gave the government a substantial edge. The defendants had three strikes against them at the start: some were of the Catholic clergy; one, Eqbal Ahmad, was a dark-skinned foreigner—and he taught Americans about revolution.

In selecting witnesses to bolster the kidnaping charge, the prosecution chose to regard Sister Jogues Egan, one of the trio at the Connecticut beach house, as an interested listener, thereby freeing her from the disability of being a coconspirator and leaving her legally free to testify, under subpoena and immunity, against her friends. When she refused to testify, even after a grant of immunity, the government had her prosecuted for contempt. Even then she refused to budge.

The prosecution spared neither manpower nor money in the development of the testimony on which they hoped to convict the defendants of the serious charges the grand jury had presented. Judge R. Dixon Herman, who received the accusation, was a native of the region and represented its prevailing wisdom.

After the indictments were filed, Elizabeth McAlister, Jogues Egan and Eqbal Ahmad appeared at my office to discuss the possibility of my representing them. They were on a mission to select not only competent but also suitable lawyers, ones whose sentiments on the war were parallel to their own and who could be expected, whenever possible, to project an antiwar position and the political viewpoint of the defendants. The interview lasted several hours. It was clear that my past record in civil rights cases was not enough to justify my selection. Professor

Ahmad seemed aloof and less than enthusiastic, but I got the impression that Elizabeth McAlister and Jogues Egan felt that an Irish antiwar radical might best understand their commitment. There were few of us around. The committee had previously consulted Leonard Boudin, and I told them I had worked with him on other cases and I would be comfortable with this constitutional expert as my cocounsel, but I warned that I would not take on the case if there were more than two lawyers. I had to alter that position later when I agreed to work with Leonard and Ramsey Clark.

Before the final selection was made, however, arrangements were set up for the lawyers under consideration to talk with Philip and Daniel Berrigan, who by then had been transferred to the federal penitentiary in Danbury, Connecticut. Clark and I had decided to give our services without fee. Boudin had fixed a very modest figure. Phil wanted to know why a lawyer should be paid anything in an antiwar case. Boudin, with commendable patience, explained that while Clark and I had successful practices and could therefore afford to devote a part of our lives to such cases, his practice was exclusively in the civil rights and civil liberty areas. That explanation satisfied Phil, and all three of us undertook the defense. We were assisted by a battery of talented lawyers, including Tom Menaker, Diane Schulder (now the wife of N.Y. Attorney General Robert Abrams), Charles Glackin, William Cunningham, S.J., Terry Lenzner, who had previously worked for the Department of Justice, and Jack McMahon, a Public Defender of Newark, who were retained to do the investigation. (Later Lenzner joined us at the counsel table.) The investigative work proved to be most helpful.

The defense was by no means impoverished. Funds were raised throughout the United States. A special defense office was set up in Harrisburg and was crowded with young volunteers. Seminarians from various religious orders came to demonstrate their commitment to the defendants. A special hostel was arranged to house the defendants, the lawyers and the clerics lending moral support to the cause. Volunteers and nuns arranged for the meals. All interested parties contributed to the after-dark social session, and in the evenings the Irish contingent invariably came to the fore, after civil rights songs and antiwar songs, with Irish rebel songs. Liz McAlister excelled with "Roddy McCorley," the hero of Antrim, her ancestral home, and "The Men behind the Wire." Both Boudin and Clark lived in this convent. But long ago I had decided that while a trial is in progress it is prudent to avoid undue association with clients outside the courtroom. I was constrained to join in the singing but left when the singing ended.

Phil Berrigan had been transported in chains from Danbury to Harrisburg. We met with him outside his cell the first day of the trial. All lawyers were searched on their way to the room assigned to them and their clients. We felt sure that the room was bugged, and that fear greatly restricted our conversation. I attended all working conferences but avoided the prayer meeting held outside Phil Berrigan's cell each day after court. Clark never missed one.

As we entered the court to commence the trial, the atmosphere was tense—full of suspicion and hostility. Judge Herman's attitude toward the defense was curt and antagonistic, although he tried to hide it. Ramsey Clark was reserved, dignified and effective. The fact that he had been the Attorney General of the United States under Lyndon B. Johnson was most impressive, but galling to the prosecution. Leonard Boudin, then a professor of constitutional law at Harvard, displayed a special brilliance, particularly during arguments on constitutional questions. Throughout the trial I clashed with William Lynch, the conservative Irish Catholic who had been specially assigned to the prosecution of his radical coreligionists, superseding the local federal prosecutor. I instinctively felt he was gearing up to cross-examine the several nuns and priests so as to disassociate .them from the main body of

Catholics, who favored "law and order." Lynch had temporarily relinquished his post as head of the Organized Crime Unit of the Department of Justice to prosecute this case. For my own part, I looked forward to the time when I could cross-examine the informer and, I hoped, rip the mask of law, order and respectability off the Department of Justice.

Judge Herman, for all his hostility to the defense, was aware of the strength of the argument that the publicity surrounding the case, generated by J. Edgar Hoover, made it next to impossible for the defendants to get a fair trial. To weaken the effect of this objection on appeal, the judge extended wide latitude to the lawyers in questioning the prospective jurors. We were permitted to inquire extensively about their beliefs and their attitudes toward the government and the charges. Some three-hundred testified that they were inclined to accept the government's position on most matters, including the war and the present prosecution, and they were excused. But we had little faith in the jury that was finally selected.

The government relied heavily on the written admissions of Elizabeth McAlister and Philip Berrigan as contained in the purloined letters exchanged between them. In addition to incriminating evidence the letters contained many expressions of affection that indicated that a love affair had developed between the priest and the nun. Because they were unmarried at the time of the trial, I felt that these passages, which were irrelevant to the charges anyway, would be prejudicial. A remnant of my early upbringing made me more sensitive than my colleagues to this hazard. They were not disturbed by the prospect of having the passages read to the jury, but they acquiesced in my concern. I spoke to Lynch about it and he agreed to eliminate the passages. It was the only thing on which he and I agreed during the course of the trial. (Later I concluded my judgment in this connection was faulty, and I read some of the more sensitive passages during summation.)

At the outset each lawyer was assigned to represent several

defendants so as to ensure representation at all times during the trial of each defendant, even in the event of the absence of one or more lawyers. I was assigned to represent Elizabeth McAlister, the Scoblicks and Eqbal Ahmad. As is inevitable in cases in which so many lawyers and clients have deep feelings about the charges, things did not run smoothly all the time. Counsel had some sharp differences with their clients. Just before we got to Harrisburg, Ahmad had said he was going to try his own case. I thought the result would be disastrous and advised my clients that if he persisted I would withdraw from the case. Later on, toward the end of the prosecution's case, the major defendants insisted on testifying. They felt they could explain how immoral the war was. It took the joint efforts of all counsel to convince them that by taking the stand they must supply to the government evidence it could not otherwise present to the jury. Furthermore, the rules of the court, which would be strictly enforced by the judge, would prevent them from discussing the war.

The prosecution presented various pieces of testimony, mostly documentary, but the presentation was perfunctory, and the courtroom—jury, judge, defense and prosecutors—knew all of it was prologue. We knew the government's case would depend on Boyd Douglas, and we awaited the appearance of the man who had been chosen by the F.B.I. to act as courier between Phil Berrigan and Liz McAlister.

Douglas, a fellow prisoner at Lewisburg and an inveterate con man, had convinced Berrigan that he was a sincere opponent of our Vietnam adventure and was ready to follow the cleric in efforts to halt the immoral war. Thereafter, by arrangement with the F.B.I., he had smuggled correspondence between Phil and Elizabeth in and out of prison, but not until he had first supplied an exact copy of each letter to "Mollie," his F.B.I. agent employer. Mollie meanwhile had arranged for Douglas to take courses at an outside university in order to justify his comings and goings and also to afford him an opportunity to do further mischief as an antiwar activist poseur.

After days of routine testimony, Lynch dramatically called Douglas to the stand. Painstakingly the prosecutor went over with him, bit by bit, line by line, all the things that Phil Berrigan and Liz McAlister had said to him, and what his contacts had been with the Scoblicks, Neil McLaughlin and Joseph Wenderoth. Sitting at the counsel table was Mollie, Douglas' mentor.

After several days of this, Lynch read the letters, emphasizing matters that were incriminating and breezing almost inaudibly past those that might be explanatory or exculpatory. Finally Lynch relinquished Douglas with a triumphant "Gentlemen, your witness."

The recently developed rules giving the defense access to the records and statements of government witnesses were of tremendous value in preparing for the examination of Douglas. I had spent several nights going over his testimony and matching it with his regular reports to Mollie. Because the reports had been submitted randomly, they contained numerous statements at odds with the indictments and the theory of the case. Moreover, I felt no scruple, as my clients and my colleagues did, in attacking his character. To them Boyd was a weak person who had had bad breaks as a boy and was being used by the F.B.I. Phil Berrigan refused to believe even at that late date that Boyd was not a true convert to peace. To me, however, he was an informer who had betrayed the confidence good people had placed in him. He had deliberately led them into a position that made an indictment and jail inevitable. I had studied every crime of which he had been convicted, every swindle in which he had been implicated and the manner in which he had committed it. I had studied every line of every report he had made to agent Mollie, and every bit of testimony he had given to the grand jury. As I started the examination I had at my fingertips an account of every cent he had received from Mollie and what it was for. It was my hope in this way to establish that he was clever enough to entrap those who had trusted and confided in him.

Painstakingly we went over every bit of this evidence. I traced his career from one bank swindle to another. He made no attempt to deny that he had stolen from banks and insurance companies, but made every effort to charm the jury, some of whom appeared to be smitten with him. The fact that he had collected handsomely from the expense account of the F.B.I. seemed to fascinate them, and what I had hoped might be the coup de grace—his demand for $50,000 from Mollie to start a new life in the West—seemed only to amuse them. Pressed by Judge Herman, who had treated Douglas with kindness and even respect, giving him ample opportunities to escape from the traps I had set, I resolved to play the one card that might impress the jury and change their romanticized view of a delightful rogue to an image more nearly approaching the truth.

In the background was an attractive girl, reared in a small town, an easy prey for Douglas. As I began to scratch at the subject, Lynch sought to run interference. What follows is the court transcript of that colloquy.

By Mr. O'Dwyer:

Now, with respect to Betsy Shandel, did you urge her to go to demonstrations?

Mr. Lynch: Can we be more specific, Your Honor.

By Mr. O'Dwyer: (continuing)

Q Any demonstrations, any demonstrations at all?
A I told Betsy Shandel that people were coming down from the Catholic Left.
Q Did you tell her in those words? Did you say, "Betsy, people are coming down from the Catholic Left"?
A If I knew who was coming down, I would tell her, yes.
Q No, did you tell her people are coming down from the Catholic Left?

A No, I may not have in that exact tone.

Mr. Lynch: Objection. That is not questioning, this is badgering.

The Court: It is getting pretty argumentative, Mr. O'Dwyer.

By Mr. O'Dwyer: (continuing)

Q In any event, you told her people were coming down to demonstrate outside of the penitentiary?
A I did.
Q And you urged her to go to the demonstrations?
A I believe I left that up to her. If she wanted to go, I didn't make her go. It was up to her. If she wanted to go, she went.
Q I am asking you if you urged her to go.
A Well, the only way—you must be saying did I tell her to go to the demonstrations.
Q No, did you ask her to go?
A I may have asked her, yes.
Q On the 6th of July, of 1970, were you shown pictures of demonstrators outside of the penitentiary?
A I was.
Q And did you point out Betsy Shandel as being one of the demonstrators? Did you identify her photograph to the F.B.I.?
A I am sure I did, if she was there.
Q And did you describe her as a student at Bucknell to the F.B.I.?
A The F.B.I. knew that.
Q Did you describe her to them as a student at Bucknell?
A Yes, yes, well—well, yes, I did.
Q Did you ask her to marry you?
A Possibly.
Q Was it before or after you pointed her picture to the F.B.I.?
A I don't recall.

The trial lawyer must be prepared for each answer of a hostile witness. If the answer is disadvantageous, he must conceal his concern. He must not raise his voice. By speech and behavior he must give the impression the response was expected and move without delay to a new subject so that the jury does not have time to dwell on its implications.

On the other hand, an advantageous reply calls for a pause. I rested my eye on Douglas, and for a while neither moved nor spoke. There was complete silence in the courtroom. All attention was focused on the witness. The jury had an opportunity to look at a man who had induced a young woman into an area of danger and prevailed on her to join an unpopular movement and participate in activities he knew were under F.B.I. surveillance, in both cases using a pose of earnestness, protestations of love and proposals of marriage, only to betray her to the F.B.I., which was paying him for these services.

Nor did the F.B.I. emerge with clean hands before the jury. The prosecution knew it had not heard the end of it, and I knew that the relationship between the agency and its disreputable informer would be an important part of the summation. I knew then that in my summation I would quote, verbatim, every word of the last few minutes of testimony.

During the trial most of the faces of most of the jurors had seemed expressionless; some, obviously bored, painfully suppressed yawns. When Douglas took the stand, however, they had come alive. The foreman and others seemed to enjoy the story of his escapades, his spending sprees with his ill-gotten money. I turned now to see if my own reaction to his testimony was reflected in their faces. There were two single young women in the jury and several young parents of growing families, all solemn. The foreman turned his chair around, away from the witness. I looked for a moment again at the others. Only rarely can a lawyer sense what effect his presentation has made. But this time I felt the testimony was significant enough to turn the trial around. For the first time since our arrival in Harrisburg I felt happy that we were presenting our case to a jury made up, for the most part, of conservative Pennsylvania Dutch fundamentalists.

The trial went on for a few more days—Boudin making intermittent motions that the judge and the prosecutor had difficulty following. Ramsey's final presentation established him to be genuinely outraged at the behavior of the Department of Justice and the F.B.I.

At the end of the government's case we rested without calling either a priest or a nun to the witness stand. It was a bold stroke—it took the judge and prosecution by surprise. We had taken the precaution of having the defendants indicate around the courtroom and in the detention pen that we would be calling them as witnesses, so that if the room was bugged the "buggers" would be placed at a disadvantage. I think they were. All that was left was the summation and charge and the jury's vindicating verdict. Liz McAlister and Phil Berrigan were convicted of smuggling letters in and out of prison in violation of prison rules, a charge no one had ever seriously disputed. The kidnaping and other serious charges fell of their own weight, and the Harrisburg Seven case was consigned to history.

I did not wait for the victory party but headed straight toward the highway to warm, friendly, understanding Gotham. The trip was long enough to permit reflection on the events of the past few years, culminating in the incredible performance of J. Edgar Hoover, the man whom even Presidents feared; long enough to dwell on the trial, the jury and the devotion ever present even in a remote area in Pennsylvania to the basic principle of fair play; long enough to silently apologize to the people in the eleven counties whom I had patronizingly doubted; long enough for me to feel proud of my adopted country and grateful that I was privileged to serve in its courts of justice to protect its most noble heritage.

Back in my office the next morning, I accepted the congratulations of a few friends in the antiwar and civil rights movements, and I waited for the next case that I knew would come.

A few days after the end of the Berrigan trial several Irishmen came to the office. They had been subpoenaed to testify before a federal grand jury in Fort Worth, Texas. No charge had been brought against them, but it was rumored that they were involved in the sale of guns in Mexico, arms destined for Northern Ireland. Federal agents for some time had been harassing Irish men and women in the New York area, persons they suspected of helping the Irish Republican Army. Among those so persecuted were five septuagenarians who governed the Irish Northern Aid Committee, which had collected well over a million dollars in a single year. As required, they had filed an accounting with the government as foreign agents.

In due course a government action had been commenced against the committee, directing it to produce its books for inspection. I had appeared in court in opposition and had appealed from an adverse court ruling. The court action kept the agents at bay for a while.

While that litigation was pending, the Texas subpoenas were served. By this time the entire Irish community was up in arms about the events in Northern Ireland and several protests had been staged in New York and elsewhere. When difficulties arose—whether through an arrest for picketing the Irish consulate or British Information Services or for conducting a sit-in at Irish Airlines or BOAC—whatever they might be, those in trouble found their way to our law office. No fee had ever been charged in a civil rights case handled by O'Dwyer and Bernstien, and the Irish defense was no exception.

Having just come off the Harrisburg case, in which government harassment had been an everyday occurrence, I was keenly aware of what the government's officials were up to. It was the same Department of Justice that had contrived to try nuns and priests in a Ku Klux Klan stronghold, which now had chosen Fort Worth as the appropriate jurisdiction to subpoena before a grand jury a group of New York Irish Americans. (Subsequently it was established in a congressional hearing that New York and Fort Worth had equal claims to jurisdiction.)

I had not known any of the five before they were subpoenaed. None had had a station-house, let alone court, experience. Their way of life and professional activities would not normally have brought them into conflict with law enforcers. Ken Tierney was a physiotherapist; Tom Laffey a real estate salesman; Matthias Reilly a bus driver; Danny Crawford a painter; and Paschal Morahan a carpenter. Three of them were married and had children, and all were either United States citizens or had filed papers to become citizens.

In the Berrigan case, William Cunningham, S.J., had been one of the defense counsel. A studious but self-effacing man, he was overshadowed by the aggressively brilliant Leonard Boudin. But even under those circumstances his authority on constitutional law was unmistakable. He came to the office and brought Doris Peterson with him. Both were colleagues of Bill Kunstler at the Center for Constitutional Rights. Both agreed to help my partner Frank Durkan, who was to head the defense team.

Frank called the prosecutor to find out why our clients were being obliged to go to Fort Worth. "I want to question your clients," was all the official would say. Thereupon I explained to the five that there were several alternatives available to them. They might go willingly to Texas and answer all questions put to them by the government. That course might, however, entail embarrassing complications. All of them had attended several social functions in aid of the Catholic minority in Northern Ireland. "Should you testify," I warned them, "you will undoubtedly be called upon to testify about those in attendance at such gatherings and be required to supply names and addresses of those whom you know to have participated. Those, in turn, including your family and friends, are then subject to harassment. Should you testify but balk at listing your friends, it is the same as refusing to testify in the first place. If the government then gives you immunity from prosecution in return for your testimony and you still refuse to answer the questions put to you, you are subject to imprisonment for contempt of court."

Civil rights advocates had been invariably caught in this trap during the McCarthy period. The classical question was "Are you or have you ever been a Communist or a member of the Communist party?" If the client answered truthfully "no," a bevy of government informers was usually waiting to contradict him, and a perjury indictment and conviction would surely follow. The ruse had caught many an innocent in its web. It was not for espionage but perjury that Alger Hiss was imprisoned. Being charged with perjury before a Texas jury and a Texas judge specially selected for the occasion presented an ominous picture. In Texas the sentences in even trivial cases were often harsh beyond belief. Kids had been given six-year sentences for smoking one joint of marijuana. That very month a draft resister in a Texas court had got seven years for telling the court that he did not believe in the war and that he was opposed to it and would not serve.

The five Irishmen and Mary Kennedy, the lone female subpoenaed, had not come to my office with any hint of bravado. Concern showed plainly on their faces. All were ordinarily law-abiding citizens, politically a bit on the conservative side. But when they left to break the disquieting news to family and friends (they were to return later to give us their decision), I knew what their decision would be. A year or two in prison for contempt of court was devoutly to be preferred to informing on friends. They really had no choice at all.

Our inquiry during the next few days confirmed our worst fears. We were to appear before a nest of Nixon Democrats. Moreover, when we did so, everything we had expected occurred. Mary Kennedy, the pretty secretary of the Northern Aid Committee, refused to testify and was released. But the five men were judged in contempt and jailed for an indefinite period. "If you cooperate, you will be set free," said Judge Leo Brewster. "You have the key to the jail in your pocket."

Frank Durkan, Doris Peterson and Bill Cunningham tried every court in the circuit to appeal Judge Brewster's ruling, all to no avail. The prisoners were consigned to oblivion in the Tarrant County jail. The total space that was the home, church, dining room, toilet, and sole recreation area of its occupants measured 16 feet by 7 feet. The prisoners were too far from New York to see family and friends, and their only visitor other than counsel was a young Baptist clergyman who acted as chaplain. There was no Catholic service of any kind.

Immediately after my first visit I lodged a complaint with the court. It was late afternoon when I got to the judge's chambers. "Judge Brewster has gone fishing," his secretary told me. I left my complaint with her. "There is a civilized federal facility at Segoville, a ten-minute ride from the court," I said. "These men are federal-court prisoners and should be in a federal facility. Besides, Tarrant County jail is in and of itself a violation of the cruel and inhuman punishment provision of the U.S. Constitution."

Before I left Texas I visited the U.S. marshal. He was a decent man who readily agreed that the jail was inhuman. He merely protested that no one had previously made a complaint. Fortified with his forthright condemnation of the jail, I held a press conference at the airport on my return to New York, and thereafter enlisted the help of New York's congressmen. The five were promptly transferred to Segoville Penitentiary.

The order committing the five to jail had not set any time limit, and the judge's authority to keep them confined extended for the life of the grand jury, which had a year and a half to go. It was customary for prisoners, even those charged with serious crimes, to be released on bail pending appeal, but bail was denied to the five by Judge Brewster. The Circuit Court of Appeals sustained its controversial colleague.

Justice William O. Douglas was the only member of the

Supreme Court who could be expected to look with favor on our application for bail, but we had to wait till the Supreme Court was in summer recess before we could make the request to him. Immediately after the court disbanded, Judge Douglas retired to his rustic summer retreat in the state of Washington. As was required by the rules, the clerk of the court mailed the bail application to him. At the end of a deer path leading to the judge's cabin the mailman on the route deposited the legal papers in a designated crotch of a tree. The judge traveled on horseback over that narrow trail each morning to pick up his mail. His reply was, in turn, placed in the same crotch to await the return of the mailman, who then posted it to the clerk of the Supreme Court in Washington, D.C. In due course the prisoners were released on $10,000 bail. Douglas's intervention was responsible for reducing the jail time from eighteen months to ten.

I returned to Texas for our final appearance before Judge Brewster. With a sigh of relief he added his signature to the release document, and his signature on the bail bond brought an end to the case. No indictment was ever brought in. The bail fund, raised overnight in New York saloons, was oversubscribed.

CHAPTER FOURTEEN

Council President

EARLY IN 1973 Comptroller Abe Beame dropped by my office. "I'm a candidate for mayor," he said. He did not elaborate. He did not ask for my support nor did he ask what my plans were. His announcement came as no surprise. It had been rumored for some time that he contemplated a second run for the office. His brief talk with me was in the best political tradition, for if you tell a man in private about your plans, you are likely to either neutralize him or make him an ally.

I knew, however, that the last thing Beame wanted on his ticket was a Jewish candidate for president of the City Council. If Harrison J. Goldin became the Democratic candidate for comptroller and Beame won the Democratic primary, the ticket would be exclusively Jewish if Sanford Garelik ran for reelection to the Council presidency in November. Such a racially unbalanced ticket would be regarded as a serious handicap. That gloomy picture changed, however, when Garelik let it be known that he too intended to seek the Democratic nomination for mayor. Garelik's decision left a vacancy for the office of

Council president, and I began to talk about it with friends.

In assessing my chances of success, I had to consider that I would not get party backing in a primary contest. The best I could hope to get was the total support of the Reform, or New Democratic Coalition (N.D.C.), wing (and that represented less than 25 percent of the Democratic vote) and perhaps here and there an old-guard leader who had labor or minority connections. Otherwise neutrality was the most I could expect.

I anticipated strength among minorities, but minorities had exceedingly low registration and the cost of bringing out their vote would be high. I could count on an adverse editorial from *The New York Times* and the *Daily News,* and I could hope for a favorable one from the *Post, El Diario, El Tiempo,* the *Amsterdam News,* many of the foreign-language newspapers, the *Village Voice* and the Irish weeklies. As to editorial support from radio and television stations, that factor was then too new to assess.

Notwithstanding my previous service on the Council, I would have found it difficult if not impossible to oppose a black candidate, and I inquired among the likely ones, including Percy Sutton. None was interested in the office. I checked on whether there was likely to be a woman with reasonable political credentials, including Bess Meyerson, who had been prominently mentioned. None surfaced.

I then wrote to political and labor leaders asking whether they would encourage me to become a candidate. The responses brought few surprises in the political field but many in the labor field. Responses from the liberal Democrats were favorable, as I had expected, but I received twice as many responses approving my candidacy from minor labor leaders as I had ever previously received. I gathered that after some years of somnolence the unions were again becoming politically active on the local level. As older unions and leaders grew tired, new, progressive ones were entering the field. Many of them were still struggling to establish themselves and thus were more sensitive to my candidacy than were those grown opulent with the passage of time. Only a small fraction of the unions of city workers supported me. But backing was promised by such diverse groups as the teamsters' and construction unions, the Building Service Workers, the United Electrical Workers, longshoremen, and certain craft guilds. Support was also indicated by leaders of the ethnic communities, and most surprisingly, after I made my announcement on February 5, a special committee of Irishmen sprang up to counter the opposition in Irish communities.

My partner, Oscar Bernstien, then eighty-eight, and I put up $50,000 and set up machinery to solicit contributions. Charlie Keith, who was retiring from his real estate business, agreed to manage the campaign. In his earlier days Charlie had been one of those whom we called "premature anti-Fascists" and had served with great distinction in the Abraham Lincoln Brigade in Spain. He questioned whether his participation would be an asset in wooing the city's Irish.

"It's a new day, Charlie," I said. "We were right on Vietnam and right on the F.B.I. and right on the C.I.A., and now the alcohol revenuers are chasing Irish gunrunners, and Irish women are in Belfast jails, and the whole civil rights thing is clearer now. They probably won't notice you. And besides, the spotlight will be on the mayoralty race.

Linda Fisher again consented to handle the public relations campaign.

Our first hurdle was the N.D.C. convention, and we worked hard to put it on early. Timing was important. It was unlikely that anyone from that stable would successfully contest my candidacy, but I was taking no chances. With my friends in the N.D.C. guiding me, we saw to it that an early convention took place, and that snuffed out any chance of opposition there.

With Beame taking the position that he was not endorsing any running mate, the Democratic political leaders, following Beame's lead, did likewise. Democratic State Assembly Leader Al Blumenthal, Harrison J. Goldin and I, coming out of the

N.D.C. Convention as its nominees for mayor, comptroller and Council president respectively, stood a fair chance of success. But that picture of Democratic unity changed abruptly when Herman Badillo, condemning the convention as racist, announced his own candidacy in the Democratic primary for mayor, a move that doomed any hope of electing a Democratic Reformer to that office.

As the pieces began to fall into place, Assemblyman Anthony DiFalco, son of the surrogate, announced that he was making a bid for the Council presidency. Then ten days before the deadline to file petitions, Sanford Garelik changed his mind. He had been outmaneuvered. Mario Biaggi, a much decorated former policeman, had entered the mayoral race. Garelik, who had been Chief Inspector of Police, had counted heavily on support from the same quarters. He decided to seek reelection as Council president.

Charlie Keith called a meeting to determine how we should handle the new situation. We concluded that Garelik would take Jewish votes away from me and that his entrance into the race would be helpful to DiFalco. DiFalco's camp concluded that Garelik would take conservative votes away from him and that his entrance would be helpful to me. As it turned out, we were both right to a degree. The conservative anti-O'Dwyer forces now had a choice between two opponents. But by the same token, I did not do as well in certain Jewish areas as I would have done had the contest been between DiFalco and me. A bitter antagonism soon developed between DiFalco and Garelik. It seems that before DiFalco began his campaign he had talked directly to Garelik, explaining that he was prepared to spend $60,000 on advertising provided Garelik was not a candidate for president of the Council. Garelik assured DiFalco that he was interested only in the mayor's job, but within the week declared his candidacy for president of the Council. Thereafter their criticism of each other grew pointed and personal. I explained my own attitude toward both of them at a three-way discussion on Barry Gray's radio program. "Each of my opponents," I said, "has some very uncomplimentary and harsh things to say about the other. I believe they are both right."

Seldom during the campaign were issues seriously discussed. Some reforms had been suggested in the Council (including abolishing the office of president), and Sandy Garelik made the blunder of presenting a bill to deal with absentee voting, outlining exceptions under which he would permit it. There was no law permitting absentee voting, but a custom allowing it had grown up with the passage of years. That now became an issue, and the opposition went after him. The other proposed reforms presented to the electorate by the candidates were less than earthshaking, and it really got down to how many troops could be delivered on primary day. We went to work on that.

With apologies to Caesar, New York City is divided politically into five parts, or counties, which are themselves divided into some forty-eight communities, each with a very special and distinct flavor. For me the principal disaster area is Staten Island, whose several communities make up Richmond County. At times the Conservative party has outpolled all other political parties there. In 1973 the progressive Italian leader of the Democratic party there, Dante Ferrari, had to surrender the leadership, and the mantle fell on Jim Smith, an ultraconservative Irishman, who promptly declared for DiFalco. What shall we do about Staten Island? we asked ourselves. A strategy meeting at our headquarters considered the question. The consensus at first was to surrender totally and unconditionally to my opponents, but the fact that Leo Whyte, the county treasurer, had come out in support of my candidacy and that I had always gotten fair treatment from the *Staten Island Advance* as well as from Mike Azzara, its political reporter, made us change our position. Besides, we had carried the county for Gene McCarthy in the 1968 primaries. We were, however, not inclined to spend much time there, leaving the campaign to Jim

Callaghan, a stalwart of one of the N.D.C. associations that had put up a valiant effort there in the past.

I did appear at some party functions and at a New Democratic Coalition meeting. "Staten Island has never been overly kind to me," I told one group. "I have tried to please. It hasn't worked. I have coaxed. I have told jokes. I have lavished praise on the Island's babies. I have remarked on the machismo of your men and and the beauty, charm and grace of your women. I have avoided the issues lest the memory of my past positions arouse your anger. Nothing has helped. Now, I can tell you, if I win but don't carry Staten Island, I will run two subways here, one from Manhattan and one from Brooklyn."* The threat got a laugh. In the end I lost Staten Island again, but I established that the Islanders do have a sense of humor.

Queens County has always been a confusing and confused county. There Republicans invariably win seats in the state assembly and senate and sometimes in Congress. On the other hand, there are Jewish areas in which I could be expected to do well. In 1970 I had lost there by 20,000 votes, carrying only the black community. We realized it could be the swing county in the election. It has a lively, though spotty, N.D.C. group, but a fair-housing dispute that had arisen between Jewish conservatives on one side and liberals and blacks on the other had placed my candidacy in a precarious position in the area of Forest Hills, which I had counted on to support me with enthusiasm.

Jim Barker came in to even the odds. He neutralized the vocal opposition by declaring for me early. He represented an Irish neighborhood as a Democratic district leader, and with his adjoining neighborhood in tow, he decided to "sell" to Matt Troy, the county leader, the perfect, balanced ticket: Biaggi,

*The establishment of subway lines in New York has been the forerunner of a mass movement of citizens from the lower economic strata. It is what Staten Islanders fear most.

O'Dwyer and Goldin. Something for everybody in Queens—an Irishman, an Italian, a Jew. A conservative, a liberal, and a moderate. Troy accepted the ticket and endorsed it. Queens thereby became the only county to officially endorse my candidacy.

The Brooklyn Democratic leader, Meade Esposito, was not born to the purple. He had started in the insurance business as a bondsman, the lowest rung on the ladder. In the course of his climb, politics had beckoned and he had successfully challenged the local Democratic district leader. His success opened the door to the leadership of his party in Brooklyn, the most populous county in the nation. When reformers met with local success he made them welcome and thereby disarmed the opposition, which had undermined his successive counterparts in Manhattan. I had met him occasionally throughout the years. To ask him to support me was not practical. He had been sustained by a number of Italians who also knew the DiFalco family. The best I could hope for was neutrality, and I got it. Thereafter regular organization district leaders in Jewish, black, Irish and Italian neighborhoods actively supported me. Indeed, in Canarsie, Mill Basin, Flatlands, Sunset Park and Bay Ridge, the Irish voters were so enthusiastic that Al O'Hagan and his Hibernians were meeting in common with the N.D.C. forces from swank Brooklyn Heights.

In the Bronx the situation was somewhat different. The antagonism toward Reformers was strong, for the reason that Reformers had twice challenged the organization for countywide office and twice been successful. A Reformer had toppled Charlie Buckley, the county leader, from his congressional perch, and another had denied Pat Cunningham, the next, erudite county leader, a seat in the Congress. Cunningham had appeared to remain neutral, and I expected him to permit his district leaders to follow their wishes. But only three, all in the South Bronx, announced for me, and they clearly had not been Cunningham's to deliver.

That turn of events released me from a very uncomfortable neutrality. Robert Abrams, the Reform candidate for borough president, was Cunningham's nemesis and was involved in a hotly contested race. Abrams had responded to every meeting I had called for the Fort Worth Five, and if we both won, we would be colleagues on the Board of Estimate. The next day we held a press conference and exchanged endorsements. Abrams and O'Dwyer, and O'Dwyer and Abrams, depending on where we were introduced, materially improved our vote in Bronx County. Abrams won by an overwhelming majority and I carried the Bronx by 2,000 votes.

The fifth county, New York, is correctly referred to as Manhattan, although more frequently as New York City. In 1973, when I sought the nomination there, the majority of its residents were black and Puerto Rican. Among the poor whites almost every nation was represented. The rich of all stripes were heavily Reformist. With Borough President Percy Sutton on our side, we counted on Manhattan to pull us through. And so it proved to do. I won the primary with 42 percent of the vote. Garelik, the incumbent, came in second, and DiFalco third. And with Abe Beame leading the ticket, the November battle was already won.

I took off a couple of weeks to expedite action on the Cheshire Home back in Bohola and to visit the North, where civil rights had all but disappeared as far as the Catholic minority was concerned. The war that had gone on intermittently since 1916 was now flaring up again, with British diplomacy having surrendered to the rule of the gun, the prison cell, the midnight raid, incarceration without trial and new methods of torture. The reign of terror had breathed new life into the moribund I.R.A. I was disheartened, but on my return to New York I was cheered when I found the Beame-O'Dwyer-Goldin team already well accepted.

And so the campaign proceeded all the way with the wind to our backs. And on election night they came again from far and near. More people now than had ever appeared before and cousins I had never heard of, and I acknowledged them all. It was easier that way. But the faithful came too, and they danced, and they sang, and they drank, and, for all I know, they smoked pot and called it tobacco. And all my family were around—Billy and Carole, Eileen and Tom, and Kathleen, Rory and Brian, all three of whom had worked tirelessly throughout the campaign—all except my sisters, whom illness had prevented from coming. By then there were only two remaining, and my brother Frank having died in California in 1960, I decided to return to Ireland for yet another visit.

It was difficult for May and Linda to understand that in 1945 and 1949 the people of America could heap honors on their brother Bill and could credit him with qualities they hoped, but were never sure, he possessed, for reasons that never seemed to justify the adulation. They had suffered confusion and disillusionment when the same media a few years later had to cull from their lexicons words abusive enough to describe the same kinsman. But what matter now in the twilight of life? They were entitled to know that New York's moods were neither deep-seated nor permanent and that New Yorkers in their busy lives relegate final judgments to history. And the survivors of Patrick O'Dwyer and Bridget McNicholas were entitled to taste a bit of victory again and to look back with kindness on the City that had bidden their brothers welcome when the outlook in their native land had been miserable and bleak.

People from Bohola met me in Dublin, and there was a torchlight parade and there were bonfires all along the road coming into the village and eight hundred nighthawks crowded into the parish hall. Father Martin McManus presided, and the village leaders spoke and made presentations to my sisters and to Kathleen and me. And afterward the local band ascended the platform and local singers performed and the young danced far into the night.

Later a more intimate gathering assembled in the old parish

house and Father McManus called on the guests to speak. I was called last. Father McManus' introduction revealed much of his life and his commitment. "On behalf of this parish," he said, "I want to welcome back a neighbor who has been greatly honored in his adopted country. I want first to say how grateful we are to New York. It has been a haven for us when circumstances bade us go. Of course we are happy when one of our people meets with success at home or abroad, but his is a special case, and I am not here merely to praise a man who has been elected to high office but rather to pay respects to one who in his life saw injustice to his fellow citizens, to the exploited members of the Negro race, and who took up their cause. Twenty years in Africa in close, intimate and daily contact with the people of that continent have left me with a respect and admiration for them. The ill treatment meted out to them through the centuries is reminiscent of our own history. Regretfully, in America not all our people remember that, but our guest did. I hope New York honored him for the right reason, and if it didn't, we in this insignificant community do. It is with a special feeling of satisfaction that I present the president-elect of the City Council of the city of New York."

Shades of Father John. He with the silk hat and the big stick and the tyranny. Seemed like the old house shook. A bit of warmth and compassion had taken the place of hate and greed. At last liberation had come to Bohola.

In Washington meanwhile Spiro Agnew had made a deal with President Nixon and, armed with a certificate of immunity from prosecution, had surrendered his post as Vice-President. Gerald Ford took his place, and on succeeding Nixon as President, chose Governor Nelson Rockefeller as the third Vice-President in two years. In Albany the law of succession moved Lieutenant Governor Malcolm Wilson into the governor's chair. A conservative Republican from suburban Westchester County, Wilson had lived in the shadow of Rockefeller for many years. It was this new governor to whom Mayor Beame and I had to appeal in the spring of 1974 when we visited the state capital in search of alms for an insolvent city.

According to law and custom, Mayor Beame had gone through certain rituals preliminary to his trip to Albany. The mayor had expressed his views on the budget to the press and the Board of Estimate. He estimated the shortfall between revenues and expenditures to be $1.5 billion. Hearings were then held before the city fathers, and, as usual, lobbyists for special interests demanded more money than the budget allowed. Finally the mayor went into what is colloquially called a "budget retreat"—meaning a period of seclusion—to determine how much could be trimmed from expenditures and thus from the $1.5 billion. The answer to that question emerged after our second visit to Albany, when the gap was reset at $818 million.

At a subsequent meeting a bargain was struck with the state whereby the projected deficit was to be further reduced by a state bond issue of $520 million to be repaid by earmarked city revenues. But things didn't work out as planned, and as time went on, the governor began to whittle down the areas in which the mayor could obtain the new revenues. The result was that the $520 million was not backed up by new revenues, as was first planned. The governor obliged Beame to fall back on revenues from borrowing, an untenable alternative, and in a massive attack on the budget, Comptroller Goldin pointed out that it was still $88 million over the mark.

Governor Wilson and Warren Anderson and Perry Duryea, the Republican senate majority leader and assembly minority leader respectively, had succeeded in exploiting the rift between Goldin and Beame and left them to fight it out on their own turf in the city. It turned out to be a boon for the Republicans. The 1974–75 budget was passed in an atmosphere of acrimony. The state legislature had compelled the city to impose a packet of nuisance taxes, to the great disadvantages of the city Democratic administration.

In November 1974, Congressman Hugh Carey from Brooklyn was elected governor. To those unfamiliar with New York politics that turn of events appeared advantageous for the hard-pressed city seeking state assistance. But the mayor's arrival in Albany in the spring of 1975 elicited no more enthusiasm than had his advent the year before. By that time it had become evident that the city's temporary notes, amounting to over $6 billion, would be called by the banks.

Moreover, there was one important aspect of the city's relationship with the banks about which we were kept ignorant. The shaky condition of the banks themselves was hidden from the public for more than a year and a half. Our creditors spoke and acted with the arrogance of people who had the strongest financial standing. We were urged to cut the budget to the bone, the clear implication being that if the budget were radically cut the banks would be in a position to restore the city's credit. However, while these negotiations were in progress the New York City banks discreetly unloaded on their unsuspecting customers over a billion dollars' worth of city paper. Because they had a virtual monopoly on the sale of the city bonds, they stopped the sale of new bonds while selling off their own to the public, and thus controlled their own competition. By the time they got rid of their notes and bonds the market was glutted and New York's credit had been laid to rest.

The banks contrived a defense for their arbitrary decision to abolish the city's credit. They pretended that at the time they had made the loans they had not known of the loose and sloppy accounting methods in which the city was engaged. These innocents from Wall Street proclaimed that they had been duped by wily connivers from the city, who had successfully hidden from them the nefarious manner in which the budget was balanced.

The members of the Board of Estimate met in my office to discuss the fix we were in. Later we had a meeting with Beame and pointed out that we had little choice but to do whatever was necessary to please the city's creditors, even if that meant a severe cutback in city services. We had finally concluded that there would have to be a layoff. The alternative was a bankruptcy proceeding, which by then almost everyone felt was worse.

Governor Carey meanwhile was anxious to balance his own budget, and he did not have an easy political road to travel. The Republicans had control of the senate, and there were a host of unfriendly Democrats in the assembly. Both Warren Anderson and Perry Duryea were contenders for the Republican nomination to oppose Carey in 1978. Even if Carey wanted to be sympathetic to the city, he had to be careful not to show any partiality toward it. Anyway, it was impossible to pass legislation until Anderson agreed to it, and in this context Anderson was as important as Carey. As a result, our first meeting with Carey and the legislative leaders consisted of posturing, and it ended in stalemate.

Back in New York the question of what aid we would get from the state to meet our yearly budget had to be sidetracked in the face of the need to meet a staggering debt. Short-term notes amounting to more than $3 billion were coming due during the months of July, August, September and October. The bond market was closed tight to the city and there was no angel in sight. Finally the Municipal Assistance Corporation (M.A.C.) was suggested, created and launched. The editorial writers, banks and political leaders hailed "Big Mac" as the city's savior. It was patterned after the formula that Carey had recently worked out to save the semipublic state Urban Development Corporation. In effect, it called for the creation of long-term Big Mac bonds in the amount of $3 billion, which approved by the state legislature and the governor, might be bought by the financial community. The bonds were to be secured by the city's sales tax, the city's prime revenue. The plan was designed to give the city more time to clear up its debt. I found no provision in the proposal, nor any agreement, that would commit the banks to purchase any of the bonds, and I voiced my opposition to the plan. As it turned out, the banks purchased less than one-third of the total issue, at exorbitant interest rates, and the city employees' pension funds had to pick up the rest.

At the Board of Estimate's first meeting with the board of Big Mac we were lectured by the Big Mac representatives, and particularly by Judge Simon Rifkind, on our profligacy. Immediately afterward, Judge Rifkind hired as Mac's president our former sanitation commissioner at a salary of $60,000—$5,000 more than the mayor's. His function was to tell the world of Big Mac's unusual accomplishments. In addition, a public relations representative was hired at a salary far above that of his counterparts in government agencies. From that day on, the meetings of the Municipal Assistance Corporation were closed to the elected representatives of the city and we had no say in its deliberations. But even that arrangement failed.

As the summer progressed, new demands by the banks resulted in new plans being hastily developed in Albany. Additional legislation created the Emergency Financial Control Board. The new agency was designed to gain general acceptance with the bankers, to give the governor and nonelected businessmen virtual control over the city, and thus to further the lucrative sale of city securities. The Board of Estimate and the leadership of the City Council were summoned to Albany at an hour's notice, and the E.F.C.B. legislation, the terms of the city's future servitude, was unveiled as a fait accompli. The document, soon to become law, put the city in a steel grip. It restricted all its financial activities and for all practical purposes took over its assets and dwarfed the role of its elected officials. We discussed the harshness of the terms of the legislation. We protested that under the guise of restraint the bill authorized nonelected officials to set the social policy and outlook of the city. We argued for modifications. And we failed.

There was no gainsaying that if we left Albany without

approving the bill, Anderson would not steer the E.F.C.B. through the senate; and Beame had no other way of saving the city. I also read in the governor's attitude that the groundwork was being laid for Beame's removal as mayor. I had been informed on the most reliable authority that his removal was being seriously considered, and I was advised that it would be in my own interest to take a more conciliatory stance toward the bankers. The power of the governor to remove was absolute, and the law of succession was clear. I found myself resisting the role of Brutus. Beame had no alternative but to surrender.

But even that wasn't sufficient. It shortly became clear that the city's resources were exhausted and to survive it would need to be in a position to issue long-term bonds insured by the federal government. The expression of opinion from the Senate Subcommittee on Banking and Currency and the appropriate committee in the House made it plain that the chances of getting assistance from those quarters were poor. House Speaker O'Neill said in mid-October that he could not get a majority of the House to vote to help us. In the Senate, Senator Adlai E. Stevenson III, normally regarded as favorably disposed, said that help to New York in the present circumstances would be help to the bankers, and they did not deserve it.

And so it went. My last exercise of public office was virtually no exercise at all.

CHAPTER FIFTEEN

Political Retirement

IN 1975 Conservative James Buckley, elected to the U.S. Senate with the help of many New York Democratic voters, had but a year left to his term. Bella Abzug, the Democratic congresswoman from the West Side, called to tell me she was a candidate for his seat. I told her I was entertaining thoughts along the same lines but had not made up my mind. Ramsey Clark, who had made a foreseeably vain but gallant try against Javits in 1974, was known to feel he had a distinctly better chance against Buckley. I believed that neither Abzug nor Clark could take the labor or the middle-class Catholic vote away from Buckley, and I wasn't sure I could.

I tested the water with leaders of Irish and Italian unions. The reception was good and I was encouraged. I sought out Albany County Chairman Dan O'Connell again. He was aged and fragile but talked amiably with me and with the leader of Schenectady County, whom I brought with me. He gave me his endorsement. "The only one can beat you is Moynihan," he said. "Bella Abzug was here and she's a fine woman, but upstate won't take her against Buckley no matter how bad he's been."

Pat Moynihan was our ambassador to the United Nations, where resolutions condemning Israel and the United States at that time were regularly being introduced. Pat's performances in defense had received extensive coverage in the media. His pose was colorful and his presentation spectacular. He had become an overnight success in Borough Park and Brighton Beach, Jewish enclaves that had previously voted for me. We watched his moves. He scorned the very notion that he nurtured any ambition to become a senator and suggested that, were he to be so unprincipled as to run, he should be defeated. The statement went roughly parallel to Sherman's.

I had made up my mind that in order to have a fair chance of success I would need the endorsement of the Democratic party and the support of labor. At the Democratic convention I received 83 percent of the vote—but Joseph Crangle sponsored Moynihan, and at the last minute Moynihan entered the race. As Dan O'Connell had said, Moynihan became my nemesis.

Many of the upstate leaders beholden to Crangle shifted to him. About the same time, George Meany, with whom I had seldom agreed, sent a special message to the New York labor leaders urging them to support Moynihan. The effect was devastating. It greatly reduced the funds available. The returns on primary day made Moynihan the winner and Mrs. Abzug a close second. I had lost heavily to both in the Jewish enclaves, where the highest percentages of votes were cast.

The next year Robert F. Wagner, Jr., and Andrew Stein felt that my performance at the polls in 1976 indicated I would be an easy target in my campaign for reelection to the presidency of the Council. Both young men were wealthy sons of wealthy fathers. Each commissioned a poll that pitted me against State Senator Carol Bellamy, City Councilman Carter Burden, State Assemblyman Leonard Stavisky, Wagner and Stein. The results of both polls were about the same. I received 33 percent of the vote, Wagner and Stein about 12–15 percent each and Burden, Bellamy and Stavisky 6 percent each.

Stein and Wagner thereupon abandoned the race for Council president, and each spent over $500,000 in a bitter contest for borough president of Manhattan, which is a four-year term paying $50,000 a year. Burden, Bellamy and Stavisky stayed in the race for Council president and Abe Hirschfeld, a successful builder, joined them. Burden, a descendent of Commodore Vanderbilt, spent $800,000 of his own money on television, radio and newspaper advertising. The expenditure was responsible by primary day for raising his percentage from 6 to 20 and, as most of the advertising was a concentrated attack on me, reducing my own from 33 to 30 percent, thereby making me particularly vulnerable in the runoff, in which I was decisively defeated by Senator Bellamy. Since I was an early advocate of women's rights I was in a poor position to complain. That ended my career in city government.

Oscar Bernstien had died at eighty-nine six months after my inauguration, but the firm we had built together, O'Dwyer and Bernstien, had been kept together by two of my nephews, a son-in-law and my son Brian, and on January 2, 1977, I returned to my desk at 63 Wall Street to await the next development.

I did not wait long. David Horowitz called. I had worked with him on behalf of the Irgun in 1946, 1947, and 1948. Since then he had followed a writing career. Some of David's family had died in Nazi concentration camps, and his horror of the Nazis and what they had done was his daily companion. Whenever the occasion warranted he exposed former Nazis living in the United States.

David said, "I know you didn't want to lose the election, but I think God has made you available to me."

"What's up, David?" I asked.

"I need you. I'm being sued for one million dollars for libel."

"Do you have a defense, David?" I asked.

"The best in the world," he replied.

"What is your defense?"

"Truth," he said. "He was a Nazi bastard. And I want you to make him eat the ton of papers he served on me, but I want to tell you he's got Cadwalader, Wickersham and Taft on his side."

"All right, David," I said, "come right down and tell me again the story of David and Goliath."

It was as if I had never been away.

Index